STATISTICAL TOOLS, DATA AND INSTRUMENTATION IN RESEARCH AND SCIENCE

ENV BOOKS SERIES

STATISTICAL TOOLS, DATA AND INSTRUMENTATION IN RESEARCH AND SCIENCE

Editors

Er. Chhavi Kumar 'Bharti'
M.Tech., NET
Assistant Professor
ARSD College, University of Delhi (India)

Dr. Prasann Kumar
Division of Research and Development
Lovely Professional University
Jalandhar - 144 411 (Punjab)
(India)

&

Dr. Pawan Kumar 'Bharti'
Society for Environment, Health Awareness of
Nutrition & Toxicology (SEHAT)
B-225/5D, Top Floor, Subhash Gali, Road No. 7, Block B
Ashok Nagar, Shahdara, Delhi - 110 093
(India)

DPH

DISCOVERY PUBLISHING HOUSE PVT. LTD.
INDIA

Published by:
Namit Wasan

DISCOVERY PUBLISHING HOUSE PVT. LTD.
4383/4B, Ansari Road, Darya Ganj
New Delhi-110 002 (India)
Phone : +91-11-23279245; 23253475; 43596065
E-mail : discoverybooksindia@gmail.com
discoverypublishinghouse@gmail.com
namitwasan9@gmail.com
web : www.discoverypublishinggroup.com

First Edition: **2020**

ISBN: 978-93-88854-51-1

Statistical Tools, Data and Instrumentation in Research and Science

Printed at:
Infinity Imaging Systems
Delhi

Preface

Statistics is the discipline that concerns the collection, organization, displaying, analysis, interpretation and presentation of data. In applying statistics to a scientific, industrial, or social problem, it is conventional to begin with a statistical population or a statistical model to be studied. Populations can be diverse groups of people or objects such as "all people living in a country" or "every atom composing a crystal". Statistics deals with every aspect of data, including the planning of data collection in terms of the design of surveys and experiments.

When census data cannot be collected, statisticians collect data by developing specific experiment designs and survey samples. Representative sampling assures that inferences and conclusions can reasonably extend from the sample to the population as a whole. An experimental study involves taking measurements of the system under study, manipulating the system, and then taking additional measurements using the same procedure to determine if the manipulation has modified the values of the measurements. In contrast, an observational study does not involve experimental manipulation.

The present book updates the subject content of Statistical tools and techniques used in scientific research, significance of scientific data set in research work, Correlation and regression through SPSS and Matlab; Biological data base; Statistical package for the social sciences; Open educational resources & Computational biology and several advanced instruments like Energy dispersive x-ray spectroscopy, Infrared Spectroscopy, FTIR Spectroscopy, X-ray Crystallography, and SEM.

Thanks are due to publisher and contributors from various institutions and universities.

The book will be helpful for the researchers, academia working in the field of Statistical tools and techniques used in scientific research, significance of research data, data set in research work, Multiple regression analysis, Correlation and regression through SPSS and Matlab; Biological data base for quick research; Statistical package for the social sciences; Open educational resources & Computational biology and several advanced instruments used in scientific research like Energy dispersive x-ray spectroscopy, Infrared Spectroscopy, Fourier Transform Infrared Spectroscopy, X-ray Crystallography, and SEM.

–Editors

(envbooks@gmail.com)

Contents

Pages: 1-5
Statistical Tools, Data and Instrumentation in Research and Science
Edited by: **Er. Chhavi Kumar 'Bharti'; Dr. Prasann Kumar and Dr. Pawan Kumar 'Bharti'**
ISBN: 978-93-88854-51-1
Edition: **2020**
Published by: **Discovery Publishing House Pvt. Ltd., New Delhi (India)**

1 Introduction

Statistical methods involved in carrying out a study include planning, designing, collecting data, analysing, drawing meaningful interpretation and reporting of the research findings. The statistical analysis gives meaning to the meaningless numbers, thereby breathing life into a lifeless data. The results and inferences are precise only if proper statistical tests are used.

Statistics is a branch of science that deals with the collection, organisation, analysis of data and drawing of inferences from the samples to the whole population. This requires a proper design of the study, an appropriate selection of the study sample and choice of a suitable statistical test. An adequate knowledge of statistics is necessary for proper designing of an epidemiological study or a clinical trial. Improper statistical methods may result in erroneous conclusions which may lead to unethical practice.

Statistics is the discipline that concerns the collection, organization, displaying, analysis, interpretation and presentation of data. In applying statistics to a scientific, industrial, or social problem, it is conventional to begin with a statistical population or a statistical model to be studied. Populations can be diverse groups of people or objects such as "all people living in a country" or "every atom composing a crystal". Statistics deals with every aspect of data, including the planning of data collection in terms of the design of surveys and experiments.

When census data cannot be collected, statisticians collect data by developing specific experiment designs and survey samples. Representative sampling assures that inferences and conclusions can reasonably extend from the sample to the population as a whole. An experimental study involves taking measurements of the system under study, manipulating the system, and then taking additional measurements using the same procedure to determine if the manipulation has modified the values of the measurements. In contrast, an observational study does not involve experimental manipulation.

Two main statistical methods are used in data analysis: descriptive statistics, which summarize data from a sample using indexes such as the mean or standard deviation, and inferential statistics, which draw conclusions from data that are subject to random variation (e.g., observational errors, sampling variation). Descriptive statistics are most often concerned with two sets of properties of a distribution (sample or population): central tendency (or location) seeks to characterize the distribution's central or typical value, while dispersion (or variability) characterizes the extent to which members of the distribution depart from its center and each other. Inferences on mathematical statistics are made under the framework of probability theory, which deals with the analysis of random phenomena.

A standard statistical procedure involves the test of the relationship between two statistical data sets, or a data set and synthetic data drawn from an idealized model. A hypothesis is proposed for the statistical relationship between the two data sets, and this is compared as an alternative to an idealized null hypothesis of no relationship between two data sets. Rejecting or disproving the null hypothesis is done using statistical tests that quantify the sense in which the null can be proven false, given the data that are used in the test. Working from a null hypothesis, two basic forms of error are recognized: Type I errors (null hypothesis is falsely rejected giving a "false positive") and Type II errors (null hypothesis fails to be rejected and an actual relationship between populations is missed giving a "false negative"). Multiple problems have come to be associated with this framework: ranging from obtaining a sufficient sample size to specifying an adequate null hypothesis.

Measurement processes that generate statistical data are also subject to error. Many of these errors are classified as random (noise) or systematic (bias), but other types of errors (e.g., blunder, such as when an analyst reports incorrect units) can also occur. The presence of missing data or censoring may result in biased estimates and specific techniques have been developed to address these problems.

VARIABLES

Variable is a characteristic that varies from one individual member of population to another individual. Variables such as height and weight are measured by some type of scale, convey quantitative information and are called as quantitative variables. Sex and eye colour give qualitative information and are called as qualitative variables.

STATISTICS: DESCRIPTIVE AND INFERENTIAL STATISTICS

Descriptive statistics try to describe the relationship between variables in a sample or population. Descriptive statistics provide a summary of data in the form of mean, median and mode. Inferential statistics use a random sample of data taken from a population to describe and make inferences about the whole population. It is valuable when it is not possible to examine each member of an entire population.

It is important that a researcher knows the concepts of the basic statistical methods used for conduct of a research study. This will help to conduct an appropriately well-designed study leading to valid and reliable results. Inappropriate use of statistical techniques may lead to faulty conclusions, inducing errors and undermining the significance of the article. Bad statistics may lead to bad research, and bad research may lead to unethical practice. Hence, an adequate knowledge of statistics and the appropriate use of statistical tests are important. An appropriate knowledge about the basic statistical methods will go a long way in improving the research designs and producing quality medical research which can be utilised for formulating the evidence-based guidelines.

INSTRUMENT

Instrument is the general term that researchers use for a measurement device (survey, test, questionnaire, etc.). To help distinguish between instrument and instrumentation, consider that the instrument is the device and instrumentation is the course of action (the process of developing, testing, and using the device).

Instruments fall into two broad categories, researcher-completed and subject-completed, distinguished by those instruments that researchers administer versus those that are completed by participants. Researchers chose which type of instrument, or instruments, to use based on the research question.

VALIDITY

Validity is the extent to which an instrument measures what it is supposed to measure and performs as it is designed to perform. It is rare, if nearly impossible, that an instrument be 100% valid, so validity is generally measured in degrees. As a process, validation involves collecting and analyzing data to assess the accuracy of an instrument. There are numerous statistical tests and measures to assess the validity of quantitative instruments, which generally involves pilot testing. The remainder of this discussion focuses on external validity and content validity.

External validity is the extent to which the results of a study can be generalized from a sample to a population. Establishing eternal validity for an instrument, then, follows directly from sampling. Recall that a sample should be an accurate representation of a population, because the total population may not be available. An instrument that is externally valid helps obtain population generalizability, or the degree to which a sample represents the population.

Content validity refers to the appropriateness of the content of an instrument. In other words, do the measures (questions, observation logs, etc.) accurately assess what you want to know? This is particularly important with achievement tests. Consider that a test developer wants to maximize the validity of a unit test for 7th grade mathematics. This would involve taking representative questions from each of the sections of the unit and evaluating them against the desired outcomes.

RELIABILITY

Reliability can be thought of as consistency. Does the instrument consistently measure what it is intended to measure? It is not possible to calculate reliability; however, there are four general estimators that you may encounter in reading research:

- Inter-Rater/Observer Reliability: The degree to which different raters/observers give consistent answers or estimates.
- Test-Retest Reliability: The consistency of a measure evaluated over time.
- Parallel-Forms Reliability: The reliability of two tests constructed the same way, from the same content.
- Internal Consistency Reliability: The consistency of results across items, often measured with Cronbach's Alpha.

Relating Reliability and Validity

Reliability is directly related to the validity of the measure. There are several important principles. First, a test can be considered reliable, but not valid. Consider the SAT, used as a predictor of success in college. It is a reliable test (high scores relate to high GPA), though only a moderately valid indicator of success (due to the lack of structured environment – class attendance, parent-regulated study, and sleeping habits – each holistically related to success).

Second, validity is more important than reliability. Using the above example, college admissions may consider the SAT a reliable test, but not necessarily a valid measure of other quantities colleges seek, such as leadership capability, altruism, and civic involvement. The combination of these aspects, alongside the SAT, is a more valid measure of the applicant's potential for graduation, later social involvement, and generosity (alumni giving) toward the alma mater.

Finally, the most useful instrument is both valid and reliable. Proponents of the SAT argue that it is both. It is a moderately reliable predictor of future success and a moderately valid measure of a student's knowledge in Mathematics, Critical Reading, and Writing.

REFERENCES

https://www.ncbi.nlm.nih.gov/pmc/articles/PMC5037948/

Winters R, Winters A, Amedee RG. Statistics: A Brief Overview. Ochsner J. 2010; 10: 213-6.

Sprent P. Statistics in Medical Research. Swiss Med Wkly. 2003; 133: 522-9.

Kaur SP. Variables in Research. Indian J Res Rep Med Sci. 2013; 4: 36-8.

Satake EB. Statistical Methods and Reasoning for the Clinical Sciences Evidence-Based Practice. Ist ed. San Diego: Plural Publishing, Inc; 2015. pp. 1-19.

http://www.fao.org/3/W7295E/w7295e08.htm

http://europepmc.org/abstract/pmc/pmc5037948

https://en.wikipedia.org/wiki/Statistics

https://www.slideshare.net/jobitonio/research-instrumentation

https://researchrundowns.com/quantitative-methods/instrument-validity-reliability/

Pages: 6-17

Statistical Tools, Data and Instrumentation in Research and Science

Edited by: **Er. Chhavi Kumar 'Bharti'; Dr. Prasann Kumar and Dr. Pawan Kumar 'Bharti'**

ISBN: 978-93-88854-51-1

Edition: **2020**

Published by: **Discovery Publishing House Pvt. Ltd., New Delhi (India)**

2

Science in Data for Science with Special Reference to its Introduction

Prasann Kumar[1,2*]; Shipa Rani Dey[1]

GRAPHICAL ABSTRACT

Keywords: Calculation, Data, Introduction, Science

[1] Department of Agronomy, School of Agriculture, Lovely Professional University, Jalandhar - 144 411 (Punjab) (India)

[2] Divison of Research and Development, Lovely Professional University, Jalandhar - 144 411 (Punjab) (India)

INTRODUCTION

Data science is a multi-disciplinary field that leverages tools in data management, Machine learning and data visualization for data driven decision making (Figure 2.1).

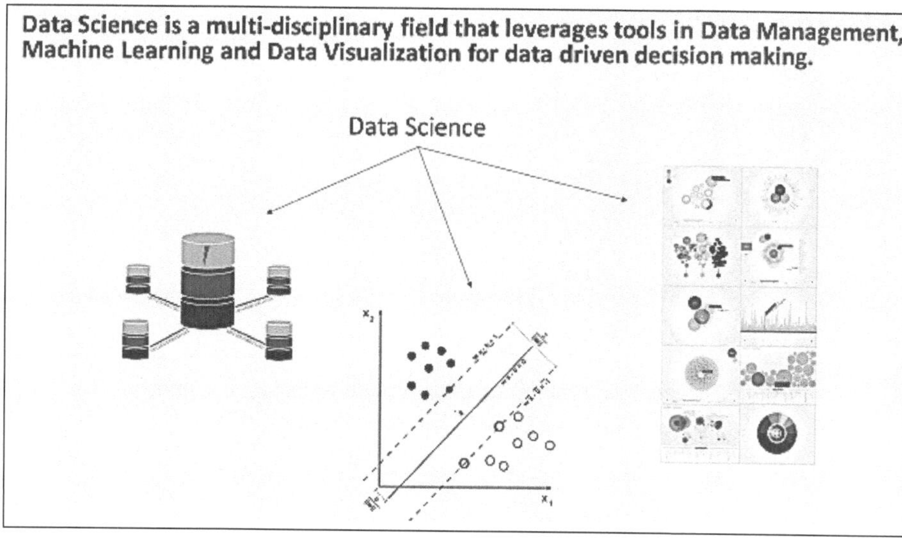

Fig. 2.1: Data science in multi-disciplinary field

Source: based on review of literature

Fig. 2.2: Netflix

Source: based on review of literature

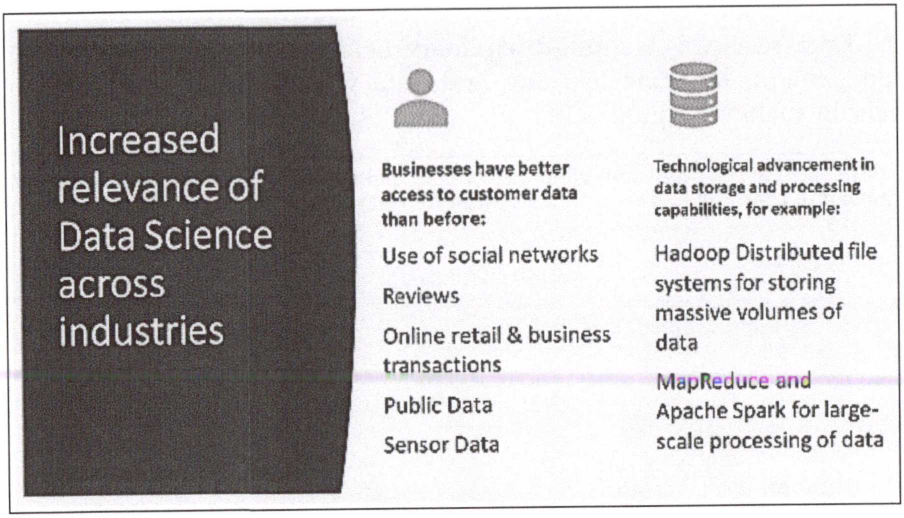

Fig. 2.3: Increased relevance of data science across industries

Source: based on review of literature

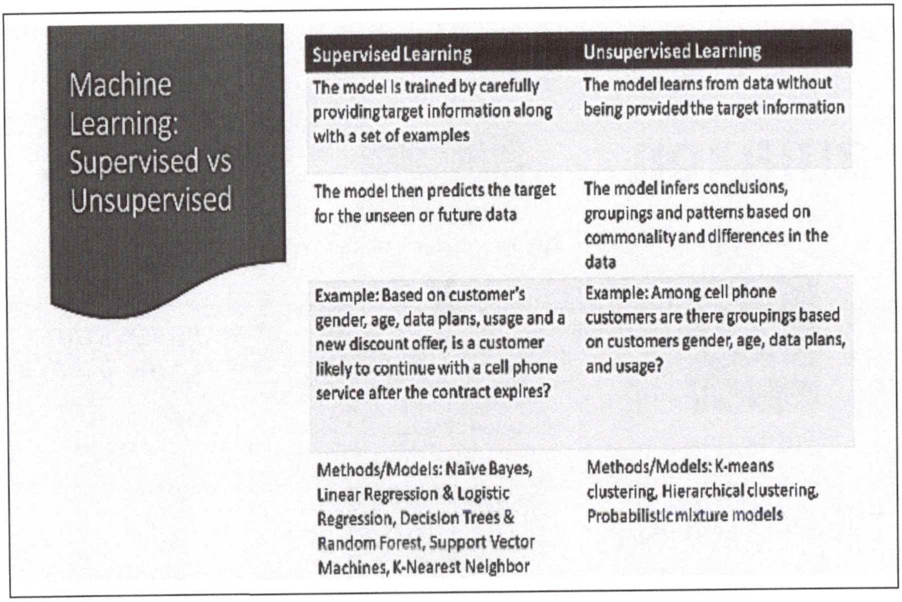

Fig. 2.4: Machine Learning Supervised vs Unsupervised

Source: based on review of literature

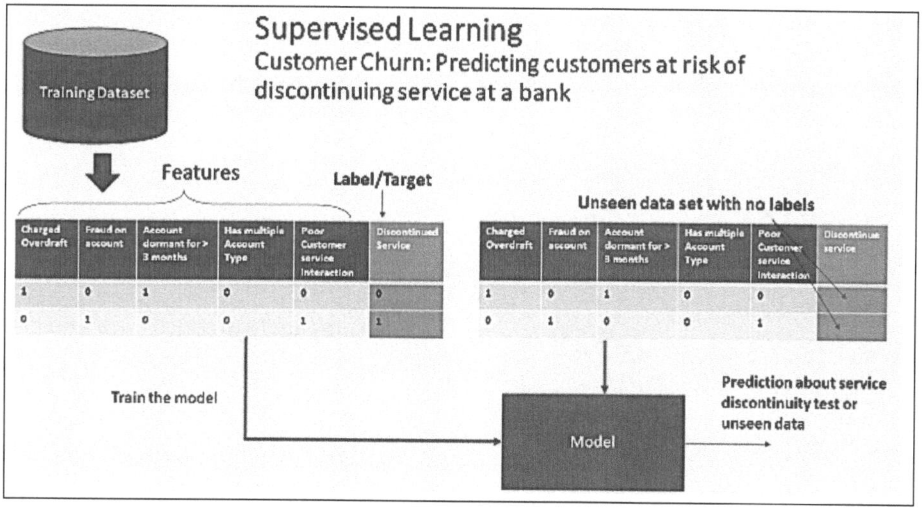

Fig. 2.5: Supervised Learning

Source: based on review of literature

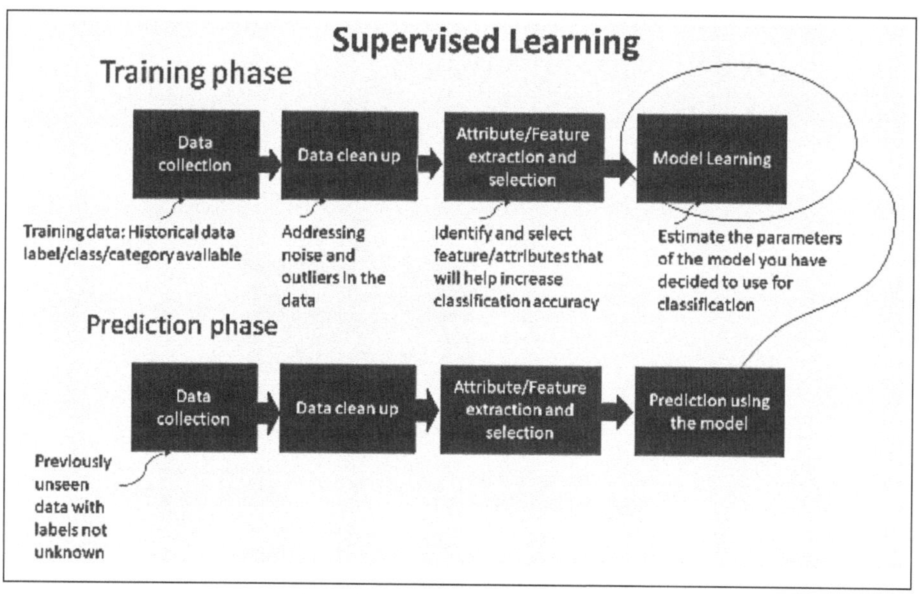

Fig. 2.6: Continuation of figure 2.5

Source: based on review of literature

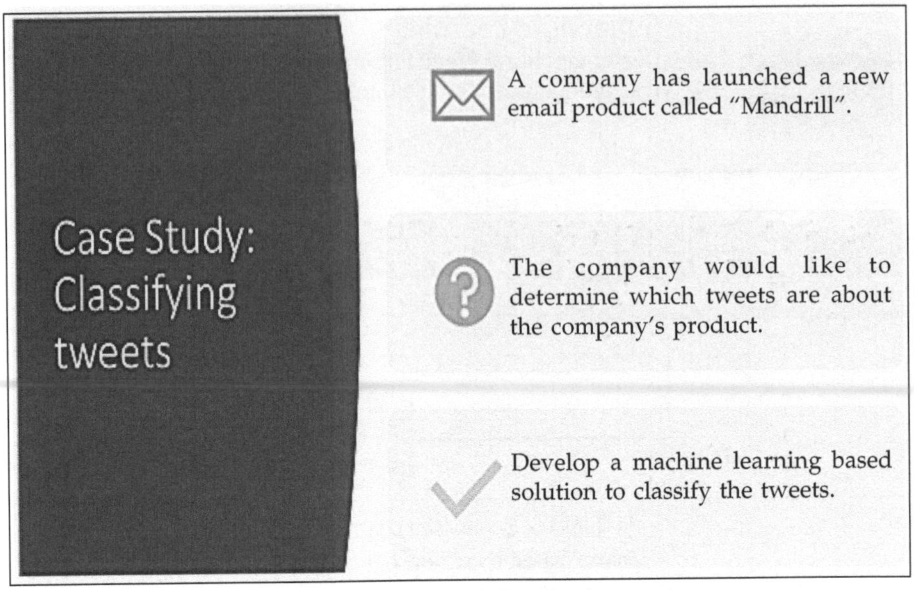

Fig. 2.7: Case Study and classification tweets
Source: based on review of literature

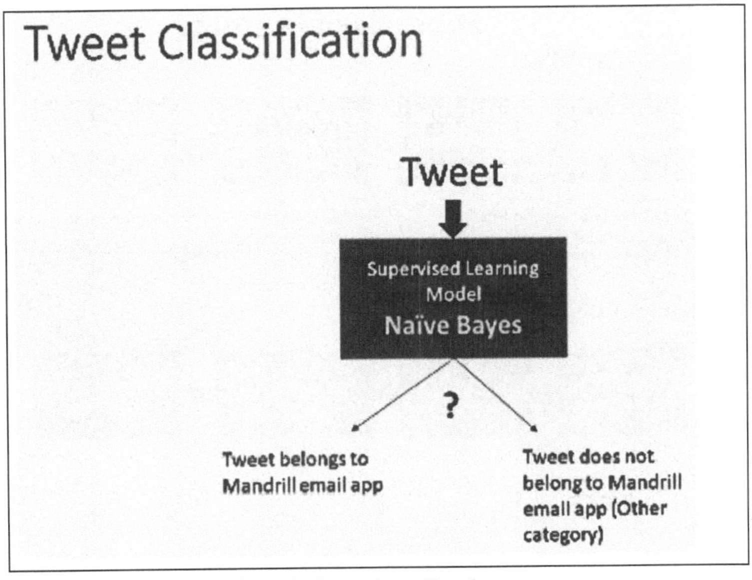

Fig. 2.8: Tweet Classification
Source: based on review of literature

Naïve Bayes Classifier for Tweet Classification

The Naïve Bayes Classifier is based on the Bayes' theorem

$$P(A|B) = \frac{P(B|A)P(A)}{P(B)}$$

- $P(A|B)$ = *conditional probability of A given B (posterior probability)*
- $P(B|A)$ = *conditional probability of B given A (likelihood)*
- $P(A)$ = *probability of A (prior probability)*
- $P(B)$ = *probability of B(total probability)*

Fig. 2.9: Naïve Bayes Classifier for Tweet Classification

Source: based on review of literature

Bayes Theorem Equations for Tweet Classification

- $P(class_{Mandrill}|tweet) = \frac{P(tweet|class_{Mandrill})P\ (class_{Mandrill})}{P(tweet)}$ **Find ?**

- $P(class_{Other}|tweet) = \frac{P(tweet|class_{Other})P\ (class_{Other})}{P(tweet)}$ **Find ?**

Note: $P(tweet) = P(tweet\ class_{Mandrill})\ P(class_{Mandrill}) + P(tweet\ class_{other})P(class_{other})$ $P(class_{other})$, the prior probability be estimated from the training data or assumed through experience

Fig. 2.10: Bayes Theorem Equation for Tweet Classification

Source: based on review of literature

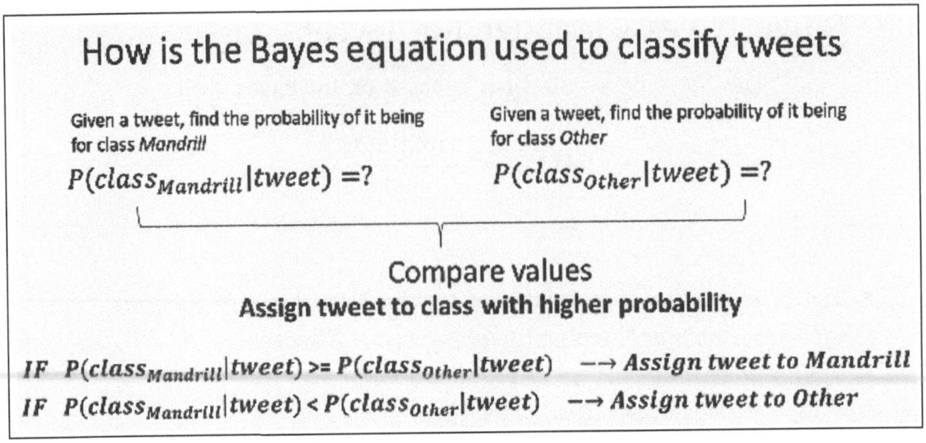

Fig. 2.11: How is the Bayes equation used to classify tweets

Source: based on review of literature

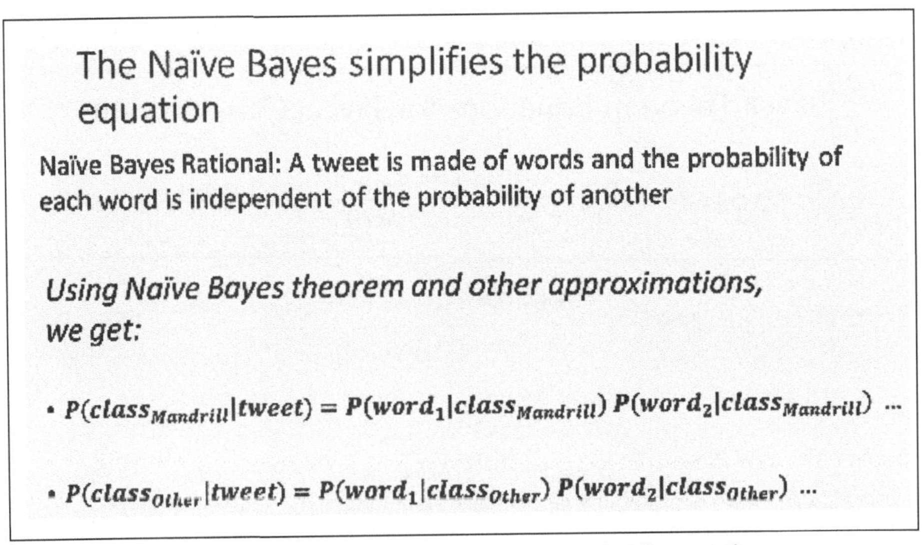

Fig. 2.12: The Native Bayes Simplifies the probability equation

Source: based on review of literature

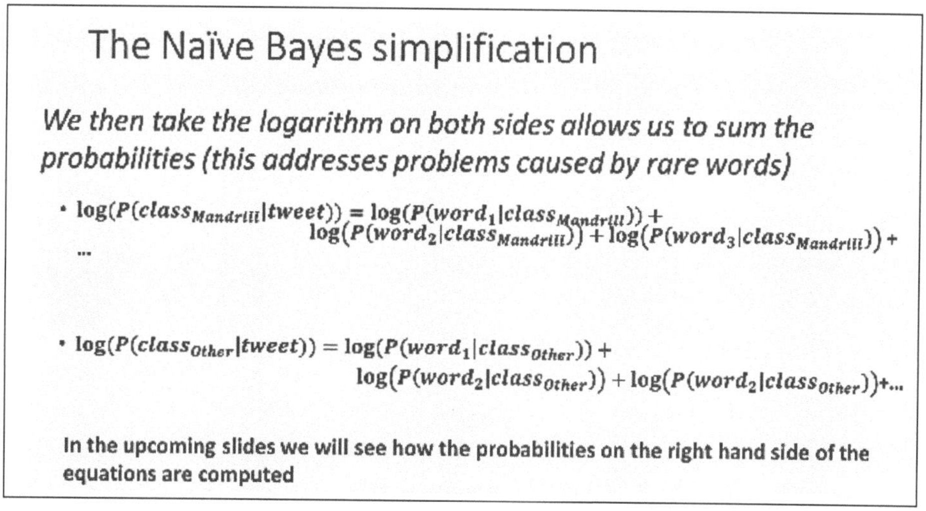

Fig. 2.13: The Naïve Bayes simplification

Source: based on review of literature

TRAINING THE MODEL

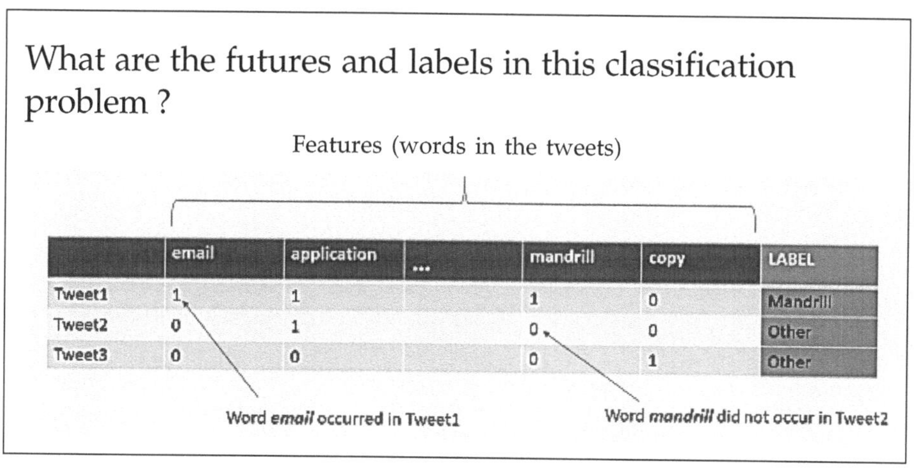

Fig. 2.14: Features and labels in the classification problem

Source: based on review of literature

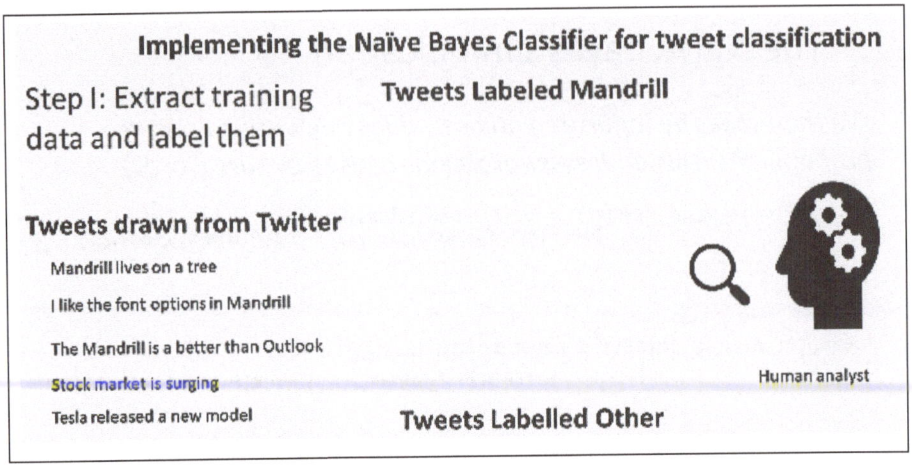

Fig. 2.15: Implementing the Naïve Bayes Classifier for tweet classification
Source: based on review of literature

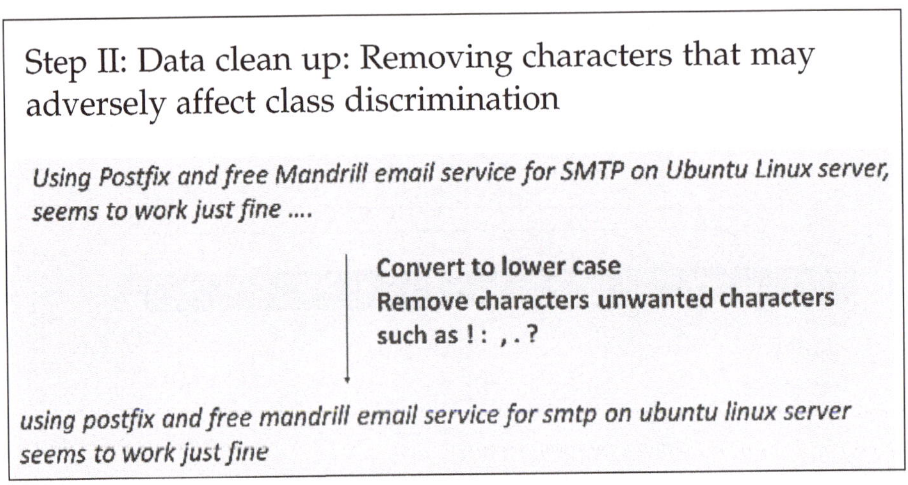

Fig. 2.16: Data clean up
Source: based on review of literature

Step III: Feature Extraction and selection: Breaking down tweets to words, filtering out unwanted words and counting their occurrences

Training Data: Class Mandrill

after looking at its website not sure what @mailchimp's mandrill does but gosh darn its #logo is nice
and we're live come hear @levelos talk about using mailchimp and mandrill for newsletters in #drupal http://bit.ly/zawi4i

.

.

.

Training Data: Class Other

@mandrill @ccp_manifest @ccpgames don't go to glasgow city
@ccpgames i hope they record the whole thing with high quality audio.
@mandrill @ccpgames plus we have a faint ccp seagull

.

.

Training Data: Class Mandrill word list and Count

Word	Count
website	580
mandrill	300
mailchimp	195

Training Data: Class Other word list and Count

Word	Count
city	580
quality	404
faint	360

Fig. 2.17: Feature Extraction and Selection

Source: based on review of literature

Step IV: Compute conditional probabilities and long probabilities

Training Data Class Mandrill Conditional Probabilities

Word	Count	P(Word|Class_Mandrill)	Log(P(Word|Class_Mandrill))
website	580	580/10000 = 0.058	-2.847
mandrill	300	300/10000 = 0.03	-3.506
mailchimp	195	195/10000 = 0.0195	-3.937

Total words in Class Mandrill training data

Training Data Class Other Conditional Probabilities

Word	Count	P(Word|Class_Other)	Log(P(Word|Class_Other))
city	580	580/20000 = 0.029	-3.540
quality	404	404/20000 = 0.0202	-3.902
faint	360	360/20000 = 0.0180	-4.017

Total words in Class Other training data

Fig. 2.18: Computer conditional probabilities and log probabilities

Source: based on review of literature

MODEL TESTING

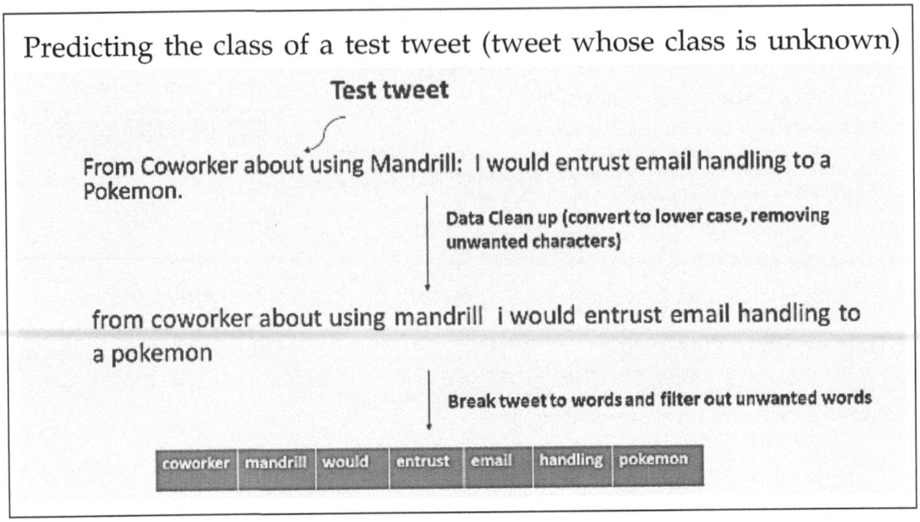

Fig. 2.19: Predicting the class of a test tweet

Source: based on review of literature

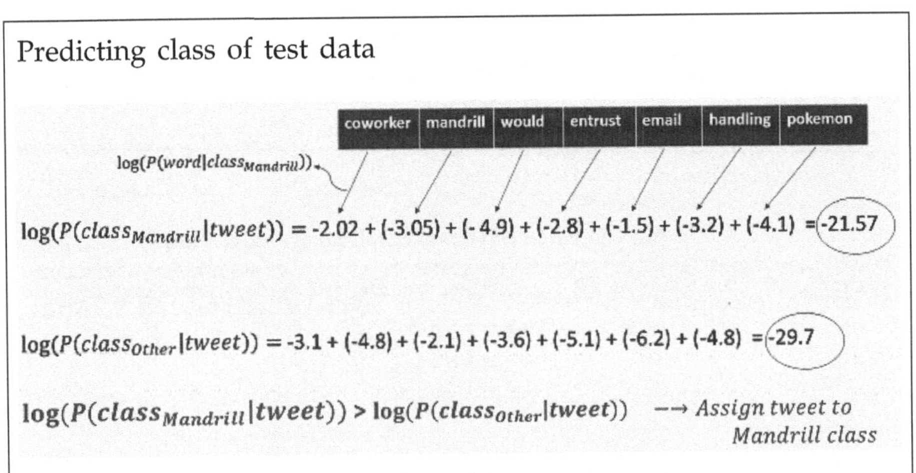

Fig. 2.20: Predicting class of test data

Source: based on review of literature

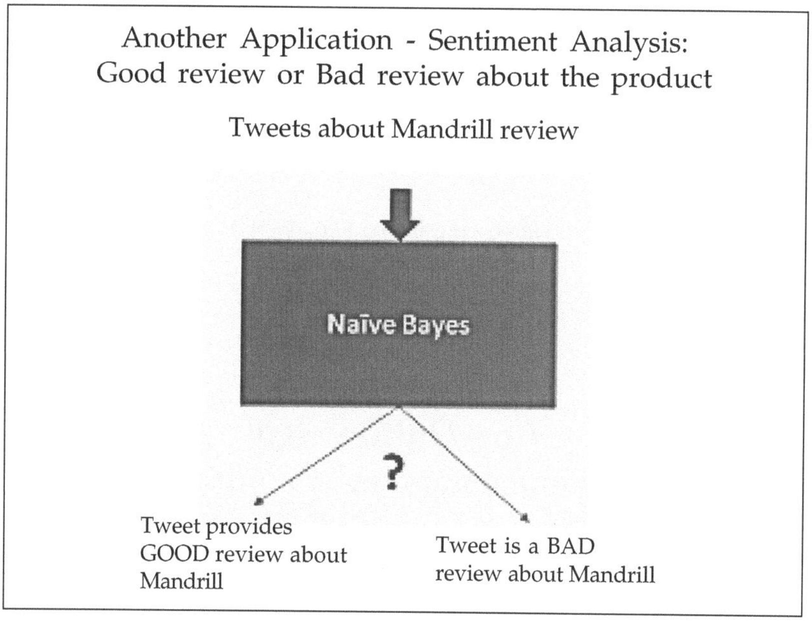

Fig. 2.21: Sentiment Analysis

Source: based on review of literature

REFERENCE

Chodhary D. Director of Graduate Engineering, Christian Brother University Memphis, TN, USA.

Pages: 18-23

Statistical Tools, Data and Instrumentation in Research and Science
Edited by: **Er. Chhavi Kumar 'Bharti'; Dr. Prasann Kumar and Dr. Pawan Kumar 'Bharti'**
ISBN: 978-93-88854-51-1
Edition: **2020**
Published by: **Discovery Publishing House Pvt. Ltd., New Delhi (India)**

3

Correlation and Regression Analysis through SPSS

Prasann Kumar[1,2*] and Shipa Rani Dey[1]

GRAPHICAL ABSTRACT

Keywords: Analysis, Correlations, Regression, Social

[1] Department of Agronomy, School of Agriculture, Lovely Professional University, Jalandhar - 144 411 Punjab (India)
[2] Divison of Research and Development, Lovely Professional University, Jalandhar - 144 411 Punjab, (India)

INTRODUCTION TO CORRELATION

- The Pearson product-moment correlation coefficient measures the degree of association between two interval (or better)-level variables.
- For example, the relationship between daily consumption of fat calories and body weight, or attitudes towards smoking and attitudes towards consumption of alcohol.

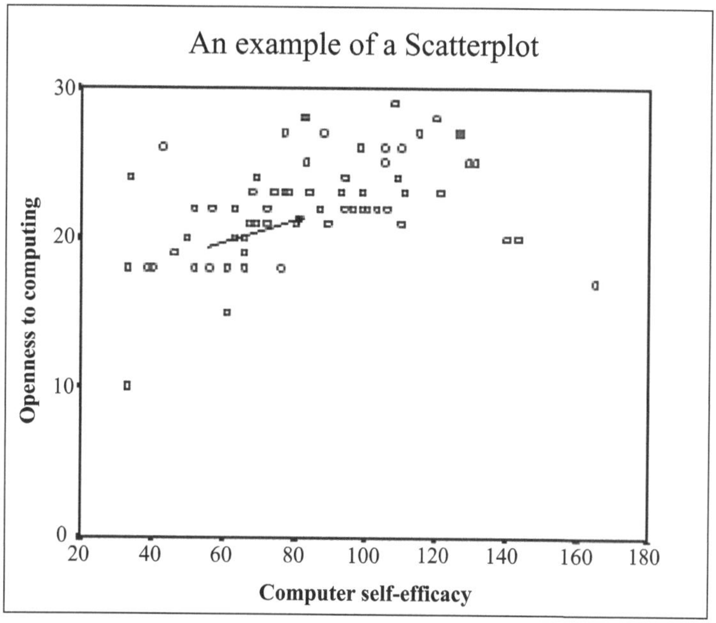

Fig. 3.1: An example of a Scatterplot
Source: based on review of literature

How is the Correlation Coefficient Computed?

The conceptual formula for the correlation coefficient is a little daunting, but it looks like this:

$$r = \frac{\Sigma(X-X)(Y-Y)}{\sqrt{[\Sigma(X-X)^2]\,[\Sigma(Y-Y)^2]}}$$

Reporting of result with SPSS-SPSS data file&-SPSS Output for Bivariate Correlation

Writing up the Results of Your Test:

- Reporting of results into paper or thesis
- (r = _, DF=_, p <_, two-tailed).

Application and significance of Coefficient of Correlation (R)

- Policy makers
- Banking
- Direction of the variables undertaken for the study
- Marketing decisions
- Concrete combinations
- Biological drugs (antipyretic drugs)

THE REGRESSION MODEL

Regression takes us a step beyond correlation in that not only are we concerned with the strength of the association.

Describe its nature with sufficient precision to be able to make predictions.

To be able to make predictions, we need to be able to characterize one of the variables in the relationship as independent and the other as dependent.

A regression equation is used to predict the value of a dependent variable, Y.

Here, Lets consider in this case a country's male literacy rate, on the basis of some constant *a* that applies to all cases, plus some amount *b* which is applied to each individual value of X (the country's % of people living in cities), plus some error term *e* that is unique to the individual case and unpredictable:

$Y = a + bX + e$ (male literacy $= a + b$ (percent urban) $+ e$)

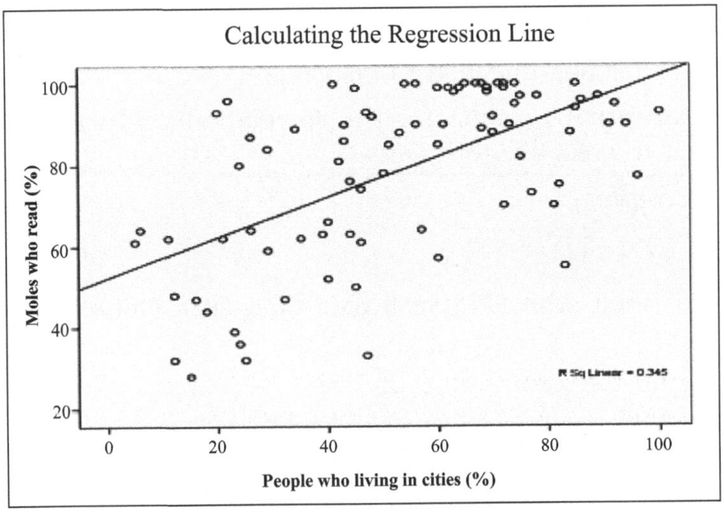

Fig. 3.2: Calculating the regression line

Source: based on review of literature)

Finding the Intercept (Constant) and Slope (β or unstandardized regression coefficient)

The intercept

Coefficients[a]

Model		Unstandardized Coefficients B	Unstandardized Coefficients Std. Error	Standardized Coefficients Beta	t	Sig.
1	(Constant)	52.372	4.378		11.961	.000
	People living in cities	.495	.075	.587	6.608	.000

a. Dependent Variable: Males who read (%)

The slope, or β

Beta weight when X and Y are expressed in standard score units

The regression equation for predicting Y (male literacy) is

$$Y = a + (b)X, \text{ or } Y = 52.372 + .495X,$$

Fig. 3.3: Finding the intercept and slope

Source: based on review of literature

More Output from Linear Regression

Model Summary

Model	R	R Square	Adjusted R Square	Std. Error of the Estimate
1	.587[a]	.345	.337	16.649

a. Predictors: (Constant), People living in cities (%)

Interpretations: ?????

Fig. 3.4: More output linear regression

Source: based on review of literature

***F* test of the regression equation**

ANOVA[b]

Model		Sum of Squares	df	Mean Square	F	Sig.
1	Regression	2104.898	1	12104.898	43.668	.000[a]
	Residual	3007.879	83	277.203		
	Total	5112.776	84			

a. Predictors: (Constant), People living in cities (%)

b. Dependent Variable: Males who read (%)

Fig. 3.5: F-test of the regression equation

Source: based on review of literature

Some more on Regression: R-squared (R^2)

It measures the proportion of the variation in your dependent variable explained by all of your independent variables in the model:

$$R^2 \equiv 1 - \frac{SS_{res}}{SS_{tot}} \equiv 1 - \frac{\Sigma(y_i - \hat{y}_i)^2}{\Sigma(y_i - \bar{y})^2}$$

$$R^2 = \frac{SS_{reg}}{SS_{tot}}$$

Fig. 3.6: Some more on Regression: R-squared (R^2)

Source: based on review of literature

Adjusted R Square:

$$R^2_{adjusted} = 1 - \frac{(1 - R^2)(N - 1)}{N - p - 1}$$

where

R^2 = sample R-square

p = Number of predictors

N = Total sample size.

It penalizes you for adding independent variable that do not help in predicting the dependent variable.

Fig. 3.7: Adjusted R Square

Source: based on review of literature

ANALYZE RESIDUALS FROM REGRESSION

An important way of checking whether a regression, simple or multiple, has achieved its goal to explain as much variation as possible in a dependent variable while respecting the underlying assumption, is to check the *residuals of a regression.*

In other words having a detailed look at what is *left over* after explaining the variation in the dependent variable using independent variable(s), i.e. the unexplained variation.

Explanation of the output: *Participants answer*

TOOLS FOR ANALYZING RESIDUALS

A histogram, dot-plot or stem-and-leaf plot lets you examine residuals:

Standard regression assumes that residuals should be normally distributed.(Shape determine –normality)

A Q-Q PLOT TO ASSESS NORMALITY OF THE RESIDUALS

Plot the residuals against each independent variables to find out, whether a pattern is clearly related to one of the independents.

Plot the residuals against other variables to find out, whether a structure appearing in the residuals might be explained by another variable (a variable that you might want to include into a more complex model.)

CONCLUSION

In statistical modeling, regression analysis is a set of statistical processes for estimating the relationships among variables. It includes many techniques for modeling and analyzing several variables, when the focus is on the relationship between a dependent variable and one or more independent variables (or 'predictors'). More specifically, regression analysis helps one understand how the typical value of the dependent variable (or 'criterion variable') changes when any one of the independent variables is varied, while the other independent variables are held fixed.

REFERENCES

https://en.wikipedia.org/wiki/Regression_analysis

https://en.wikipedia.org/wiki/Correlation_and_dependence

https://en.wikipedia.org/wiki/Outline_of_regression_analysis

https://en.wikipedia.org/wiki/Linear_regression

https://www.wikilectures.eu/w/Correlation_and_Regression

https://wiki.aapg.org/Correlation_and_regression_analysis

www.statsoft.com/Textbook/Multiple-Regression

Pages: 24-33

Statistical Tools, Data and Instrumentation in Research and Science
Edited by: Er. Chhavi Kumar 'Bharti'; Dr. Prasann Kumar and Dr. Pawan Kumar 'Bharti'
ISBN: 978-93-88854-51-1
Edition: **2020**
Published by: **Discovery Publishing House Pvt. Ltd., New Delhi (India)**

4

Multiple Regression Analysis and Assumptions

Prasann Kumar[1,2*] and Shipa Rani Dey[1]

GRAPHICAL ABSTRACT

Keywords: Assumption,Multiple, Regression, Queen, Stat

[1] Department of Agronomy, School of Agriculture, Lovely Professional University, Jalandhar - 144 411 Punjab (India)

[2] Divison of Research and Development, Lovely Professional University, Jalandhar - 144 411 Punjab, (India)

INTRODUCTION

We look at situations where several explanatory variables works together to explain the response.

The Assumptions:

1. The distribution of residuals is normal (at each value of the dependent variable).
2. The variance of the residuals for every set of values for the independent variable is equal.
   - violation is called heteroscedasticity.
3. At every value of the dependent variable the expected (mean) value of the residuals is zero
   - No non-linear relationships
4. All independent variables are uncorrelated with the error term.
5. No independent variables are a perfect linear function of other independent variables (no perfect multicollinearity)

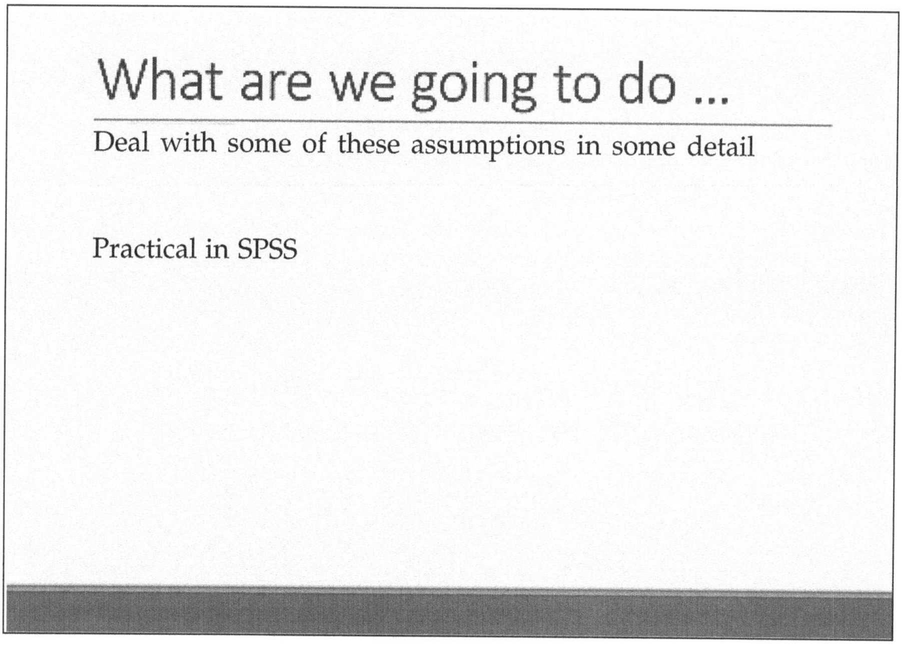

Fig. 4.1: What are we going to do?

Source: based on review of literature

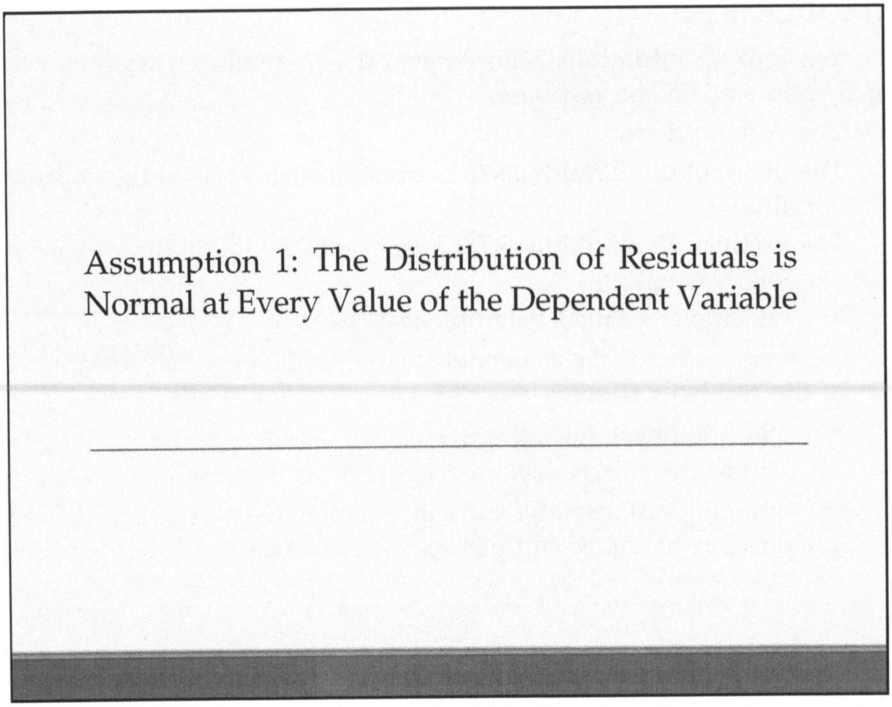

Fig. 4.2: Assumption 1

Source: based on review of literature

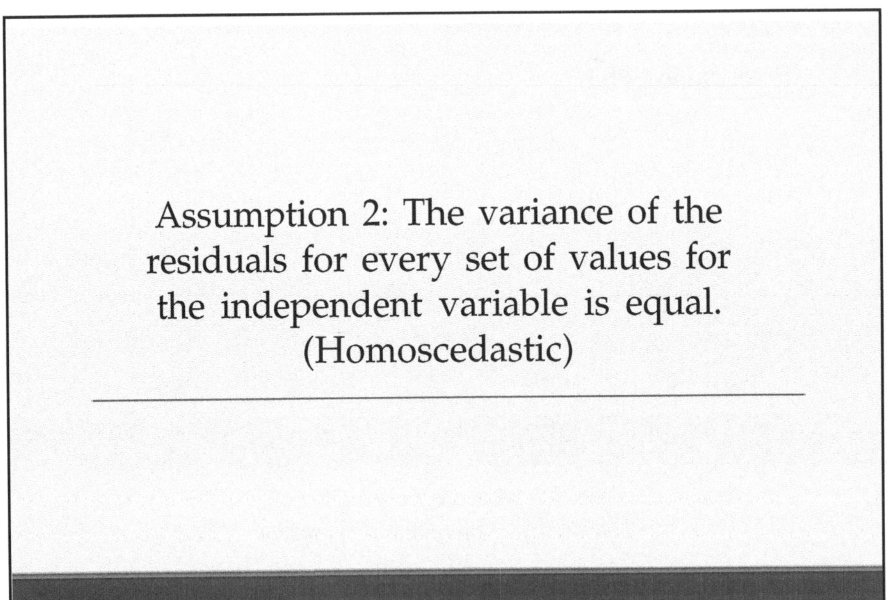

Fig. 4.3: Assumption 2

Source: based on review of literature

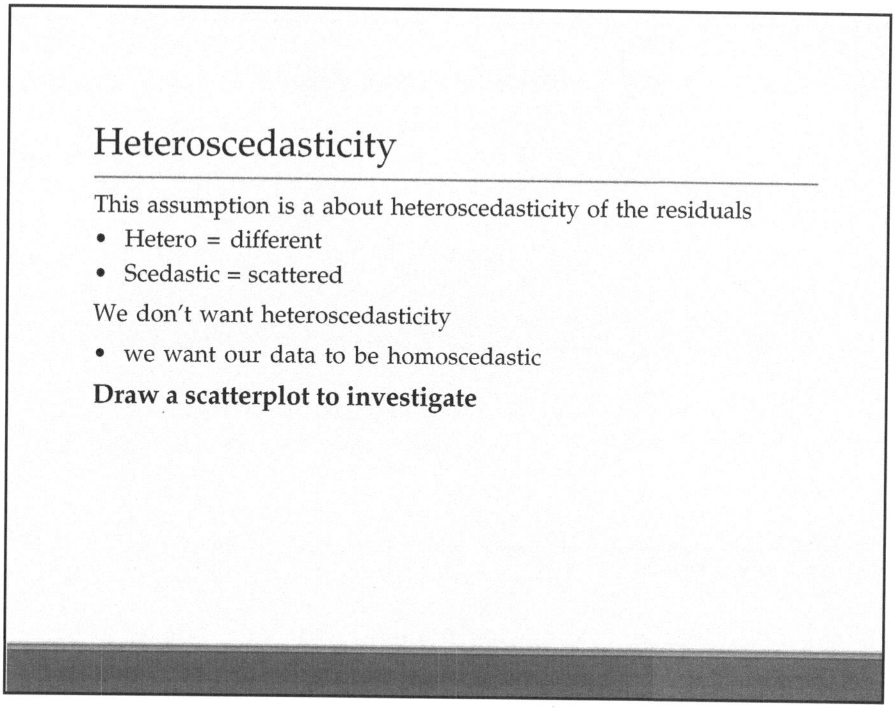

Fig. 4.4: Heteroscedasticity
Source: based on review of literature

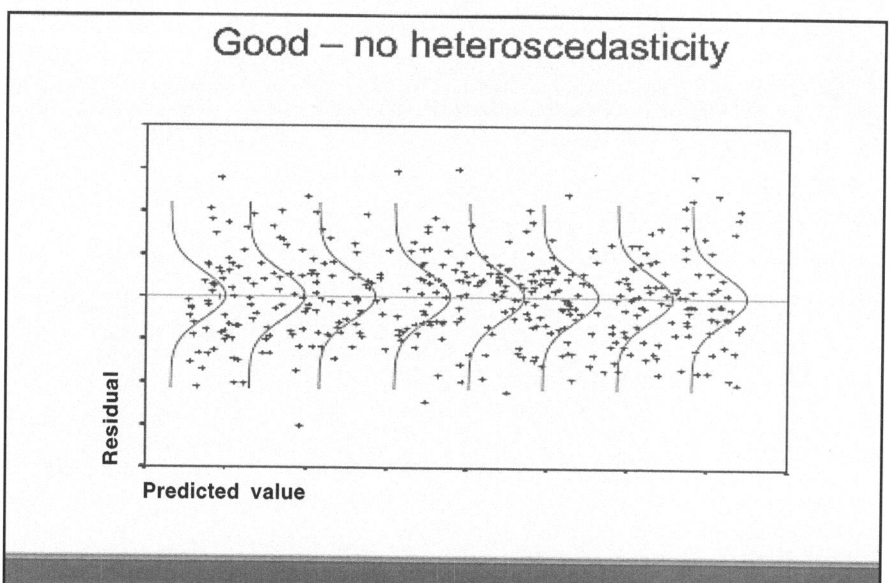

Fig. 4.5: Good-no heteroscedasticity
Source: based on review of literature

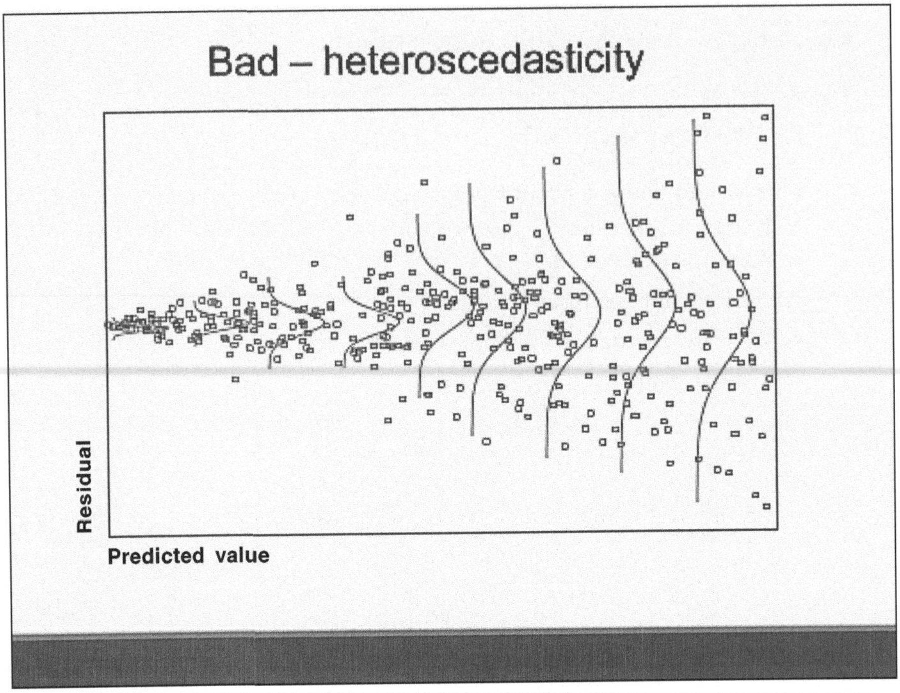

Fig. 4.6: Bad-heteroscedasticity

Source: based on review of literature

Testing Heteroscedasticity

White's test

- Not automatic in SPSS (is in SAS)
- Luckily, not hard to do
- More luckily, we aren't going to do it
  - (In the very unlikely event you will ever have to do it, look it up.
  - Google: White's test spss)

Fig. 4.7: Testing Heteroscedasticity

Source: based on review of literature

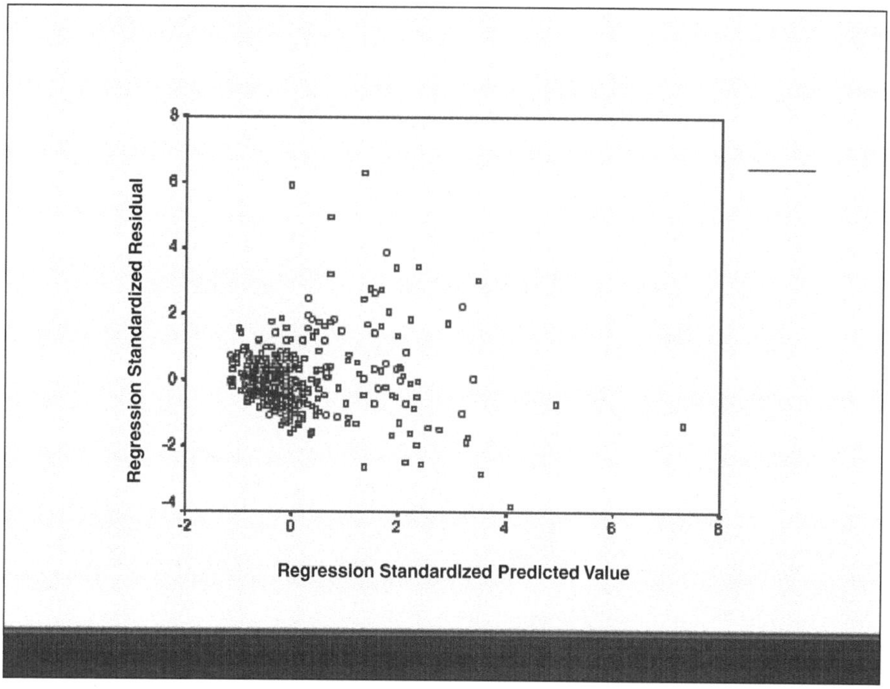

Fig. 4.8: Regression standardized Residual

Source: based on review of literature

Assumption 3: At every value of the dependent variable the expected (mean) value of the residuals is zero

Fig. 4.9: Assumption 3

Source: based on review of literature

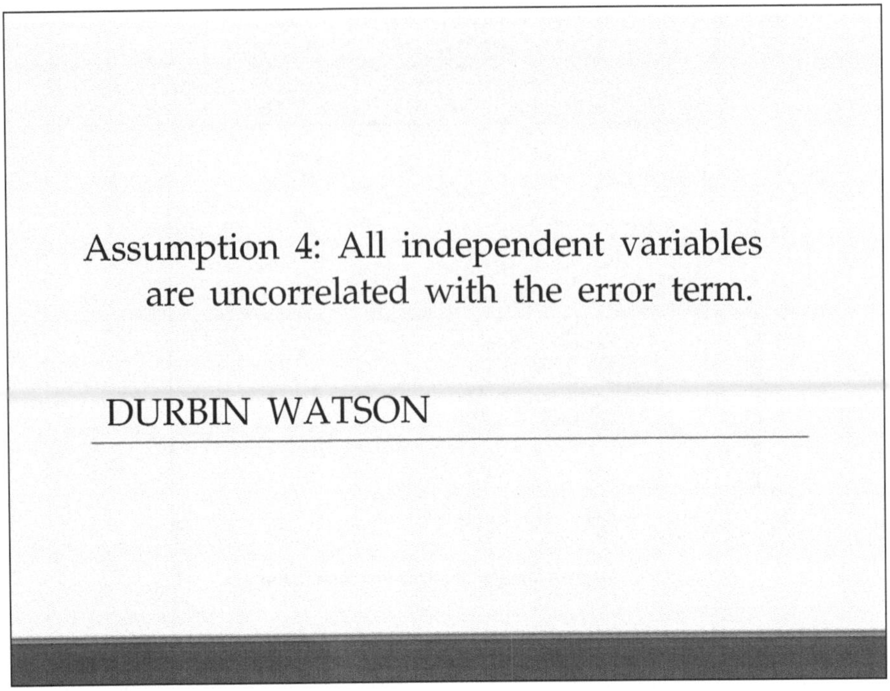

Fig. 4.10: Assumption 4
Source: based on review of literature

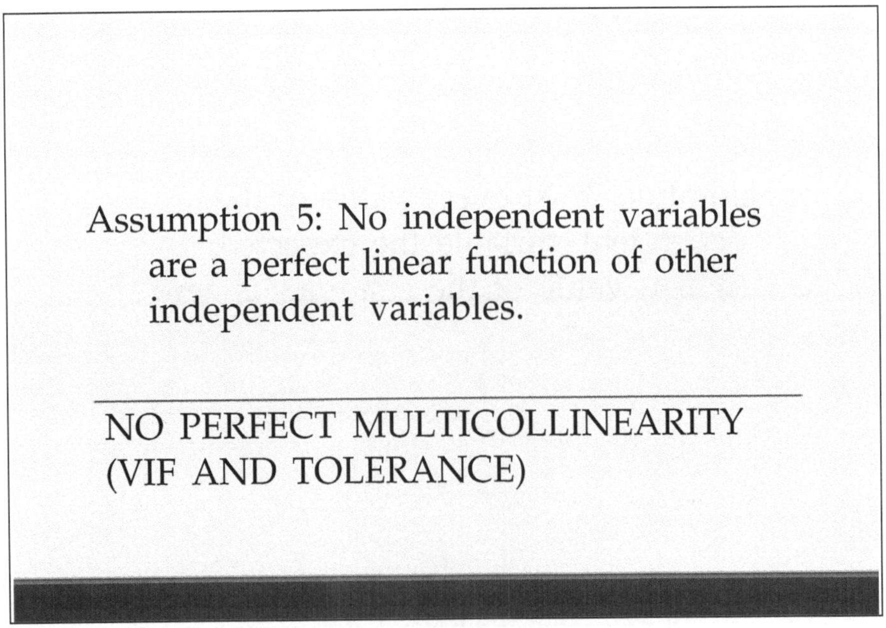

Fig. 4.11: Assumption 5
Source: based on review of literature

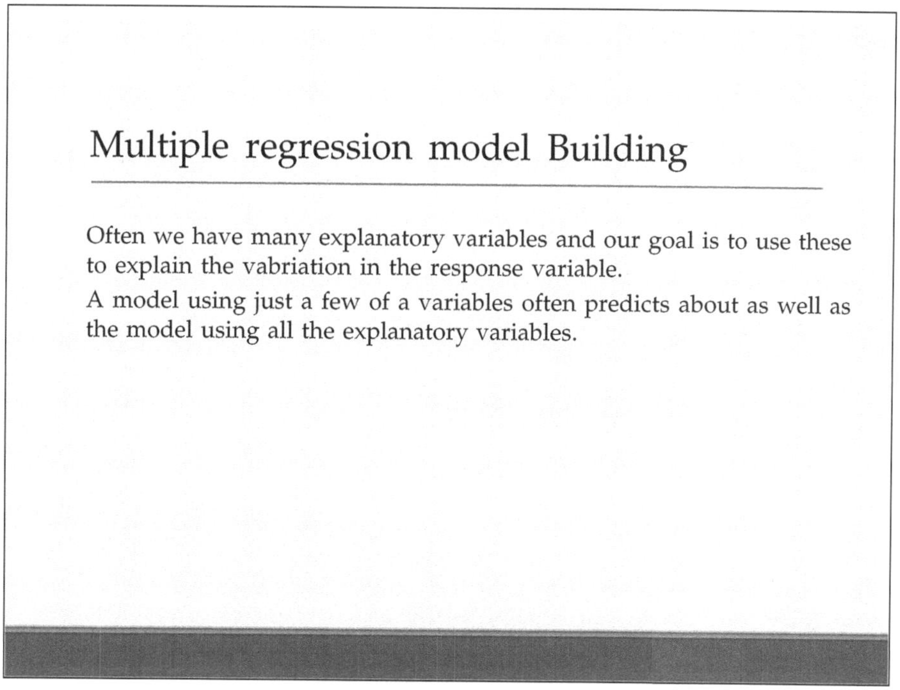

Fig. 4.12: Multiple regression model building
Source: based on review of literature

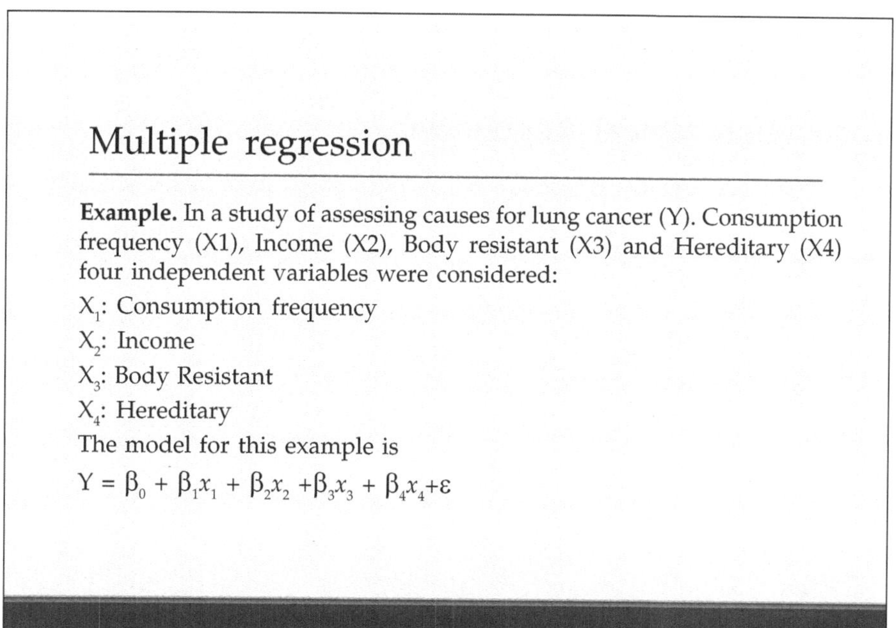

Fig. 4.13: Multiple regression
Source: based on review of literature

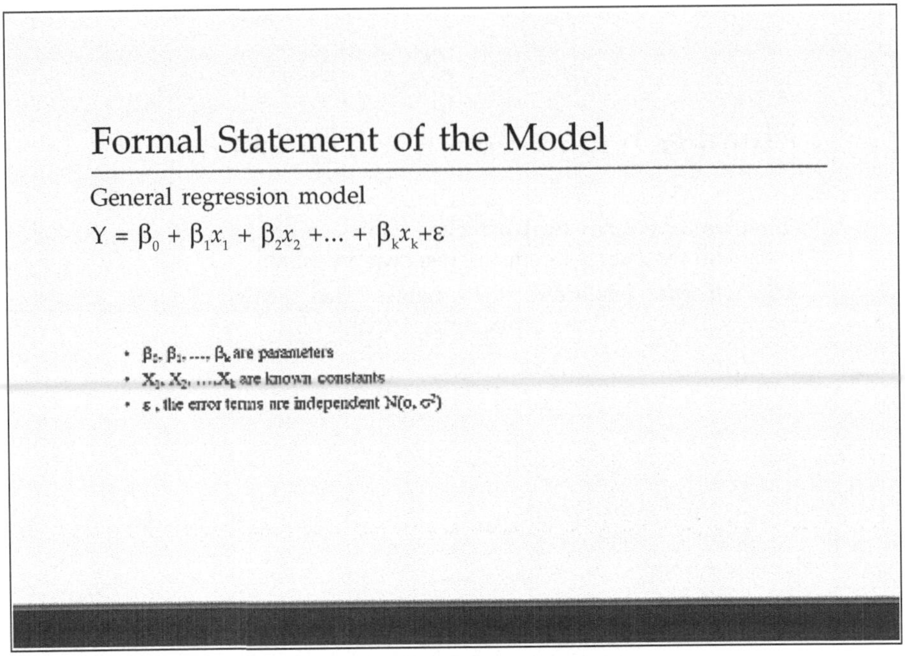

Fig. 4.14: Formal Statement of the Model

Source: based on review of literaturee

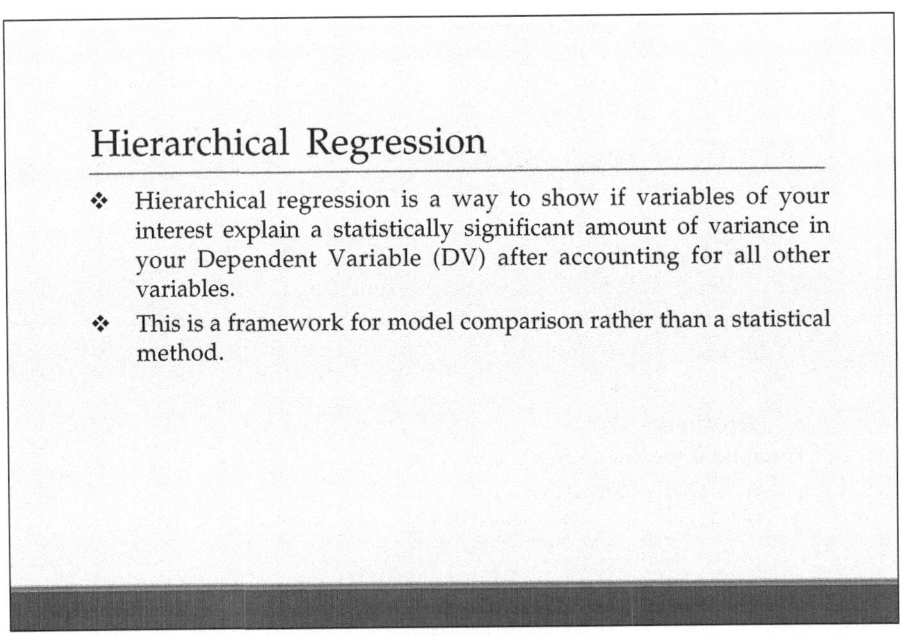

Fig. 4.15: Hierarchical Regression

Source: based on review of literatur

CONCLUSION

A research design is the set of methods and procedures used in collecting and analyzing measures of the variables specified in the problem research. The design of a study defines the study type (descriptive, correlation, semi-experimental, experimental, review, meta-analytic) and sub-type (e.g., descriptive-longitudinal case study), research problem, hypotheses, independent and dependent variables, experimental design, and, if applicable, data collection methods and a statistical analysis plan. A research design is a framework that has been created to find answers to research questions.

REFERENCES

https://en.wikipedia.org/wiki/Research_design

https://www.questionpro.com › Home › Consumer Insights › Market Research

https://libguides.usc.edu/writingguide/researchdesigns

https://explorable.com/research-designs

https://guides.lib.vt.edu/researchmethods/design-method

https://www.nyu.edu/classes/bkg/methods/005847ch1.pdf

https://cirt.gcu.edu/research/developmentresources/research.../quantresearch/approach.

https://www.scribbr.com › Knowledge Base › Starting the research process

https://scholarshipfellow.com › Blog

https://library.sacredheart.edu/c.php?g=29803&p=185902

Pages: 34-52

Statistical Tools, Data and Instrumentation in Research and Science

Edited by: **Er. Chhavi Kumar 'Bharti'; Dr. Prasann Kumar and Dr. Pawan Kumar 'Bharti'**

ISBN: 978-93-88854-51-1

Edition: **2020**

Published by: **Discovery Publishing House Pvt. Ltd., New Delhi (India)**

5

MATLAB
Tool for Research

Prasann Kumar[1,2*] and Shipa Rani Dey[1]

GRAPHICAL ABSTRACT

Keywords: Data

[1] Department of Agronomy, School of Agriculture, Lovely Professional University, Jalandhar - 144 411 Punjab (India)

[2] Divison of Research and Development, Lovely Professional University, Jalandhar - 144 411 Punjab, (India)

INTRODUCTION

- As a Programming Language
- As a Toolbox for various fields

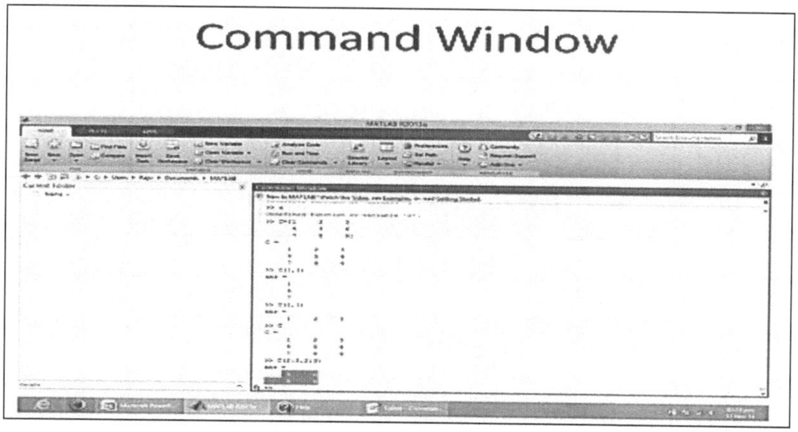

Fig. 5.1: Command Window

Source: Based on review of literature

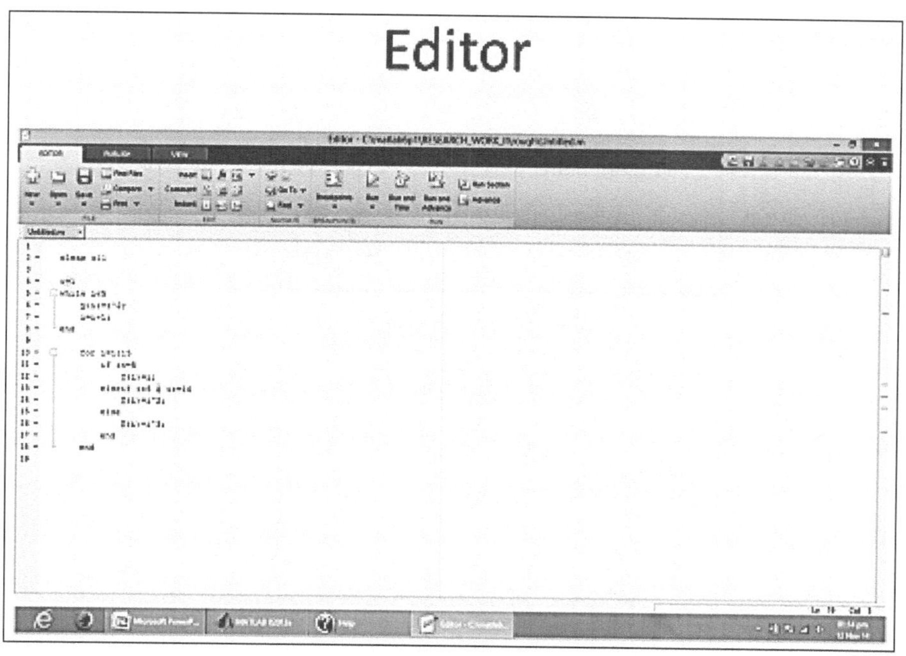

Fig. 5.2: Editor

Source: Based on review of literature

- Control system toolbox
- System identification toolbox
- Optimization toolbox
- Digital signal processing toolbox
- Robust control toolbox
- Neural Network toolbox
- Fuzzy logic toolbox etc

Fig. 5.3: Toolboxes

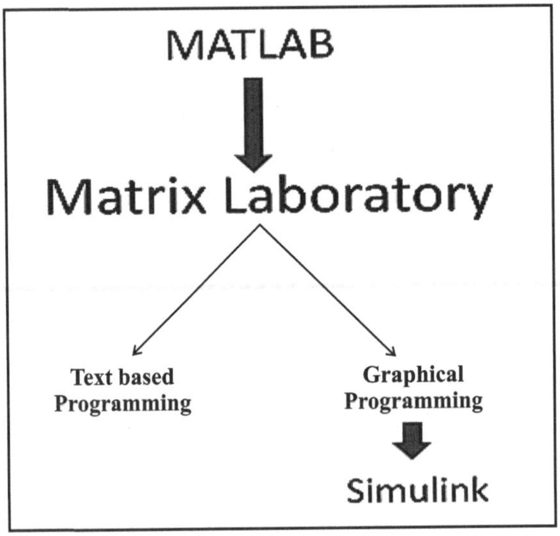

Fig. 5.4: Matrix Laboratory

Source: Based on review of literature

Matrix Manipulation

```
A=[1 2 3 4 5]
B=[10
   20
   30
   40
   50]
A*B=1*10+2*20+3*30+4*40+5*50=550
```

Fig. 5.5: Matrix Manipulation

Source: based on review of literature

Matrix Manipulation.....

```
A'=[1
    2
    3
    4
    5]
C=[ 1  2  3
    4  5  6
    7  8  9 ]
C=[1 2 3;4 5 6; 7 8 9]
```

Fig. 5.6: Continuation of figure 5.5

Source: Based on review of literature

Matrix Manipulation.....

```
D=[1 2 3; 4 6 2; 1 6 8]

E=inv(D)= [1.2000   0.0667  -0.4667
          -1.0000   0.1667   0.3333
           0.6000  -0.1333  -0.0667]
F=det(D)=30
```

Fig. 5.7: Continuation of figure 5.6

Source: Based on review of literature

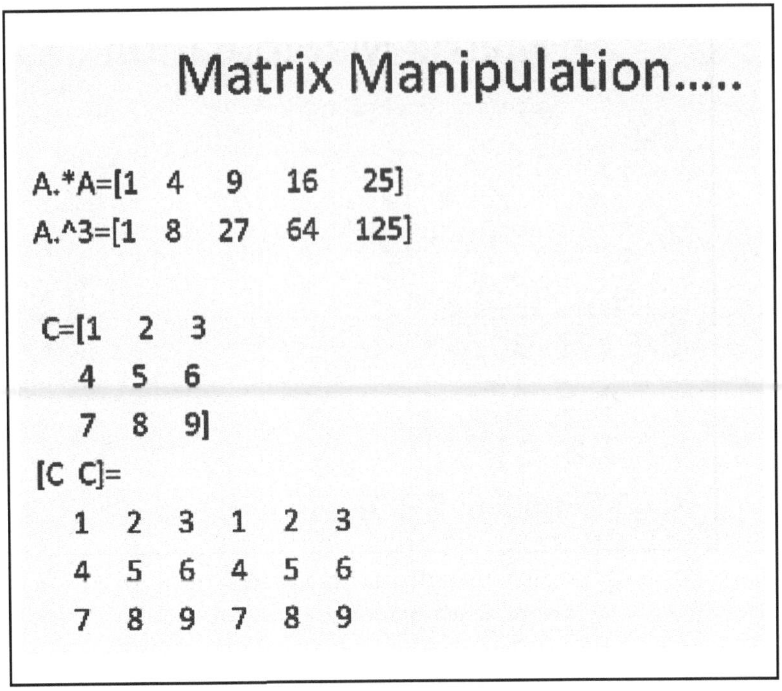

Fig. 5.8: Continuation of figure 5.7

Source: Based on review of literature

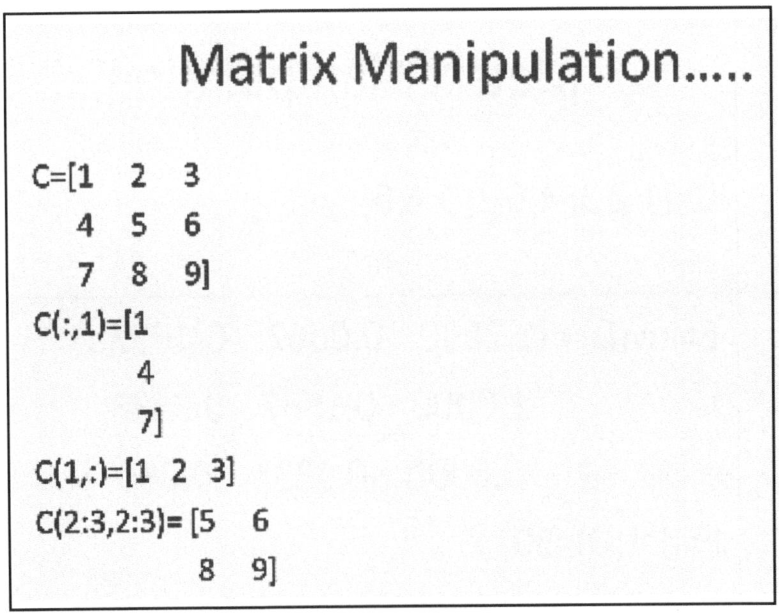

Fig. 5.9: Continuation of figure 5.8

Source: Based on review of literature

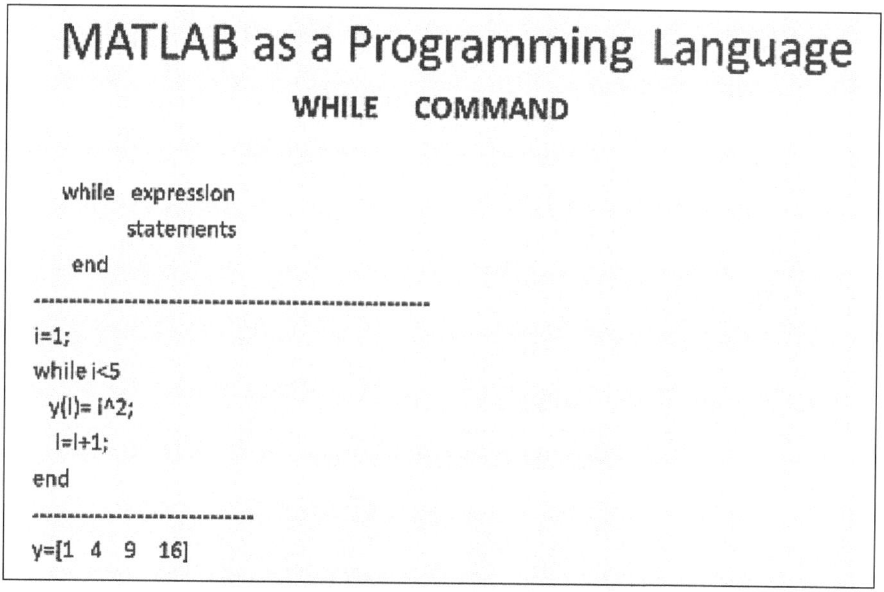

Fig. 5.10: MATLAB as a programming language
Source: Based on review of literature

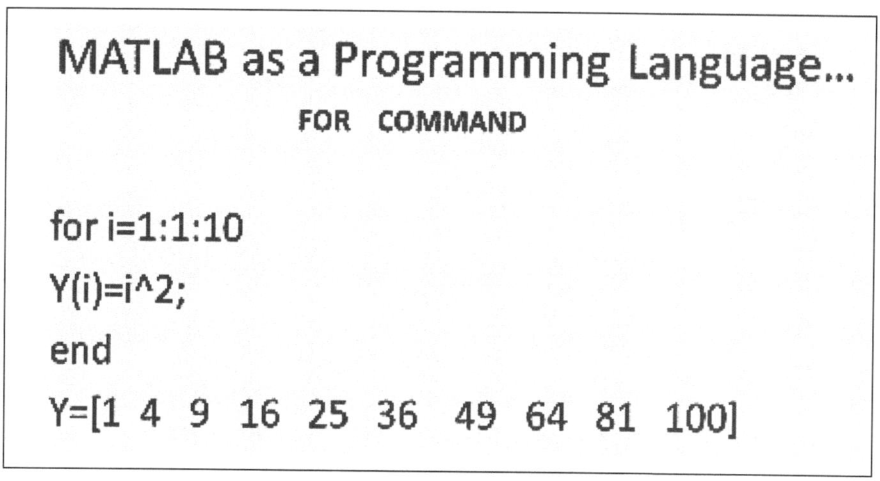

Fig. 5.11: Continuation of figure 5.10
Source: Based on review of literature

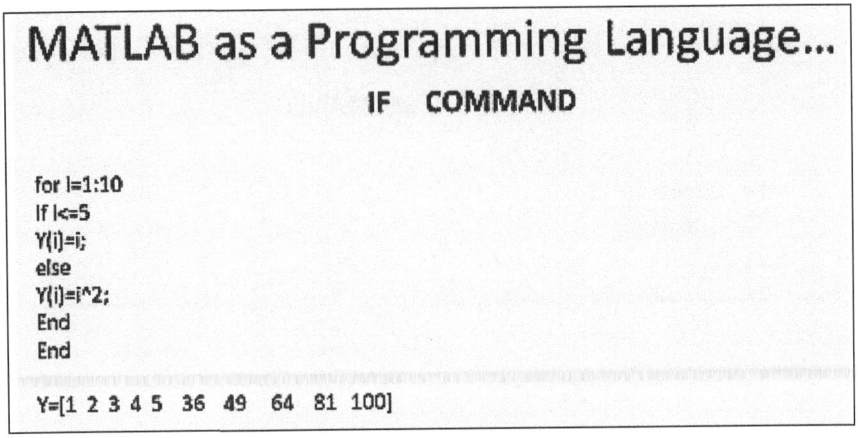

Fig. 5.12: Continuation of Figure 11

Source: Based on review of literature

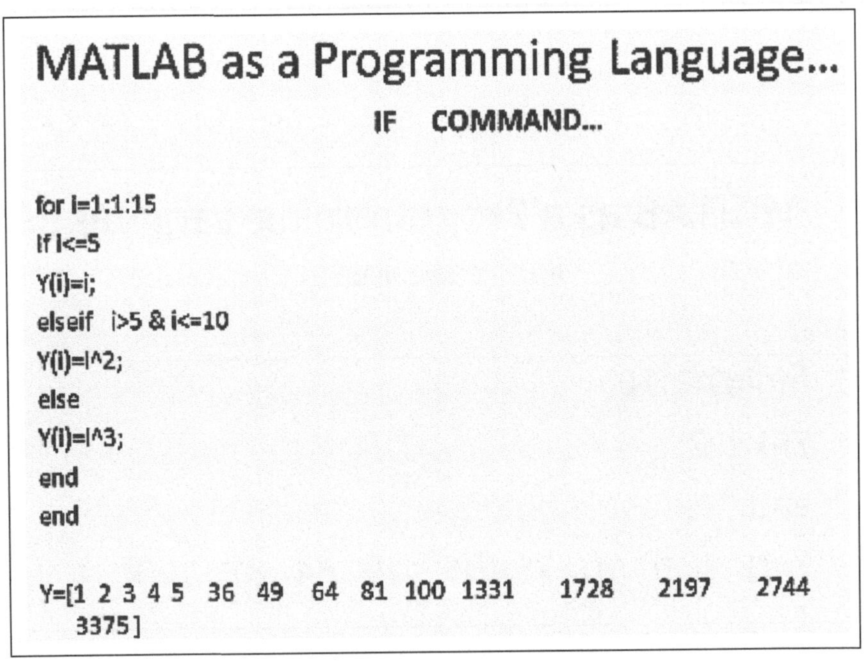

Fig. 5.13: Continuation of figure 5.12

Source: Based on review of literature

MATLAB as a Programming Language...

BREAK COMMAND...

```
for i=1:15
    Y(i)=i;
    if i==7
    break;
    end
  end
Y =
   1   2   3   4   5   6   7
```

Fig. 5.14: Continuation of figure 13

Source: Based on review of literature

MATLAB as a Programming Language...

Exit COMMAND...

```
for j=1:3
for i=1:5
  Y(i,j)=i;
  if i==4
  exit
  end
end
end
Y
```

Fig. 5.15: Continuation of 14

Source: Based on review of literature

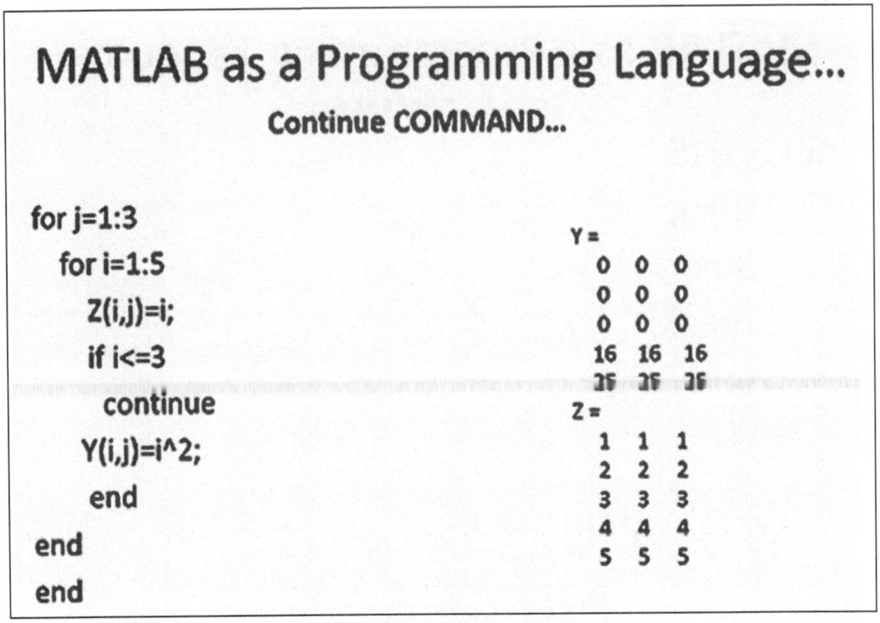

Fig. 5.16: Continuation of figure 5.15

Source: Based on review of literature

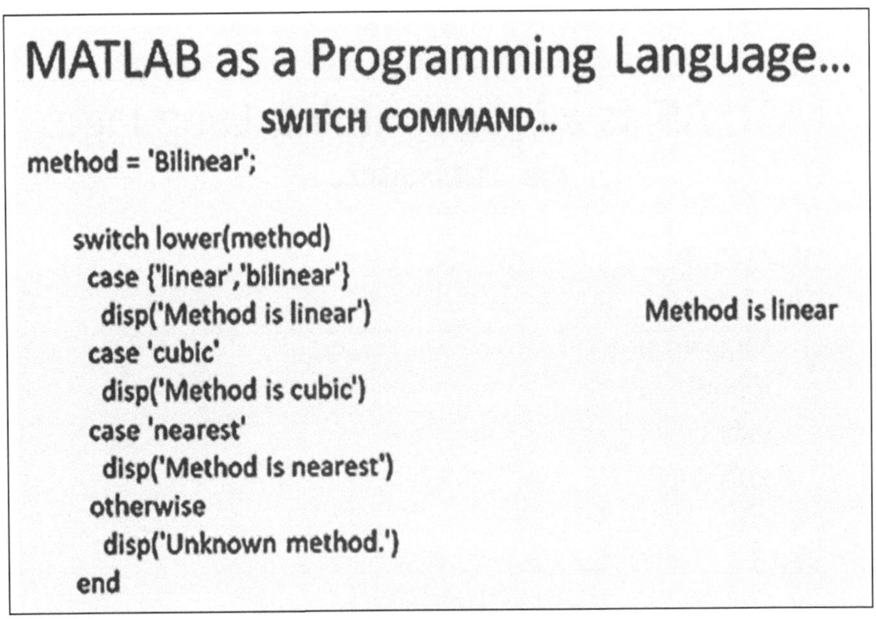

Fig. 5.17: Continuation of figure 5.16

Source: Based on review of literature

MATLAB as a Programming Language...

SWITCH COMMAND...

```
method = 'Bilinear';

  switch lower(method)
    case {'linear','bilinear'}
      disp('Method is linear')
    case 'cubic'
      disp('Method is cubic')
    case 'nearest'
      disp('Method is nearest')
    otherwise
      disp('Unknown method.')
  end
```

Method is linear

Fig. 5.18: Continuation of figure 5.17

Source: Based on review of literature

MATLAB as a Programming Language...

FUNCTION COMMAND...

```
A(:,:,1)=[i     i     i
          2*i  2*i   2*i
          3*i  3*i   3*i]
-----------------------------------------
function [AA]=fun(i)
AA=[i     i     i
    2*i  2*i   2*i
    3*i  3*i   3*i];

.........................................
for i=1:5
A(:,:,i)=fun(i);
end
```

Fig. 5.19: Continuation of figure 5.18

Source: Based on review of literature

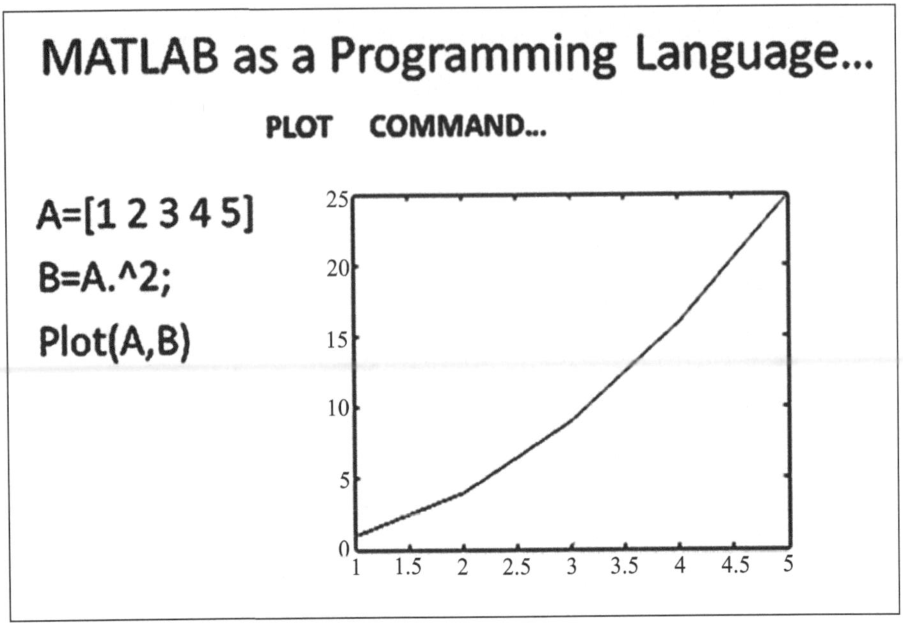

Fig. 5.20: Continuation of figure 5.19

Source: Based on review of literature

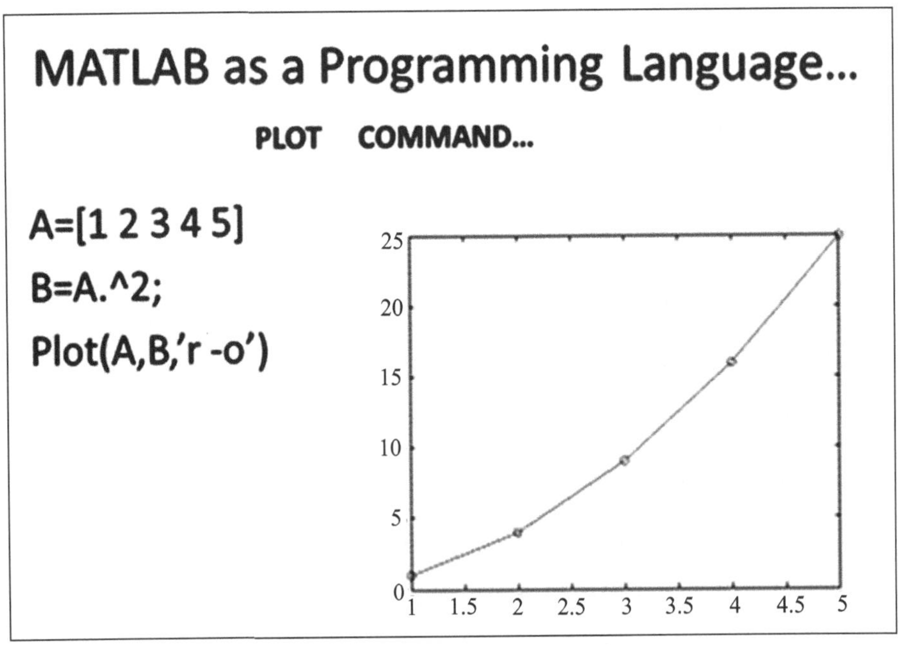

Fig. 5.21: Continuation of figure 5.20

Source: Based on review of literature

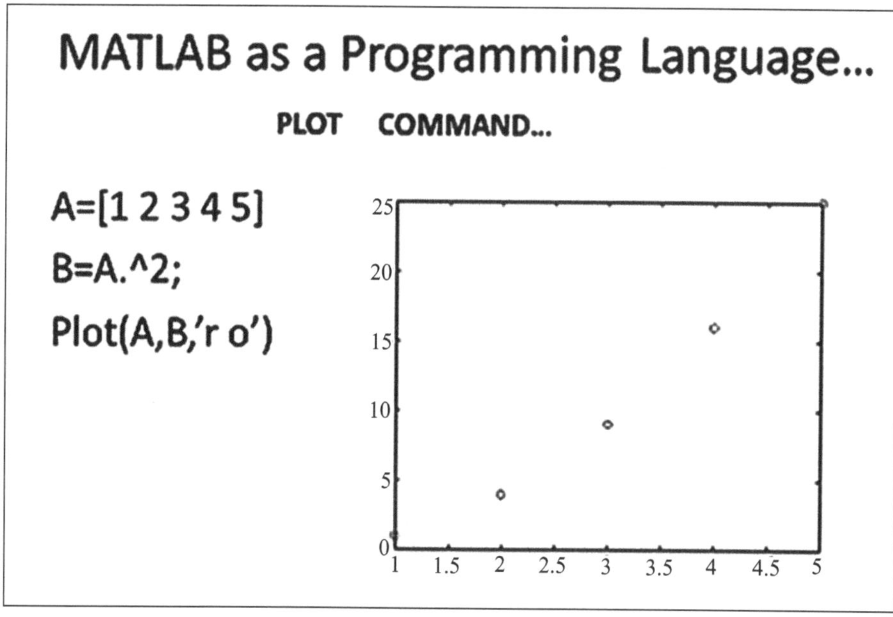

Fig. 5.22: Continuation of figure 5.21

Source: Based on review of literature

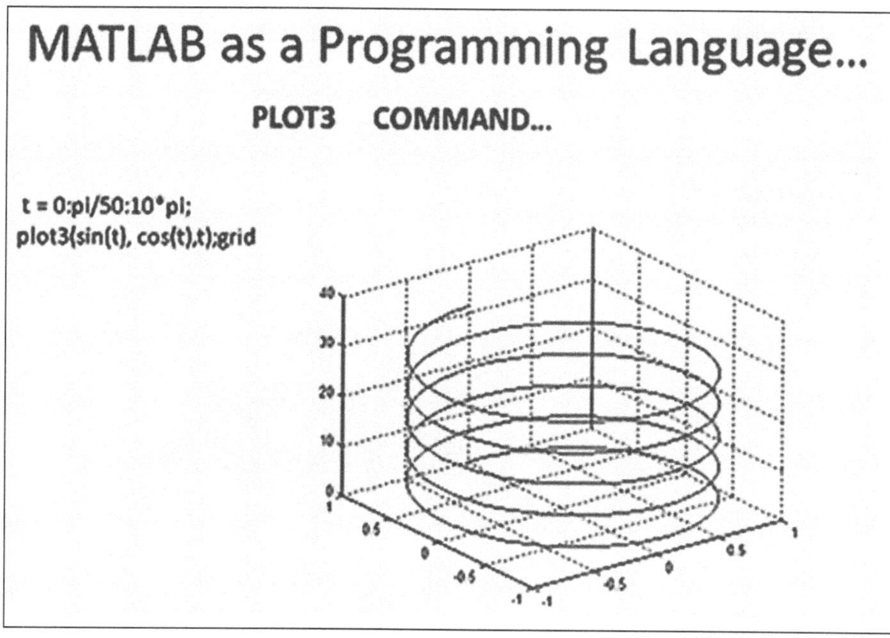

Fig. 5.23: PLOT3 Command

Source: Based on review of literature

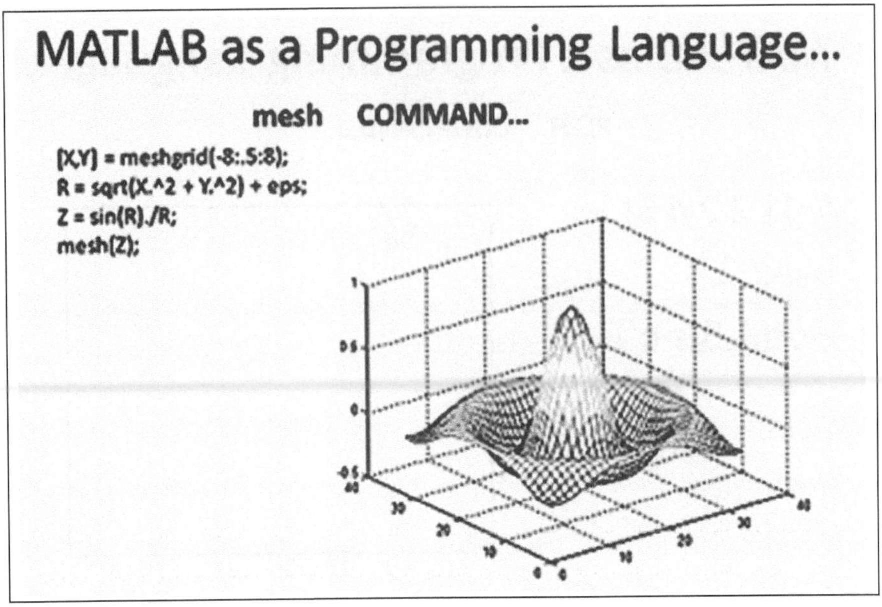

Fig. 5.24: mesh COMMAND

Source: Based on review of literature

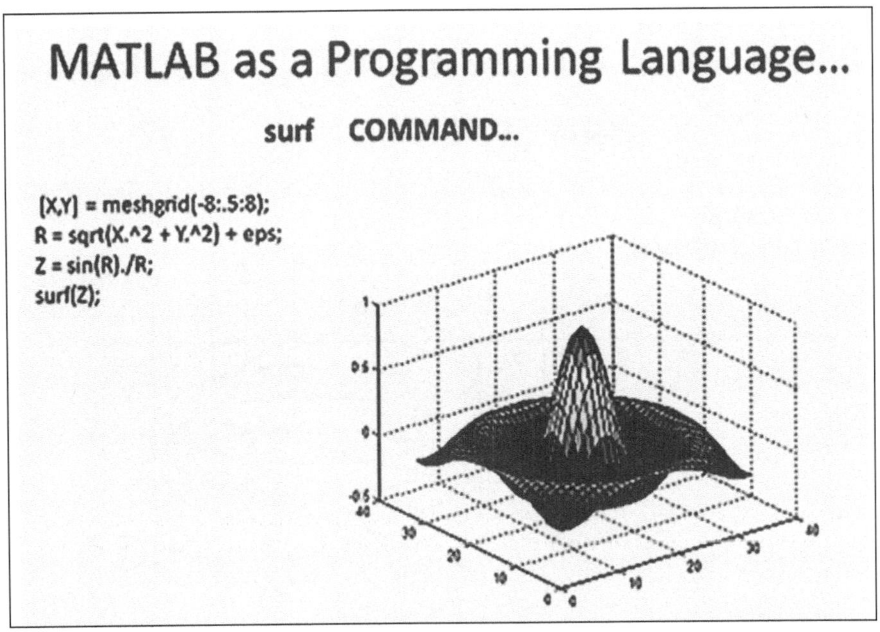

Fig. 5.25: surf COMMAND

Source: Based on review of literature

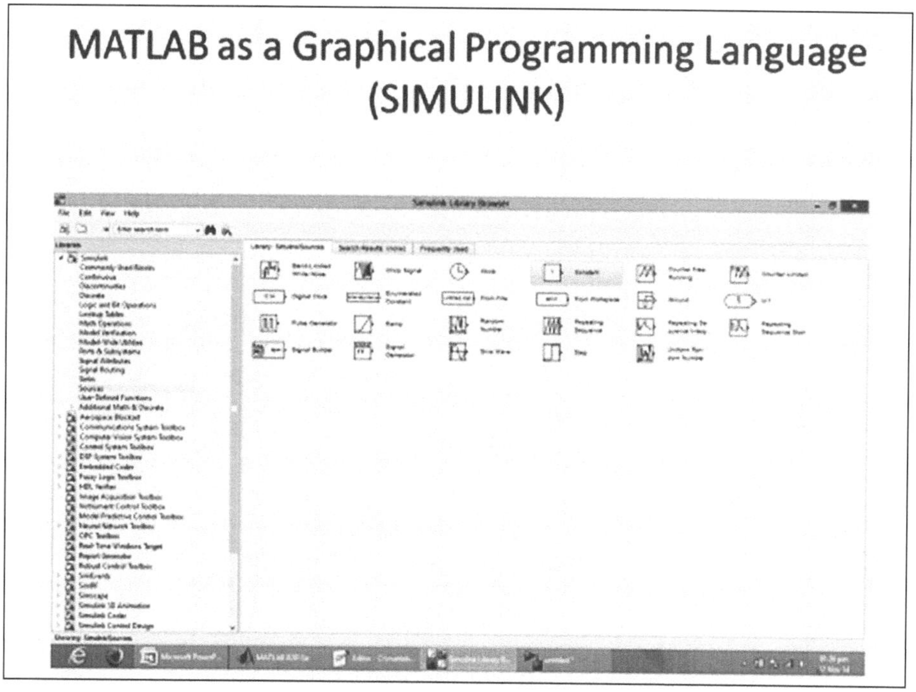

Fig. 5.26: SIMULINK
Source: Based on review of literature

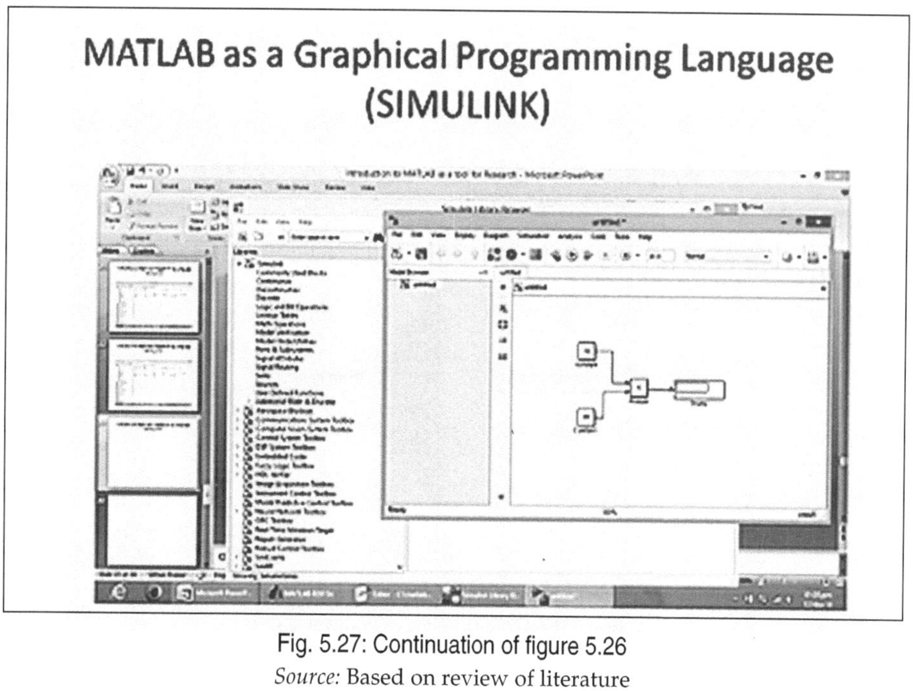

Fig. 5.27: Continuation of figure 5.26
Source: Based on review of literature

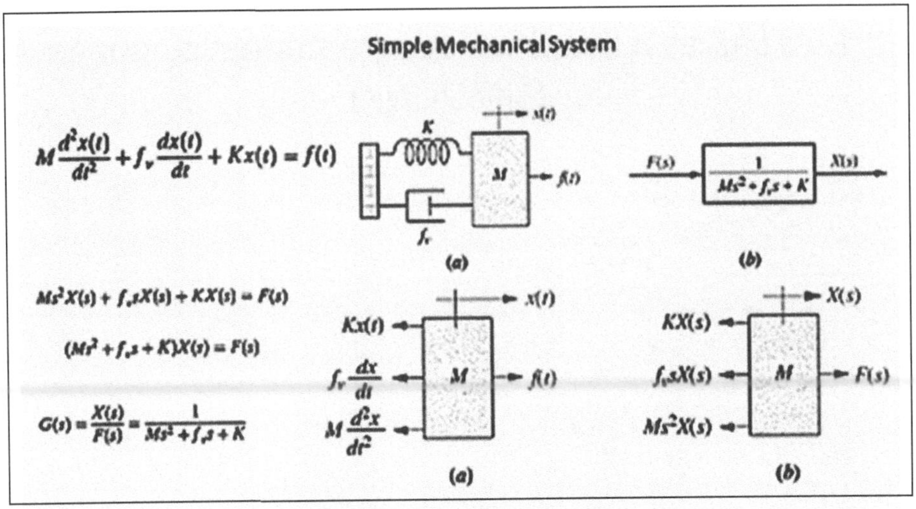

Fig. 5.28: Control System Toolbox

Source: Based on review of literature

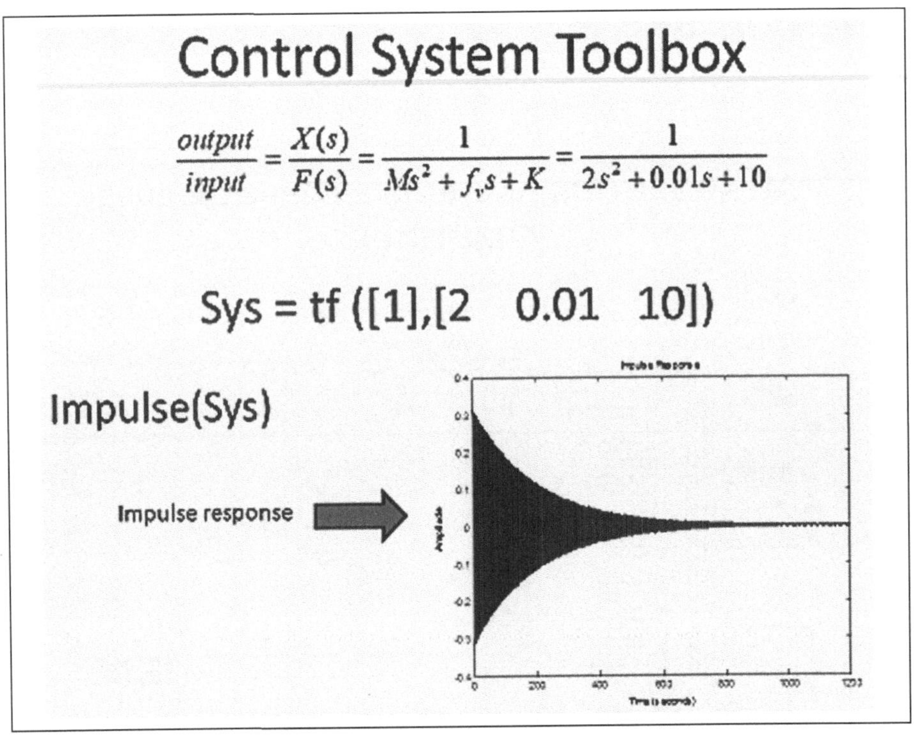

Fig. 5.29: Continuation of figure 5.28

Source: Based on review of literature

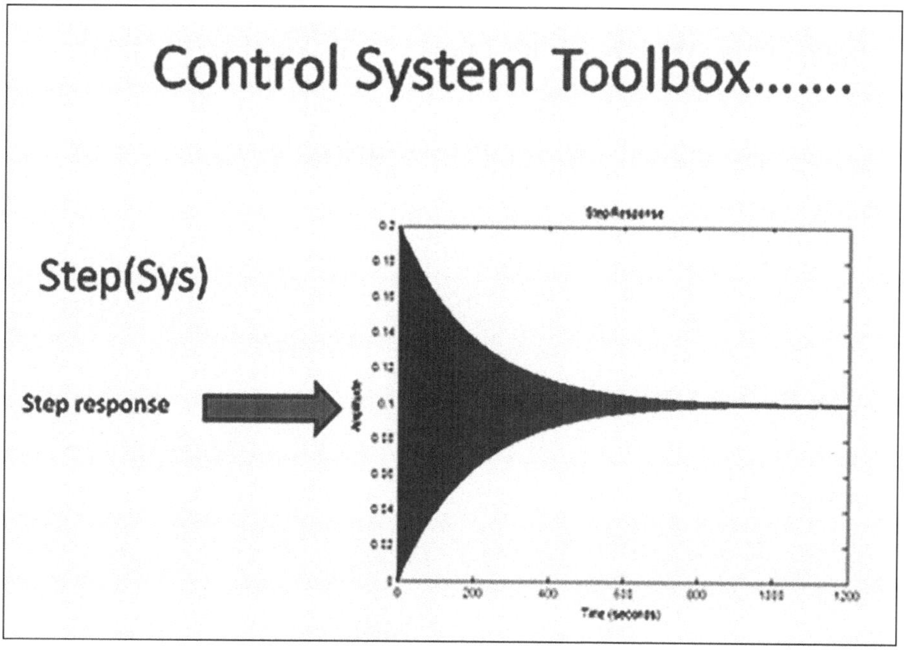

Fig. 5.30: Continuation of figure 5.29
Source: Based on review of literature

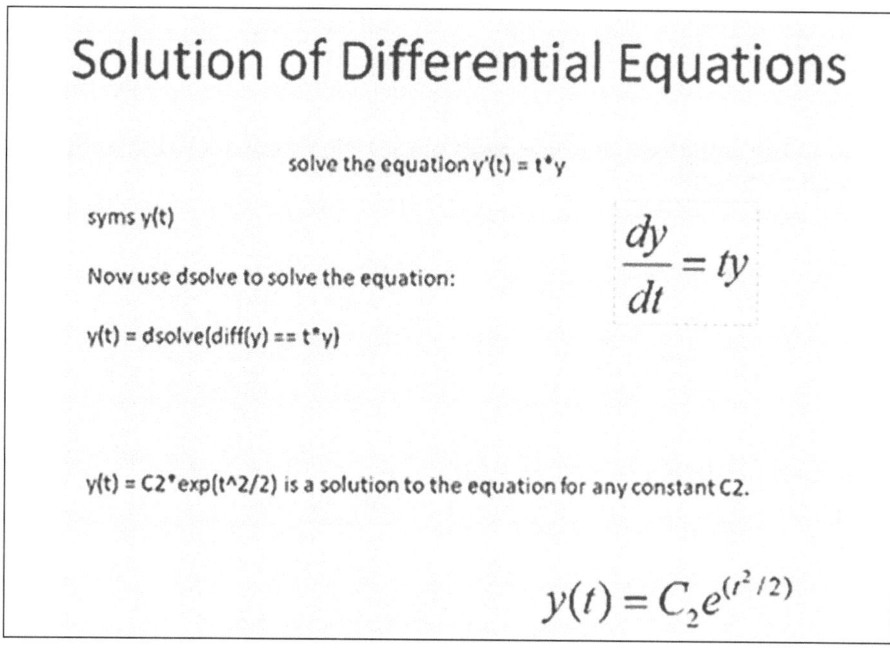

Fig. 5.31: Solution of differential equations
Source: Based on review of literature

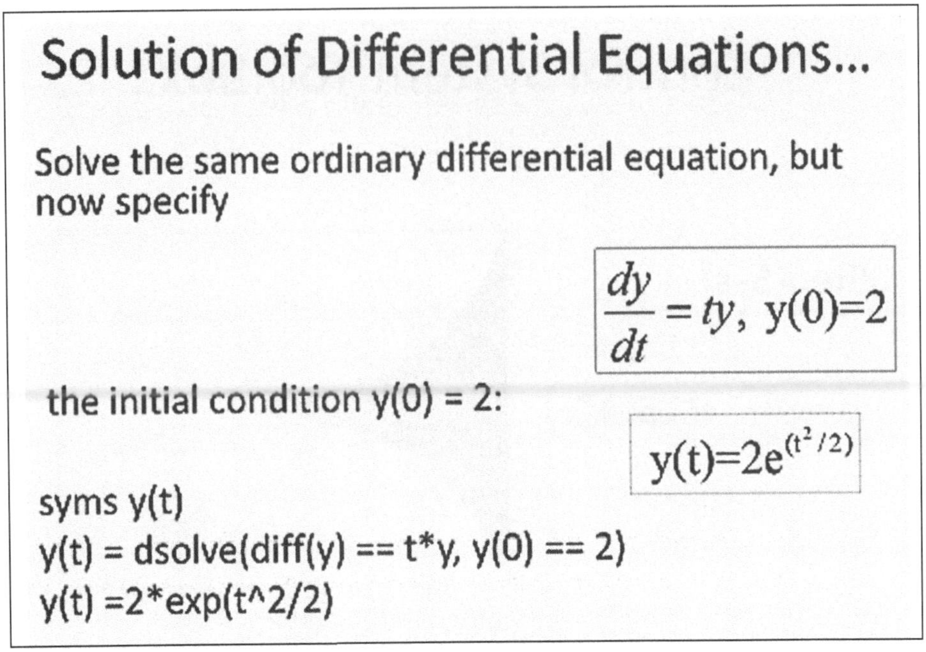

Fig. 5.32: Continuation of figure 5.31

Source: Based on review of literature

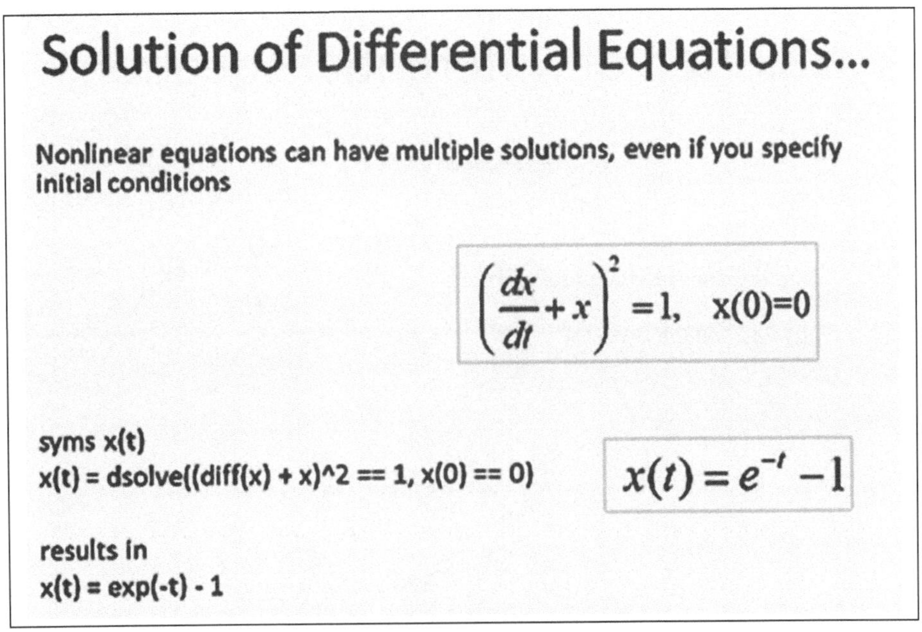

Fig. 5.33: Continuation of figure 5.32

Source: based on review of literature

Solution of Differential Equations...

```
options = odeset('RelTol',1e-4,'AbsTol',[1e-4 1e-4 1e-5]);
[T,Y] = ode45(@rigid,[0 12],[0 1 1],options);
Plot(T,Y)

function dy = rigid(t,y)
dy = zeros(3,1);
% a column vector
dy(1) = y(2) * y(3);
dy(2) = -y(1) * y(3);
dy(3) = -0.51 * y(1) * y(2);
```

$$\frac{dy_1}{dt} = y_2 y_3 \quad , y_1(0) = 0$$

$$\frac{dy_2}{dt} = -y_1 y_3 \quad , y_2(0) = 1$$

$$\frac{dy_3}{dt} = -0.51 y_1 y_2 \quad , y_3(0) = 1$$

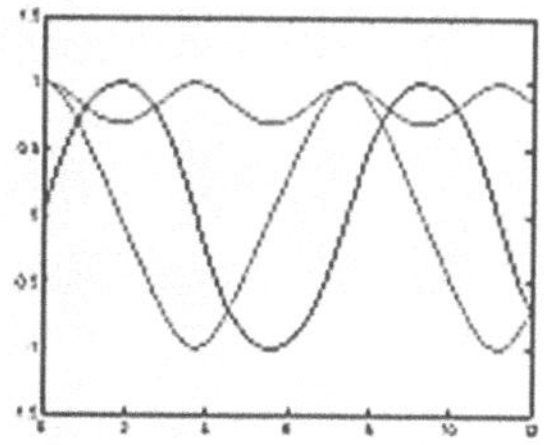

Fig. 5.34: Continuation of figure 5.33
Source: Based on review of literature

Solution of Differential Equations...

```
[T,Y] = ode15s(@vdp1000,[0 3000],[2 0]); Plot(T,Y)
```

$$\left(\frac{dy_1}{dt}\right)^{\cdot} = y_2 \qquad ,y_1(0) = 2$$

$$\left(\frac{dy_2}{dt}\right)^{\cdot} = 100(1 - y_1^2)y_2 - y_1 \quad ,y_2(0) = 0$$

```
function dy = vdp1000(t,y)
dy = zeros(2,1);   % a column vector
dy(1) = y(2);
dy(2) = 1000*(1 - y(1)^2)*y(2) - y(1);
```

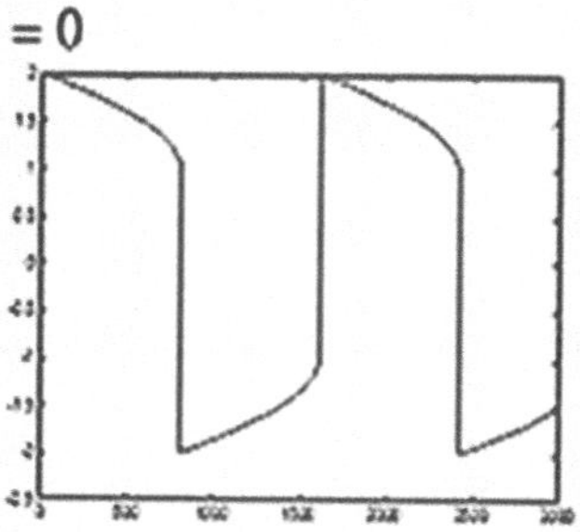

Fig. 5.35: Continuation of figure 5.34
Source: Based on review of literature

CONCLUSION

MATLAB is a high-performance language for technical computing. It integrates computation, visualization, and programming in an easy-to-use environment where problems and solutions are expressed in familiar mathematical notation. Typical uses include:

- Math and computation
- Algorithm development
- Modelling, simulation, and prototyping
- Data analysis, exploration, and visualization
- Scientific and engineering graphics
- Application development, including Graphical User Interface building

REFERENCES

https://en.wikipedia.org/wiki/MATLAB

https://cimss.ssec.wisc.edu/wxwise/class/aos340/spr00/whatismatlab.htm

https://www.mathworks.com/matlabcentral/.../121528-i-need-to-install-pso-research-to...

https://www.mathworks.com/academia/research.html

Pages: 53-68

Statistical Tools, Data and Instrumentation in Research and Science

Edited by: Er. Chhavi Kumar 'Bharti'; Dr. Prasann Kumar and Dr. Pawan Kumar 'Bharti'

ISBN: 978-93-88854-51-1

Edition: 2020

Published by: Discovery Publishing House Pvt. Ltd., New Delhi (India)

6

Biological Data base for Quick Research

Prasann Kumar[1,2*] and Shipa Rani Dey[1]

GRAPHICAL ABSTRACT

[1] Department of Agronomy, School of Agriculture, Lovely Professional University, Jalandhar - 144 411 Punjab (India)

[2] Divison of Research and Development, Lovely Professional University, Jalandhar - 144 411 Punjab, (India)

INTRODUCTION

WHAT is a database?

- A collection of data that needs to be:
  - Structured
  - Searchable
  - Updated (periodically)
  - Cross referenced
- Challenge:
  - To change "meaningless" data into useful information that can be accessed and analysed the best way possible.

For example:

HOW would YOU organise all biological sequences so that the biological information is optimally accessible?

You need an appropriate database management system (DBMS)

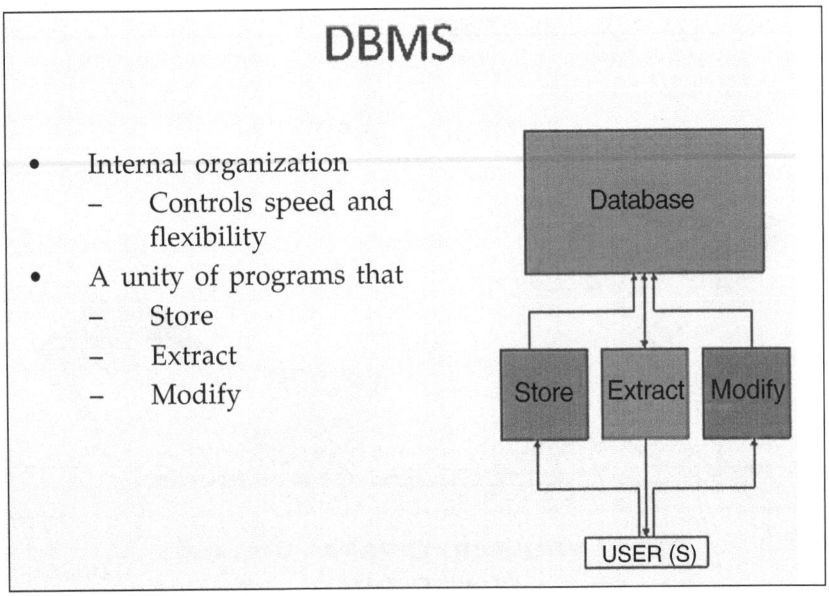

Fig. 6.1: DBMS

Source: Based on review of literature

DBMS organisation types

- Flat file databases (flat DBMS)
  - Simple, restrictive, table
- Hierarchical databases (hierarchical DBMS)
  - Simple, restrictive, tables

- Relational databases (RDBMS)
  - Complex,versatile, tables
- Object-oriented databases (ODBMS)
  - Complex, versatile, objects

Relational Databases

- Data is stored in multiple inter-related tables
- Data relationships across tables can be either many-to-one or many-to-many
- A few rules allow the database to be viewed in many ways
- Lets convert the "course details" to a relational database
- What have we achieved?
- No repeating information
- Less storage space
- Better reality representation
- Easy modification/management
- Easy usage of any combination of records

REMEMBER

The DBMS has programs to access and edit this information so ignore the human reading limitation of the primary keys.

Accessing Database Information

- A request for data from a database is called a *query*
- *Queries* can be of three forms:
  - Choose from a list of parameters
  - Query by example (QBE)
  - Query language

Query Language

- The standard
- SQL (Structured Query Language) originally called SEQUEL (Structured English QUEry Language)
- Developed by IBM in 1974; introduced commercially in 1979 by Oracle Corp.
- Standard interactive and programming language for getting information from and updating a database.
- RDMS (SQL), ODBMS (Java, C++, OQL etc)

Distributed databases

- From local to global attitude
- Data appears to be in one location but is most definitely not

- A definition: Two or more data files in different locations, periodically synchronized by the DBMS to keep data in all locations consistent
- An intricate network for combining and sharing information
- Administrators praise fast network technologies!!!
- Users praise the internet!!!

Data warehouse

- Periodically, one imports data from databases and store it (locally) in the data warehouse.
- Now a local database can be created, containing for instance protein family data (sequence, structure, function and pathway/ process data integrated with the gene expression and other experimental data).
- Disadvantage: expensive, intensive, needs to be updated.
- Advantage: easy control of integrated data-mining pipeline.

Why biological databases ?

- Exponential growth in biological data.
- Data (genomic sequences, 3D structures, 2D gel analysis, MS analysis, Microarrays ...) are no longer published in a conventional manner, but directly submitted to databases.
- Essential tools for biological research.

Fig. 6.2: Why biological data base?

Source: Based on review of literature

So why do biologists care?

Three main reasons:

- Database and data proliferation and specialization
  - Dozens to hundreds at the moment
- More and more scientific discoveries result from inter-database analysis and mining
- Rising complexity of required data-combinations
  - E.g. translational medicine: "from bench to bedside" (genomic data vs. clinical data)

Categories of databases for Life Sciences

- Sequences (DNA, protein)

- Genomics
- Mutation/polymorphism
- Protein domain/family (——> tools)
- Proteomics (2D gel, Mass Spectrometry)
- 3D structure
- Metabolism
- Bibliography
- 'Others' (Microarrays,...)
- Like any other database
- Data organization for optimal analysis
- Data is of different types
- Raw data (DNA, RNA, protein sequences)
- Curated data (DNA, RNA and protein annotated sequences and structures, expression data)

Using a database

- How to get information out of a database:
  - Summaries: how many entries, average or extreme values
  - Browsing: no targeted information to retrieve
  - Search: looking for particular information
- Searching a database:
  - Must have a key that identifies the element(s) of the database that are of interest.
    - Name of gene
    - Sequence of gene
    - Other information

Raw Biological data Nucleic Acids (DNA)

Symbol	Meaning	Explanation
G	G	Guanine
A	A	Adenine
T	T	Thymine
C	C	Cytosine
R	A or G	puRine
Y	C or T	pYrimidine
M	A or C	aMino
K	G or T	Keto
N	G, A, T or C	Any base

Fig. 6.3: Raw biological data (DNA)

Source: Based on review of literature

Raw Biological data Amino acid residues (proteins)

1-letter code	3-letter code	Amino acid
M	Met	Methionie
N	Asn	Aspargine
P	Pro	Proline
Q	Gln	Glutamine
R	Arg	Arginine
S	Ser	Serine
T	Thr	Threonine
V	Val	Valine
W	Trp	Tryptophan
Y	Tyr	Tyrosine
X	Xxx	Any amino acid

Fig. 6.4: Amino acid residues

Source: Based on review of literature

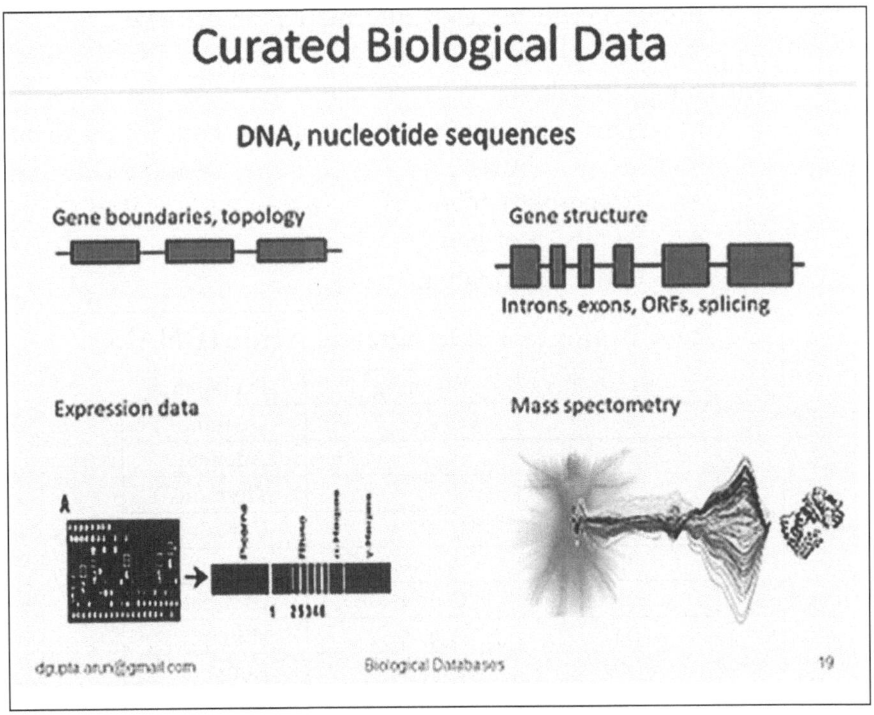

Fig. 6.5: Curated biological data for DNA

Source: Based on review of literature

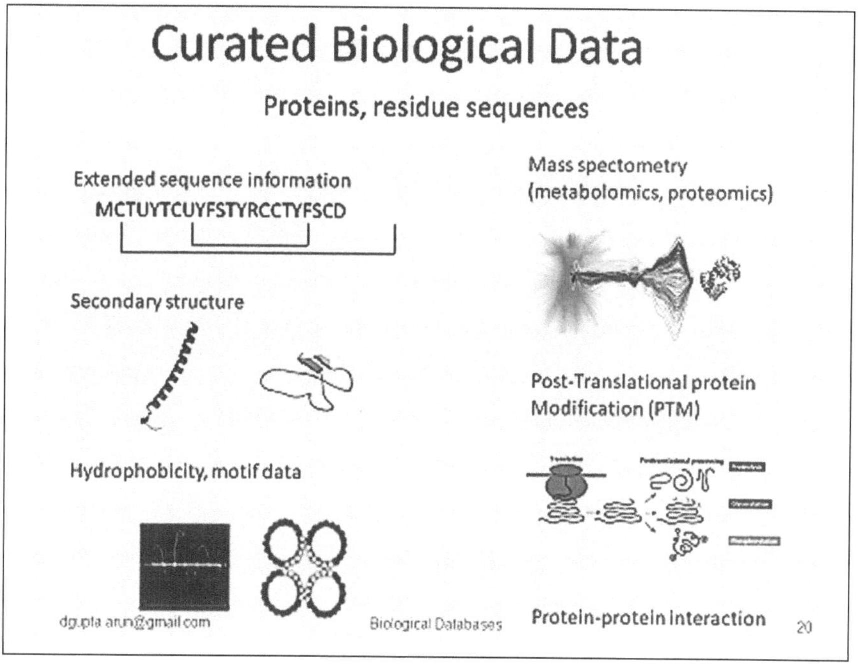

Fig. 6.6: Curated biological data for proteins
Source: Based on review of literature

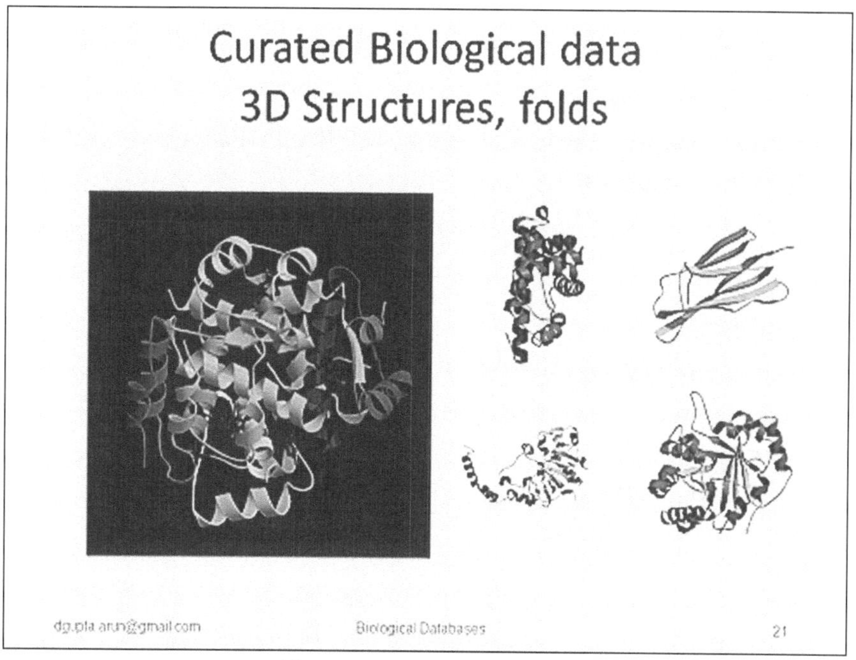

Fig. 6.7: 3D structure folds
Source: Based on review of literature

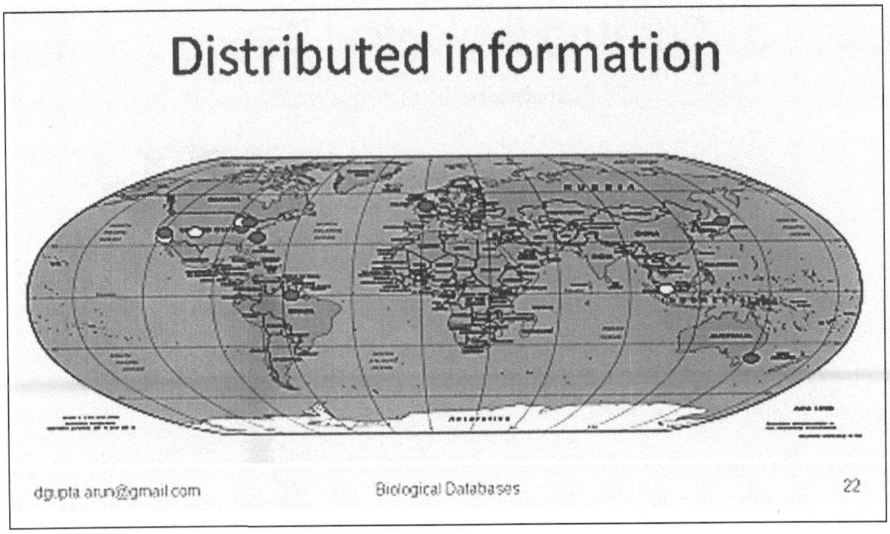

Fig. 6.8: Distribution information

Source: Based on review of literature

A few biological databases

- **Nucleotide Databases**

  Alternative Splicing, EMBL-Bank, Ensembl, Genomes Server, Genome, MOT, EMBL-Align, Simple Queries, dbSTS Queries, Parasites, Mutations, IMGT
- **Genome Databases**

  Human, Mouse, Yeast, C.elegans, FLYBASE, Parasites
- **Protein Databases**

  Swiss-Prot, TrEMBL, InterPro, CluSTr, IPI, GOA, GO, Proteome Analysis, HPI, IntEnz, TrEMBLnew, SP_ML, NEWT, PANDIT
- **Structure Databases**

  PDB, MSD, FSSP, DALI
- **Microarray Database**

  ArrayExpress
- **Literature Databases**

  MEDLINE, Software Biocatalog, Flybase Archives
- **Alignment Databases**

  BAliBASE, Homstrad, FSSP
- Data storage management:
  - flat file: text file
  - relational (e.g., Oracle, Postgres)

- object oriented (rare in biological field)
- Flat file format:
- fasta
- GCG
- NBRF/PIR
- MSF....
- standardized format ?

Ideal minimal content of a << sequence >> db

- Sequences II
- Accession number (AC)
- Taxonomic data
- References
- Annotation/Curation
- Keywords
- Cross-references
- Documentation

Fig. 6.9: Ideal minimal content of a sequence
Source: based on review of literature

Database 1: nucleotide sequences

- The main DNA sequence db are EMBL (Europe)/GenBank (USA)/ DDBJ (Japan)
- There are also specialized databases for the different types of RNAs (i.e. tRNA, rRNA, tm RNA, uRNA, etc.)
- 3D structure (DNA and RNA)
- Others: Aberrant splicing db; Eucaryotic promotor db (EPD); RNA editing sites, Multimedia Telomere Resource...

Fig. 6.10: Database 1: nucleotide sequences
Source: based on review of literature

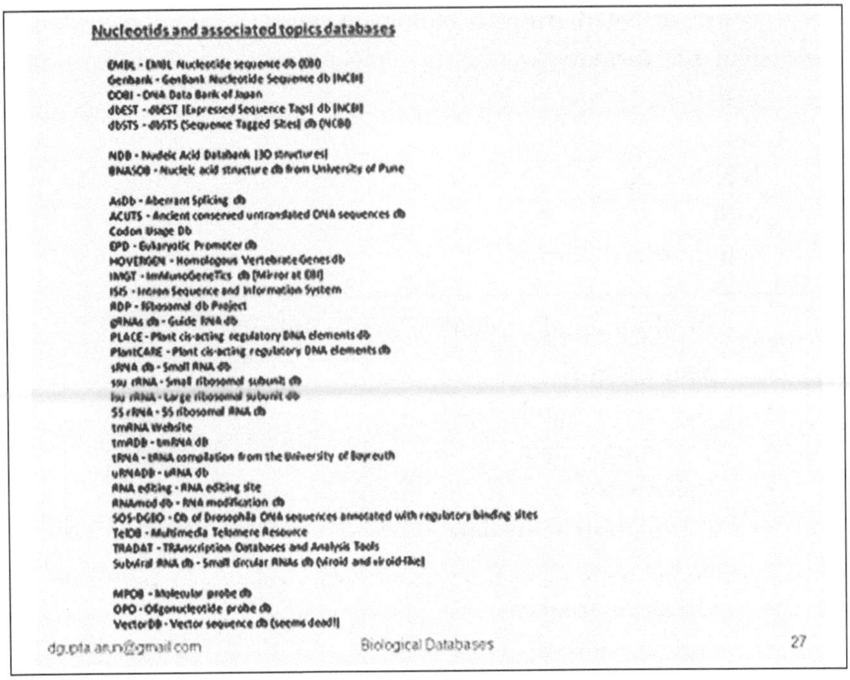

Fig. 6.11: Nucleotides and associated topic data bases

Source: Based on review of literature

EMBL/GenBank/DDBJ

- These 3 db contain mainly the same informations within 2-3 days (few differences in the format and syntax)
- Serve as **archieves** containing all sequences (single genes, ESTs, complete genomes, etc.) derived from:
  - Genome projects
  - Sequencing centers
  - Individual scientists
  - Patent offices (i.e. European Patent Office, EPO)
- Non-confidential data is exchanged daily
- Currently: approx 18×10^{10} sequences, over 92×10^{15} bp;
  - Over the last 12 months the database size has tripled

Fig. 6.12: EMBL/GenBank/DDBJ

Source: Based on review of literature

EMBL/GenBank/DDBJ

- **Archive** containing all sequences from:
  - genome projects
  - sequencing centers
  - individual scientists
  - patent offices
- Database is doubling every 8-10 months
- Sequences from >200,000 different species
- >1000 new species added every month

EMBL/GenBank/DDBJ

- Heterogeneous sequence length: genomes, variants, fragments...
- Sequence sizes:
  - max 300'000 bp/entry (!genomic sequences, overlapping
  - min 10 bp/entry
- **Archive:** nothing goes out -> highly redundant !
- full of errors: in sequences, in annotations, in CDS attribution...
- no consistency of annotations; most annotations are done by the submitters; heterogeneity of the quality and the completion and updating of the informations

Fig. 6.13: EMBL/GenBank/DDBJ

Source: Based on review of literature

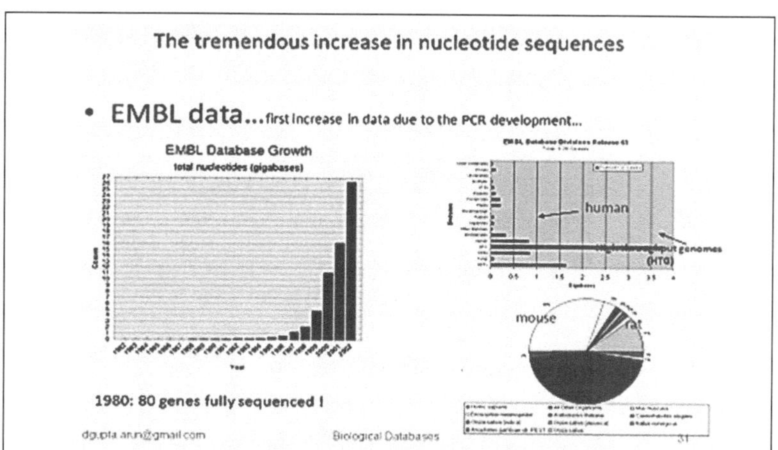

Fig. 6.14: Nucleotide sequences

Source: Based on review of literature

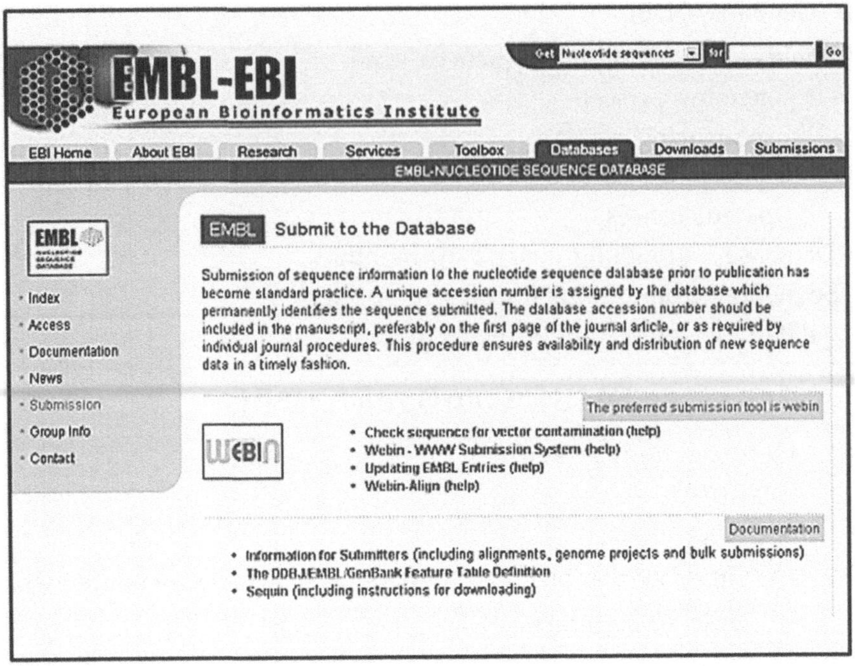

Fig. 6.15: EMBL-EBI

Source: Based on review of literature

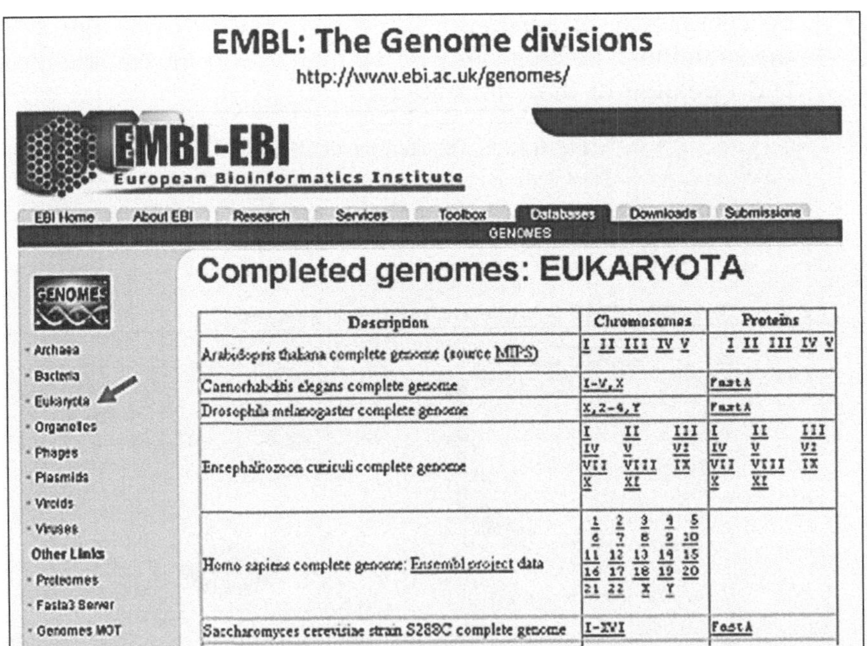

Fig. 6.16: EMBL: The Genome divisions

Source: Based on review of literature

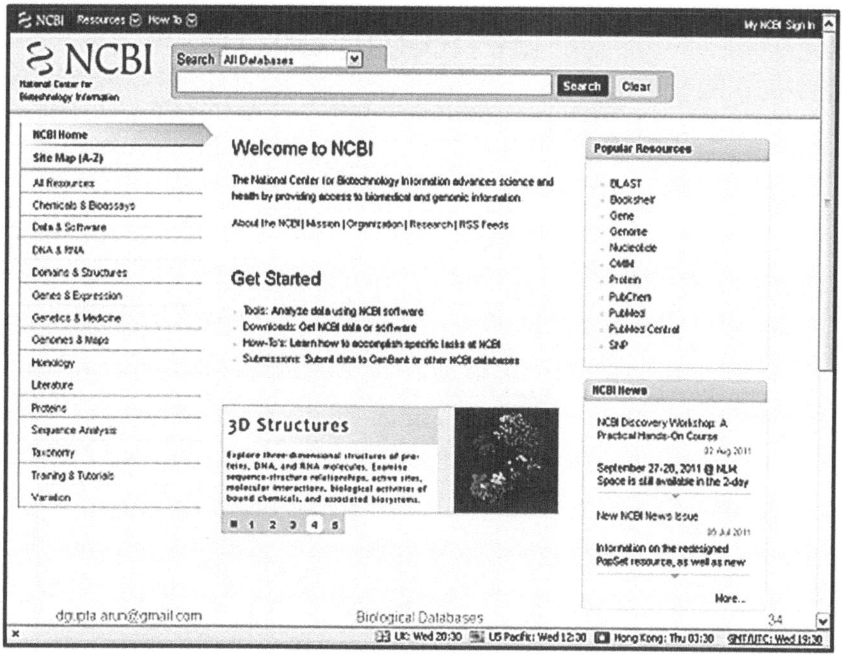

Fig. 6.17: NCBI

Source: Based on review of literature

Fig. 6.18: DDBJ

Source: Based on review of literature

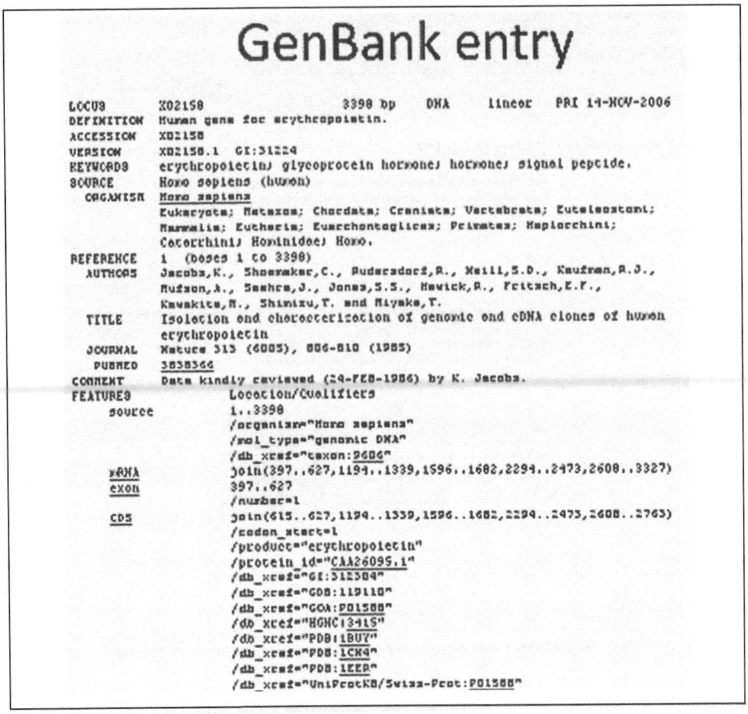

Fig. 6.19: GenBank entry

Source: Based on review of literature

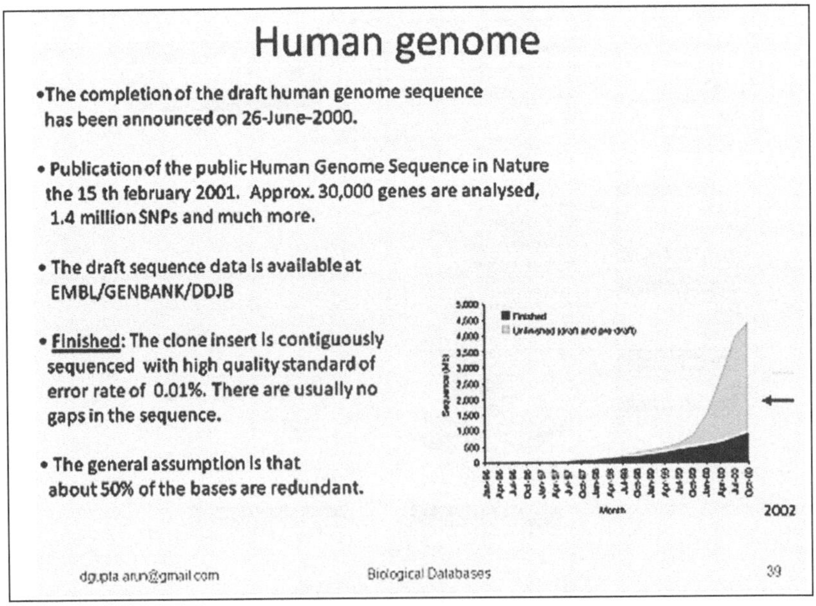

Fig. 6.20: Human genome

Source: Based on review of literature

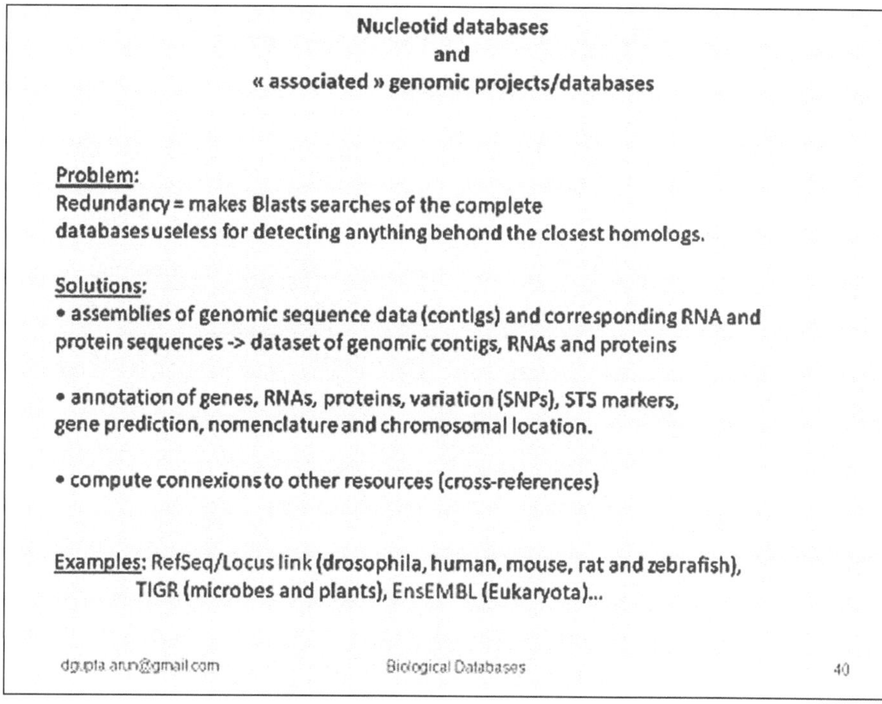

Fig. 6.21: Nucleotide databases

Source: Based on review of literature

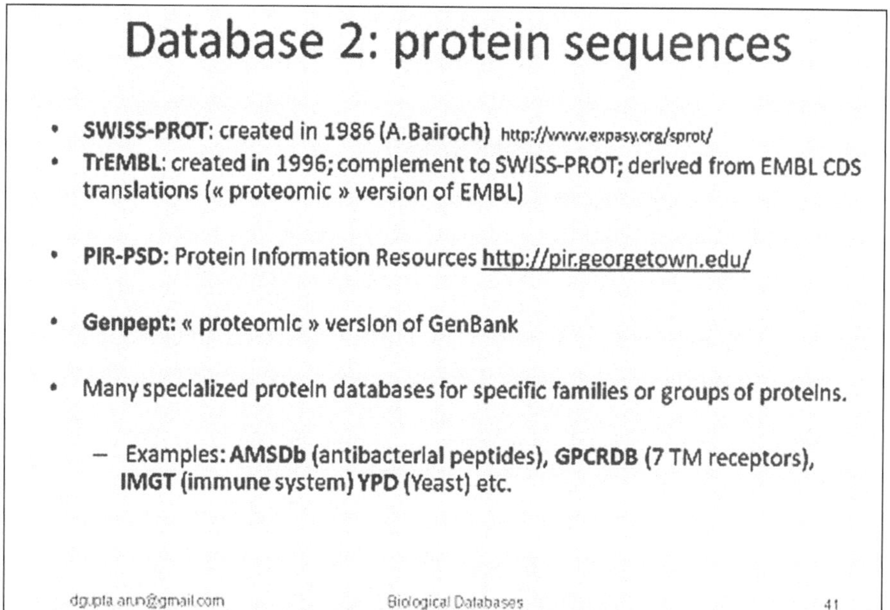

Fig. 6.22: Database 2: protein sequences

Source: Based on review of literature

Database 2: Protein sequence

What else ?

Database	Release#	Date	# of Entries
PIR	73.03	16-Aug-2002	283,224
SwissProt	40.26	13-Aug-2002	112,892
TrEMBL	21.7	09-Aug-2002	668,930
GenPept	130.0	15-June-2002	1,084,824
RefSeq		21-Aug-2002	379,148
PDF		19-Aut-2002	18,953

Fig. 6.23: Protein sequence

Source: Based on review of literature

CONCLUSION

Biological databases are libraries of life sciences information, collected from scientific experiments, published literature, high throughput experiment technology, and computational analysis. They contain information from research areas from research areas including genomics, proteomics, metabolomics, microarray gene expression, and phylogenetics. Information contained in biological databases includes gene function, structure, localization (both cellular and chromosomal), clinical effects of mutations as well as similarities of biological sequences and structures.

REFERENCES

https://en.wikipedia.org/wiki/Biological_database

https://en.wikipedia.org/wiki/List_of_biological_databases

https://bioinf.comav.upv.es/courses/biotech3/theory/databases.html

https://www.omicsonline.org/biological-databases-integration-of-life-scienc...

https://www.longdom.org/.../bioinformatics-databases-journals-articles-ppts...

https://www.enago.com/.../biological-databases-an-overview-and-future-pers..

https://www.ebi.ac.uk/training/online/.../primary-and-secondary-databases

https://www.mrc-lmb.cam.ac.uk/genomes/madanm/pdfs/biodbseq.pdf

https://www.ncbi.nlm.nih.gov/pmc/journals/973/

Pages: 69-84

Statistical Tools, Data and Instrumentation in Research and Science

Edited by: Er. Chhavi Kumar 'Bharti'; Dr. Prasann Kumar and Dr. Pawan Kumar 'Bharti'

ISBN: 978-93-88854-51-1

Edition: **2020**

Published by: **Discovery Publishing House Pvt. Ltd., New Delhi (India)**

7

Statistical Package for the Social Sciences

Prasann Kumar[1,2*] and Shipa Rani Dey[1]

GRAPHICAL ABSTRACT

Keywords: Average, Correlation, Histogram, Mean, Significance

[1] Department of Agronomy, School of Agriculture, Lovely Professional University, Jalandhar - 144 411 Punjab (India)

[2] Divison of Research and Development, Lovely Professional University, Jalandhar - 144 411 Punjab, (India)

INTRODUCTION

SPSS is a widely used program for statistical analysis in social science. It is also used by market researchers, health researchers, survey companies, government, education researchers, marketing organizations, data miners, and others. The original SPSS manual (Nie, Bent & Hull, 1970) has been described as one of "sociology's most influential books" for allowing ordinary researchers to do their own statistical analysis. In addition to statistical analysis, data management (case selection, file reshaping, creating derived data) and data documentation (a metadata dictionary is stored in the datafile) are features of the base software.

In this chapter, we are going to describes

- Using Basic Concepts of Research in Business Problems.
- Operating basic functions (file opening, data creation) through SPSS.
- Identification of metric and non metric data (scales).
- Producing frequencies, descriptive statistics, graphs and normality assessment of distribution through SPSS.

What is Research?

A systematic and scientific procedure of problem identification, data collection, compilation, analysis, interpretation, and developing implications pertaining to problem.

Types of Research

- Research can be undertaken for two different purposes :
- **Applied Research:** One is to solve a current problem faced in the work setting, demanding a timely solution.
- For e.g: a particular product may not be selling well and the manager might want to find the reasons for this in order to take corrective action. Such research is applied research.

  Examples
- Ex 1= Reason behind low sales (MKTG)
- Ex 2= High Attrition (HR)
- Ex 3= Social Science (MSJ & E) RGNF (Social Science)
- Ex 4= Videocon 2 G Spectrum
- Ex 5= Coca Cola Minute Maid low sales
- Ex 6= Study on Learning and Assessment Tools in Higher Education
- Ex7= CAW (ICSSR)

Basic Research: The other is to generate a body of knowledge by trying to comprehend how certain problems that occur in organizations can be solved.

- It is quite possible that some organizations may later on apply the knowledge gained by the findings of such basic research to solve their own problems. Eg : Research on Absenteeism by a University Professor
- Assists Higher Education Institutes and government
- Ex1 = Absenteeism (HR)
- Ex2= Consumer Brand Relationships (Emotional Aspects & Attitudinal Loyalty)
- Ex3= Consumer Trust and Internet Shopping

CONSTRUCT

- Construct is an image or abstract idea specifically invented for a given research and/or theory building purpose.
- We build constructs by combining the simpler, more concrete concepts, especially when the idea or image we intend to convey is not subject to direct observation.

SCALES

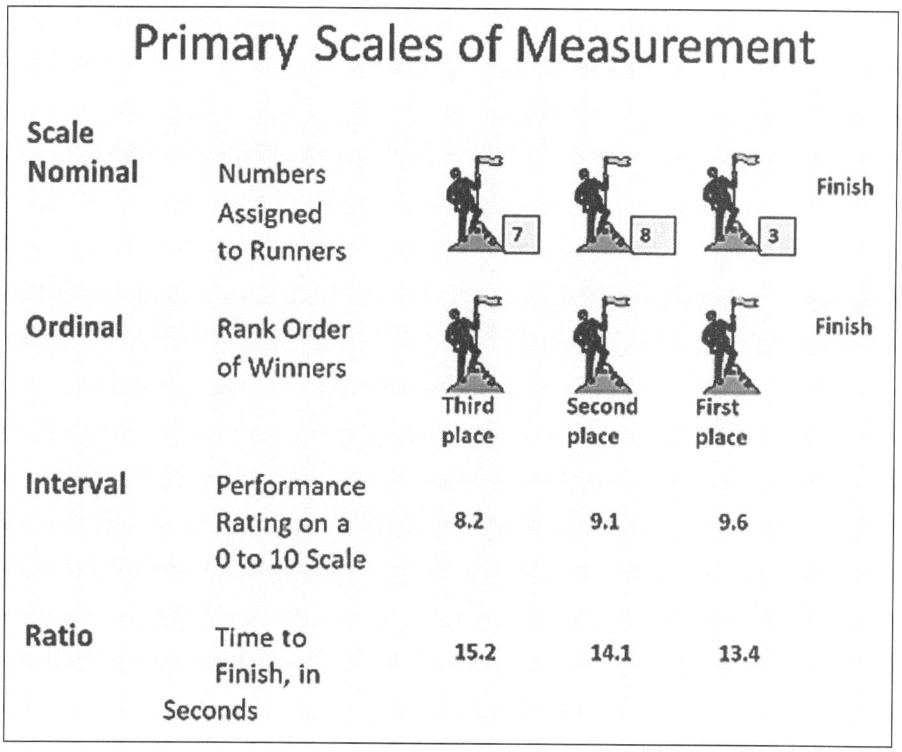

Fig. 7.1: Primary Scales of Measurements

Source: Based on review of literature

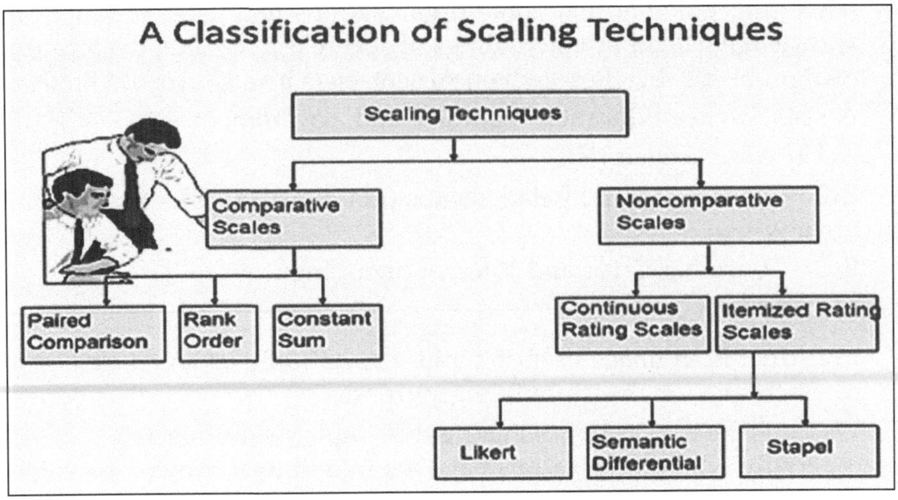

Fig. 7.2: A classification of scaling techniques

Source: Based on review of literature

Time of Self Study

Gender	Week 1	Week 2
M	45	51
M	56	53
M	67	65
M	123	105
M	89	98
M	99	96
M	115	122
M	136	125
M	102	100
M	39	39
F	124	136
F	99	87
F	135	115
F	145	156
F	89	91
F	97	100
F	112	104
F	85	79
F	156	142
F	130	119

Fig. 7.3: Time of Self Study

Source: Review of literature

Data Analysis Techniques

- Univariate
- BiVariate
- Multivariate

Need and Relevance of SPSS

- Great Discovery in Analysis
- Useful for Both Academic and Industry Problems

Practical 01

- A teacher wanted to see whether there was a difference in the amount of time boys and girls spent on their homework. He asked 10 boys and 10 girls aged 9 years to make a note of the number of minutes they spent studying over a 2 week period.

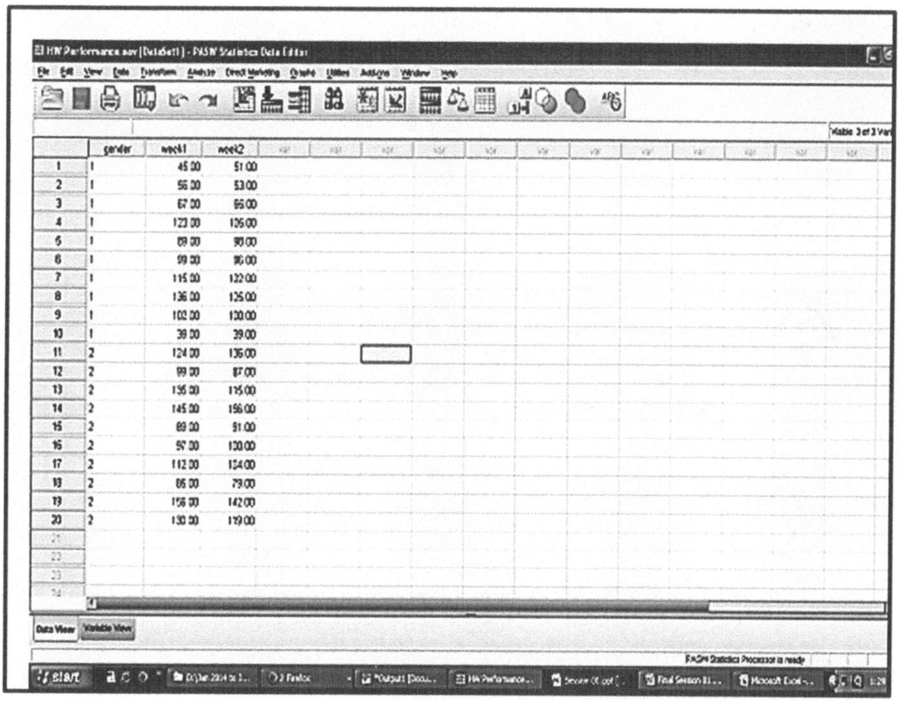

Fig. 7.4: Next step after performance in figure 7.3

Source: Based on review of literature

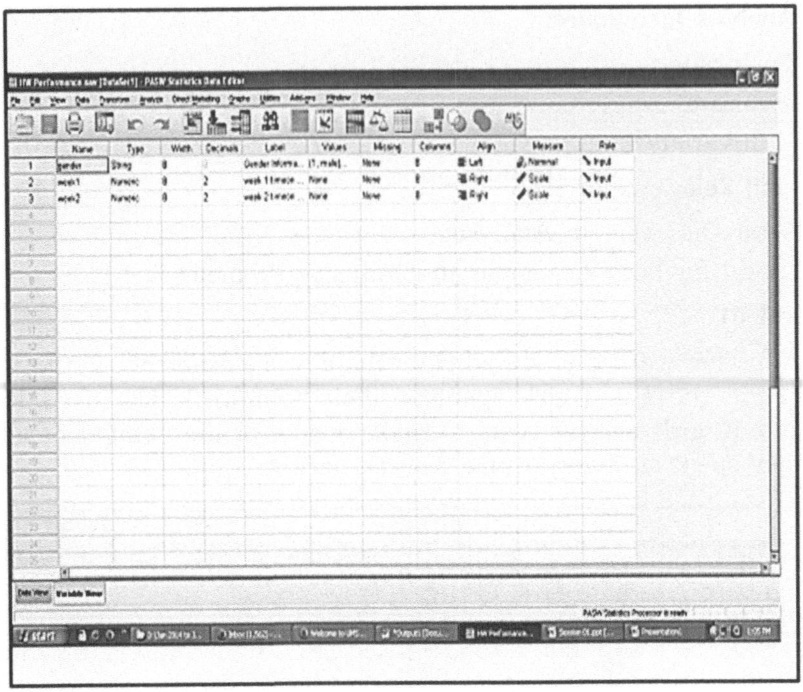

Fig. 7.5: Next steps after performance in figure 7.4

Source: Based on review of literature

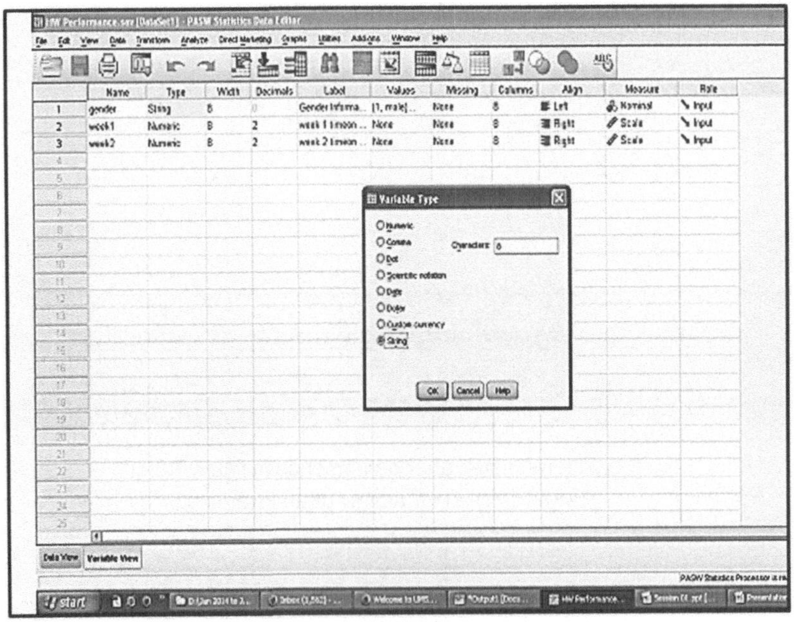

Fig. 7.6: Next steps after performance in figure 7.5

Source: Based on review of literature

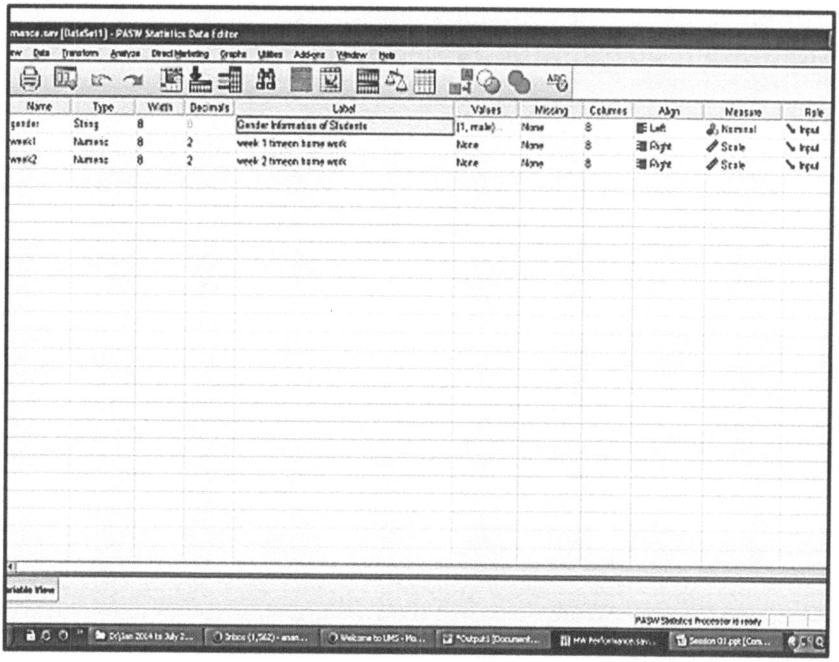

Fig. 7.7: Next steps after performance in figure 7.6
Source: Based on review of literature

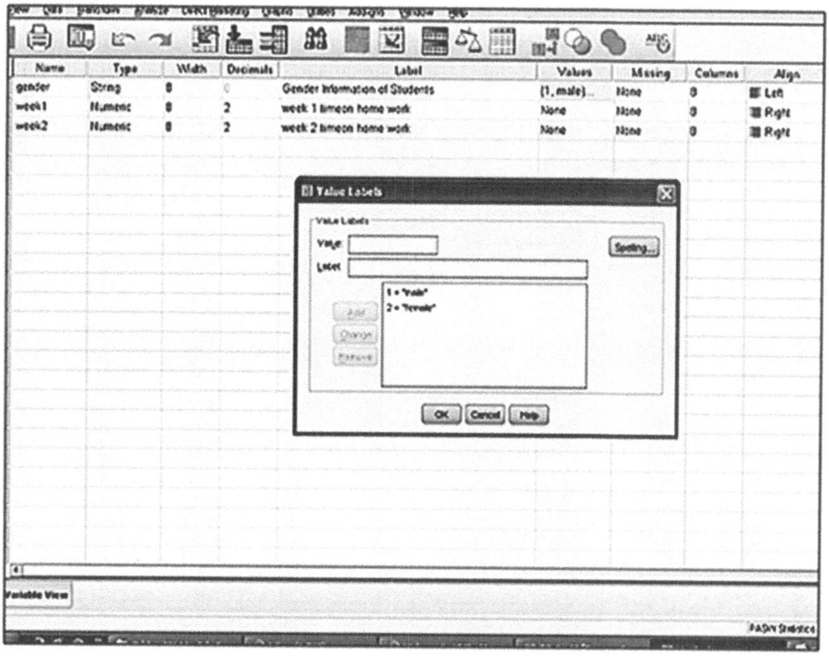

Fig. 7.8: Next steps after performance in figure 7.7
Source: Based on review of literature

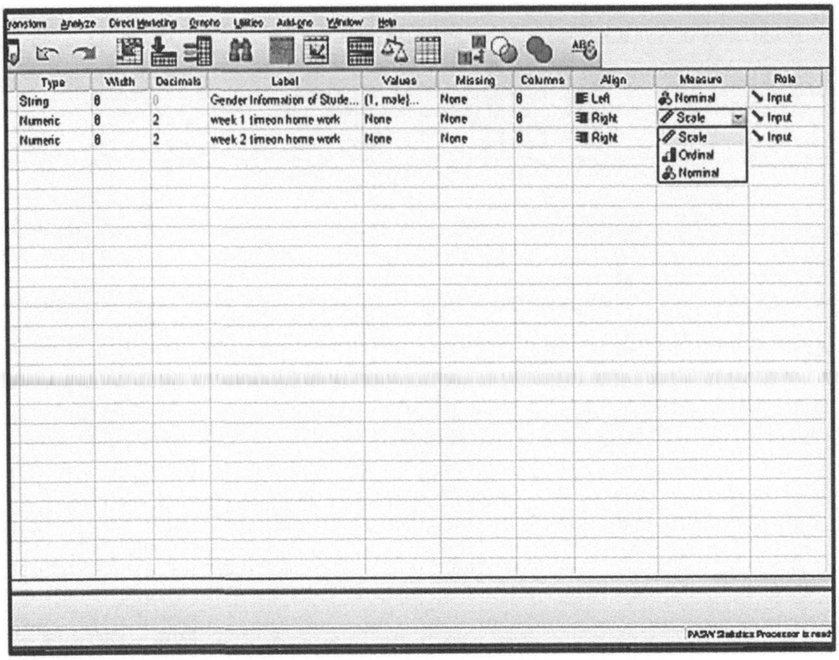

Fig. 7.9: Next step after the performance in figure 7.8

Source: Based on review of literature

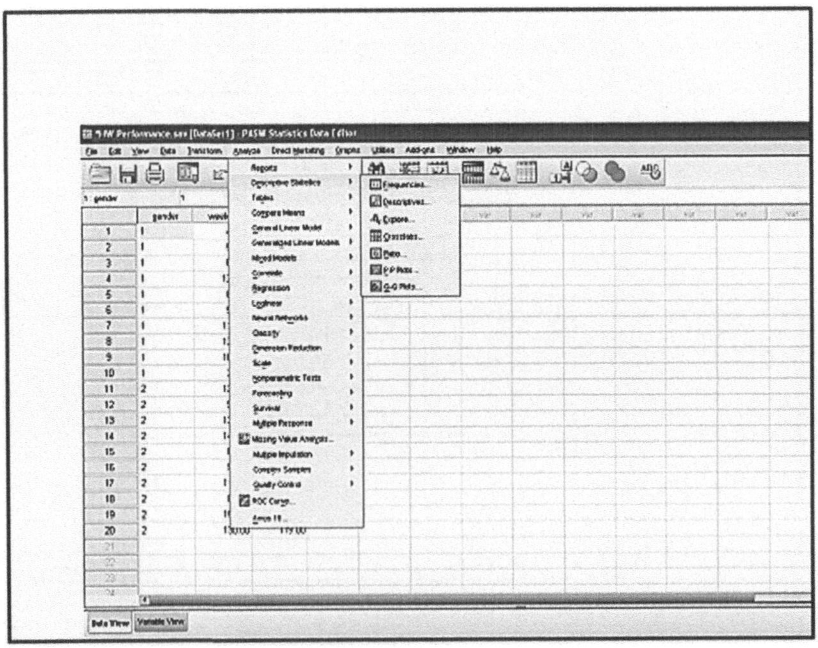

Fig. 7.10: Next step after the performance in figure 7.9

Source: Based on review of literature

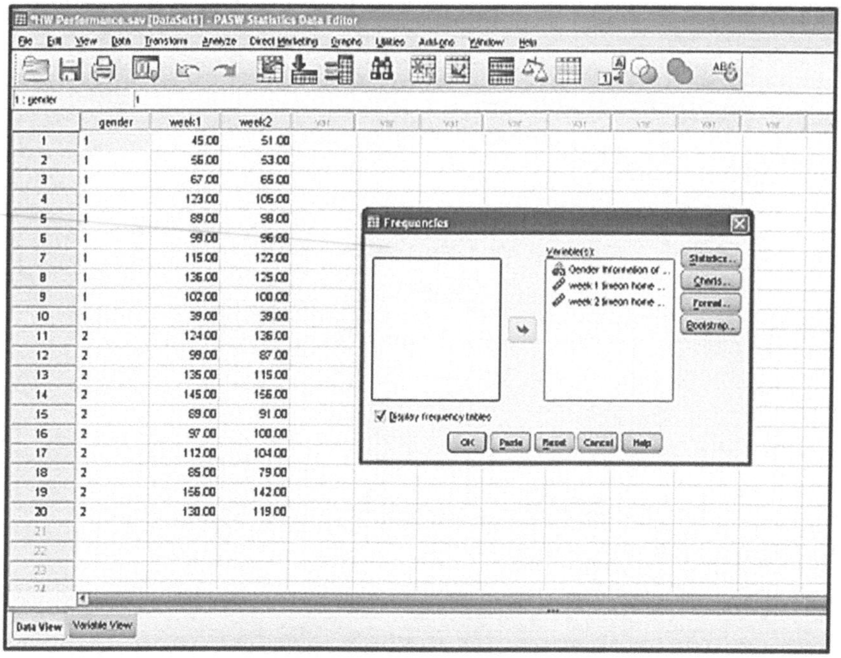

Fig. 7.11: Next step after the performance in figure 7.10

Source: Based on review of literature

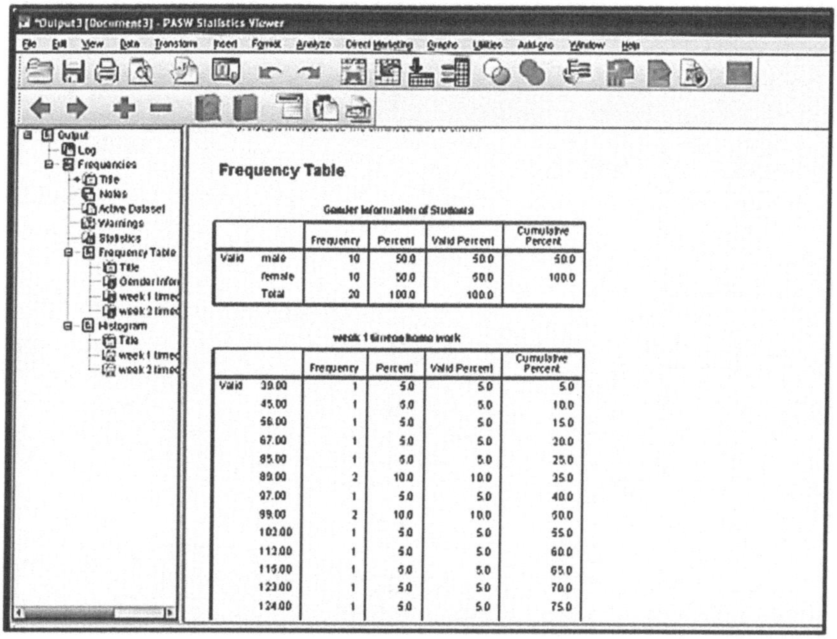

Fig. 7.12: Next step after the performance in figure 7.11

Source: Based on review of literature

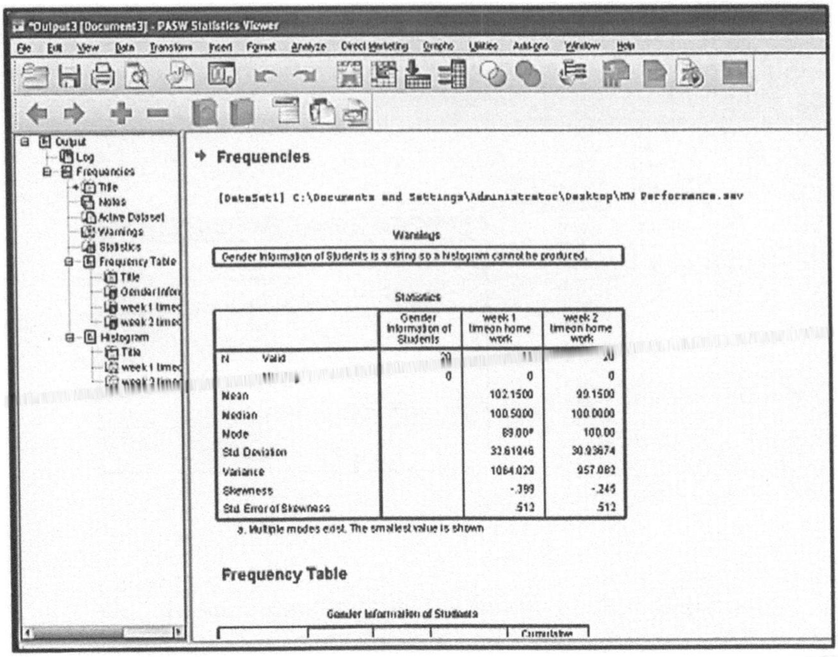

Fig. 7.13: Next step after the performance in figure 7.12
Source: Based on review of literature

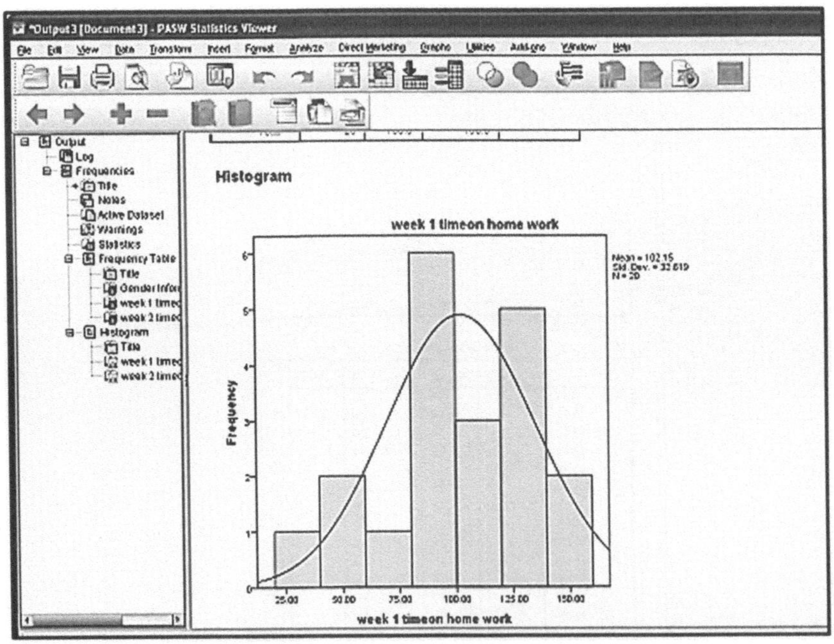

Fig. 7.14: Next step after the performance in figure 7.13
Source: Based on review of literature

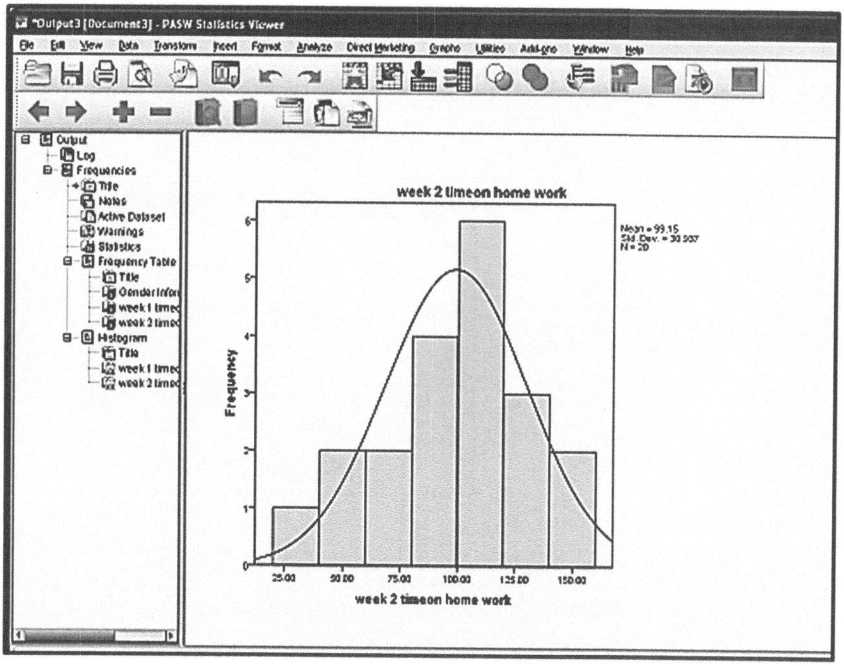

Fig. 7.15: Next step after the performance in figure 7.14

Source: Based on review of literature

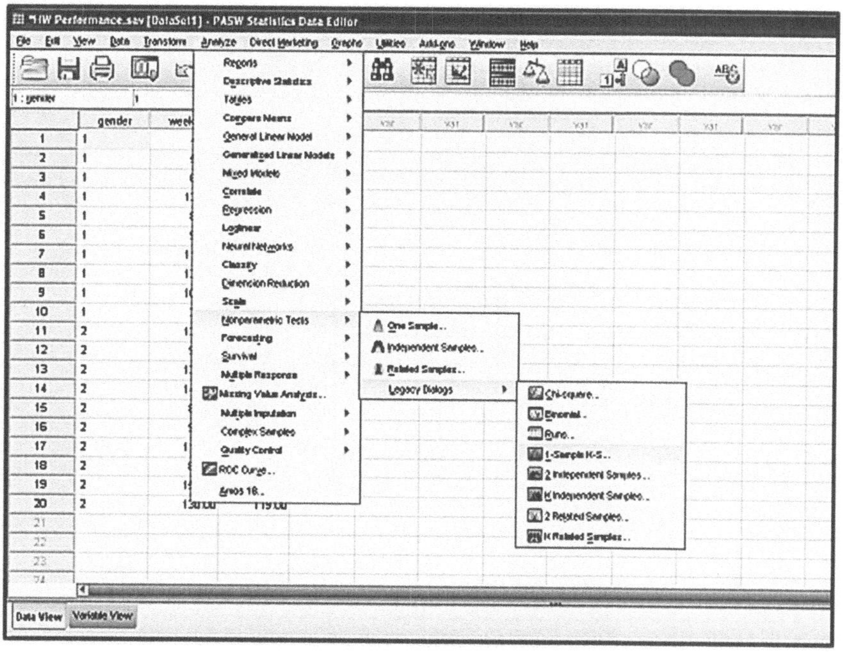

Fig. 7.16: Next step after the performance in figure 7.15

Source: Based on review of literature

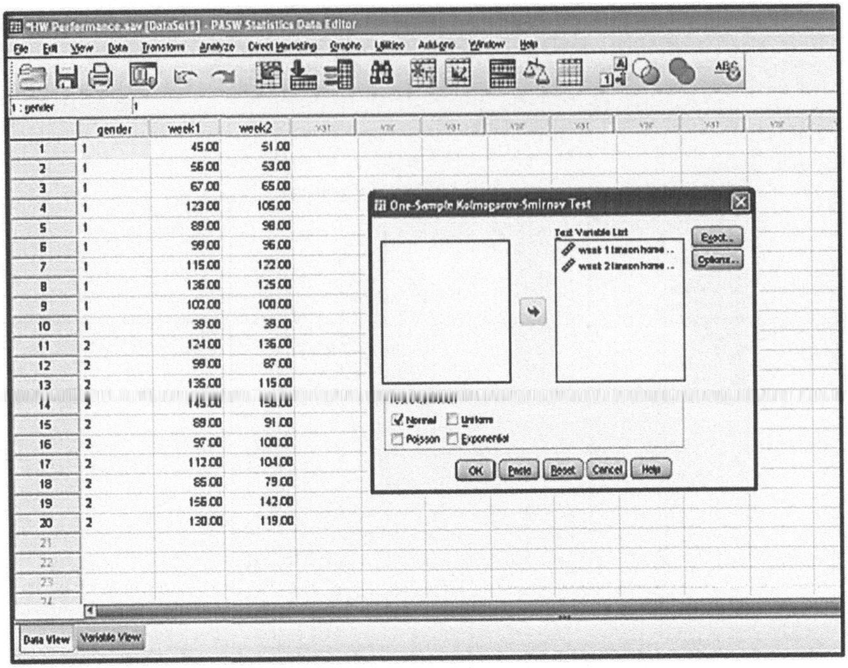

Fig. 7.17: Next step after the performance in figure 7.16

Source: Based on review of literature

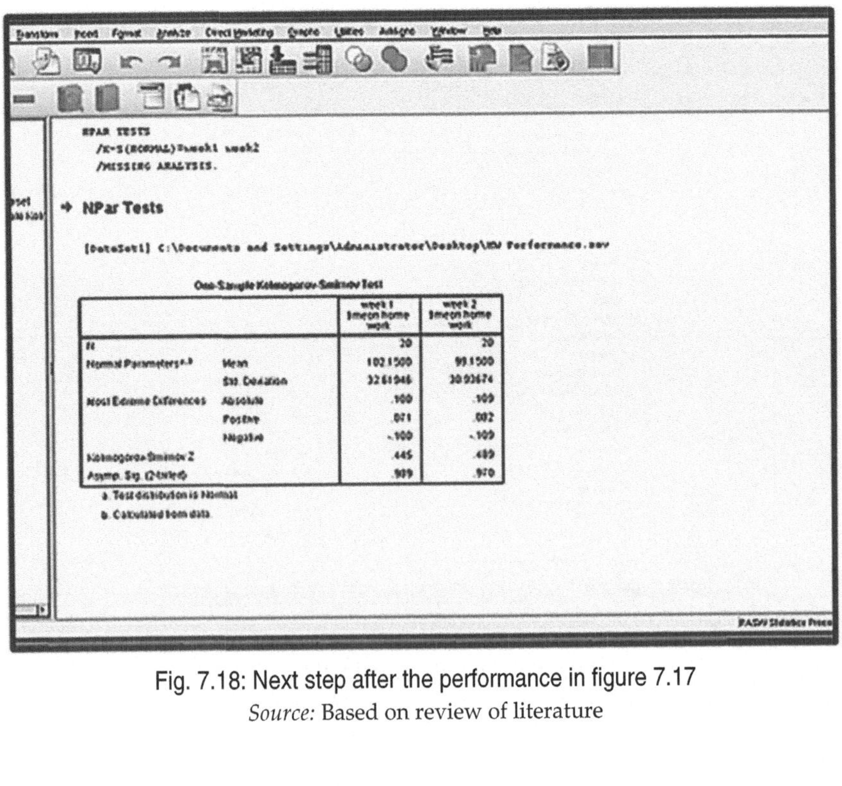

Fig. 7.18: Next step after the performance in figure 7.17

Source: Based on review of literature

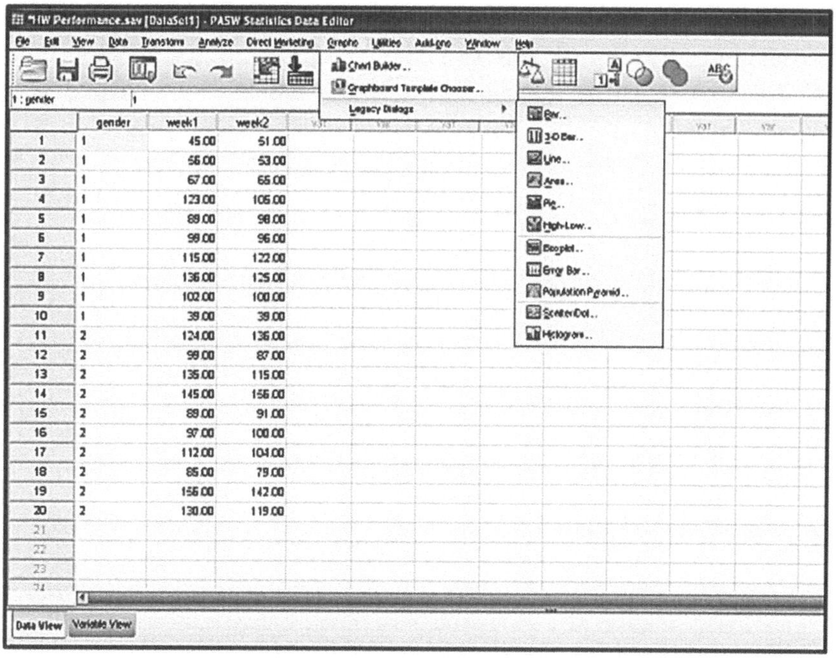

Fig. 7.19: Next step after the performance in figure 7.18

Source: Based on review of literature

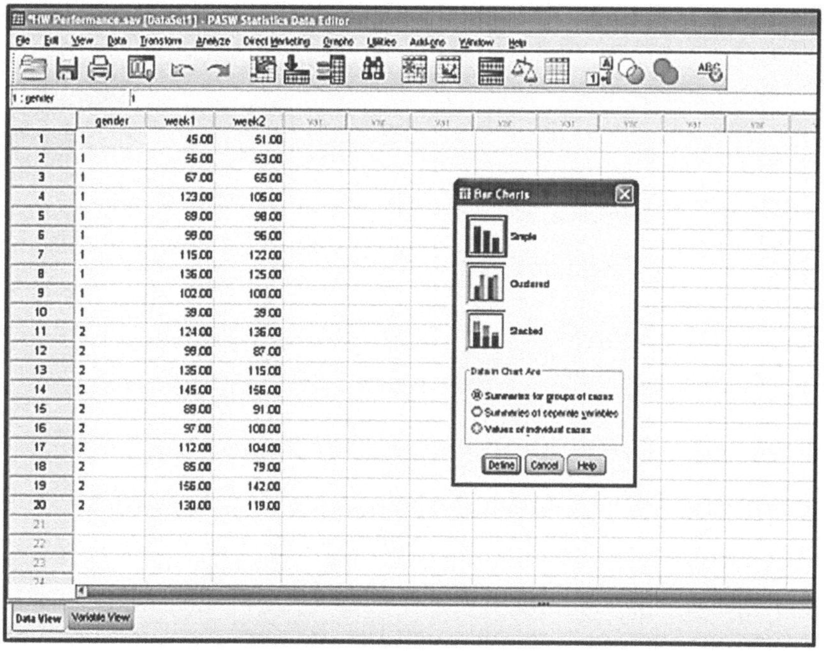

Fig. 7.20: Next step after the performance in figure 7.19

Source: Based on review of literature

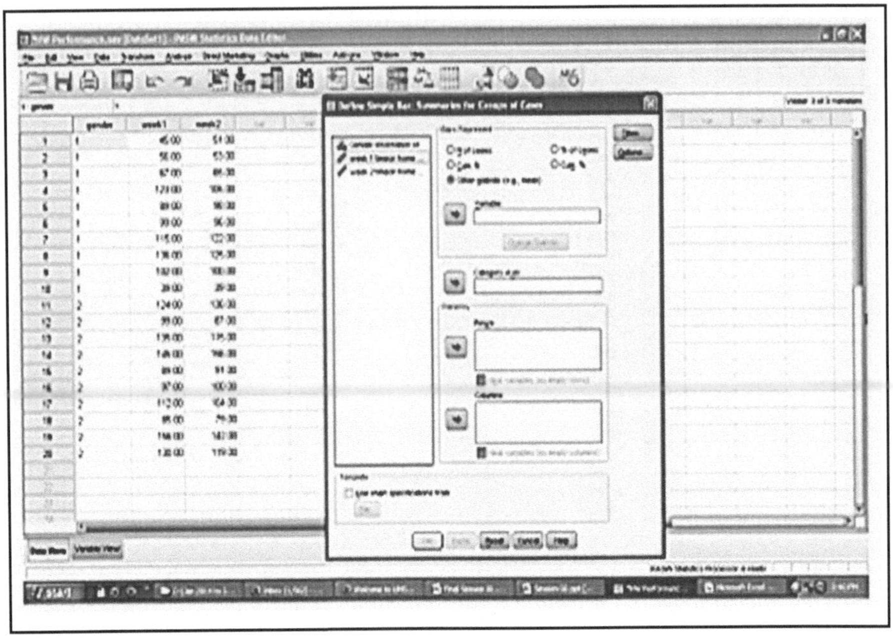

Fig. 7.21: Next step after the performance in figure 7.20

Source: Based on review of literature

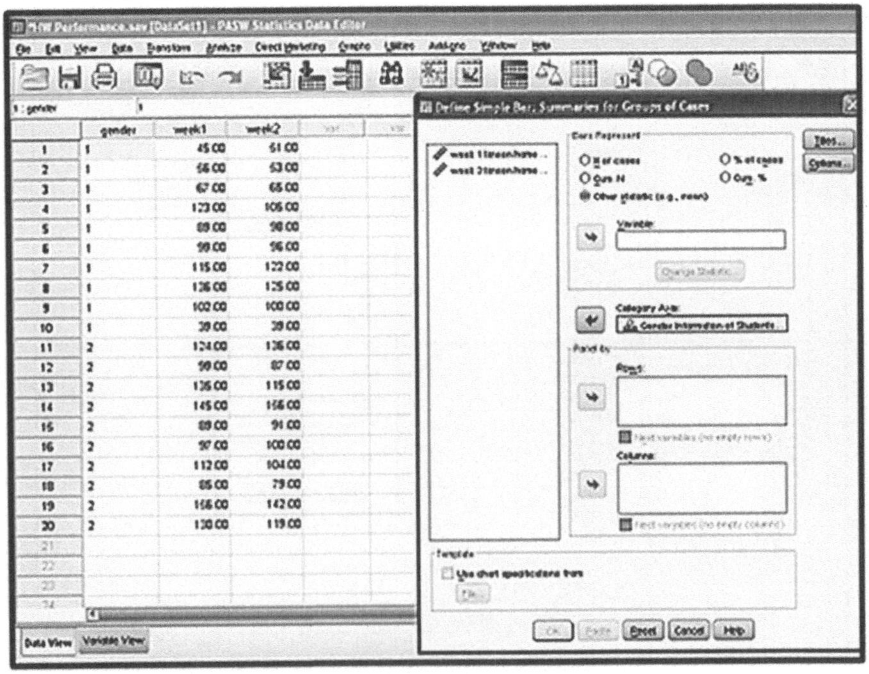

Fig. 7.22: Next step after the performance in figure 7.21

Source: Based on review of literature

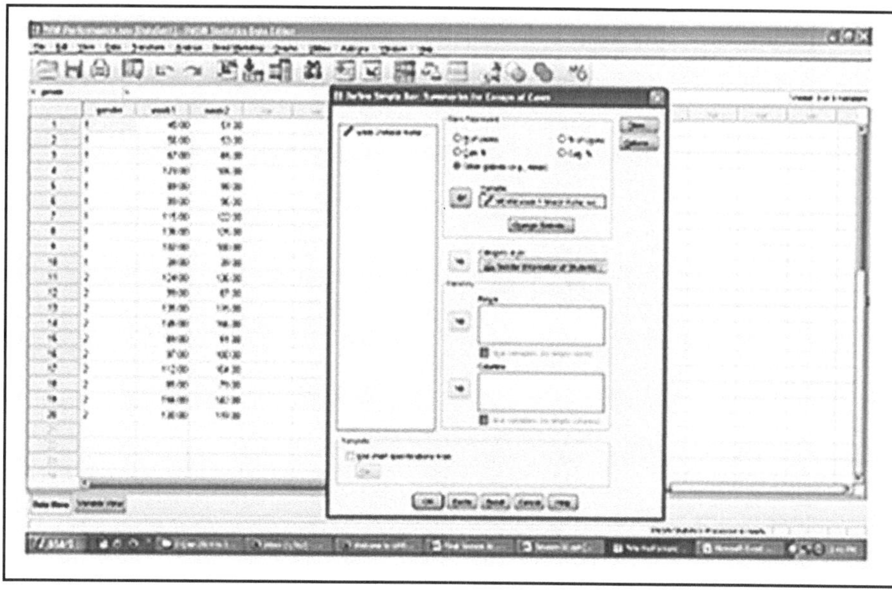

Fig. 7.23: Next step after the performance in figure 7.22
Source: Based on review of literature

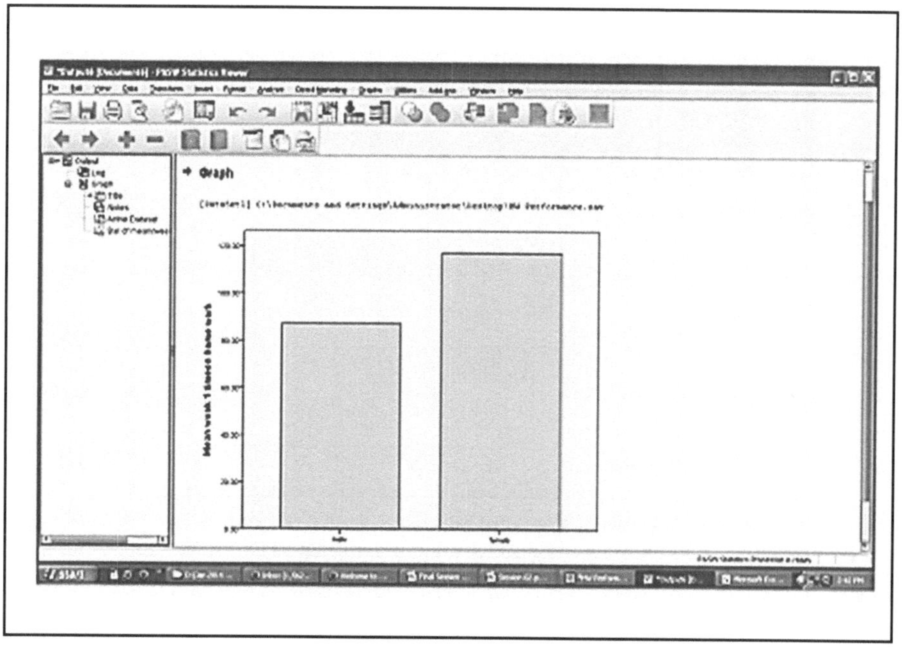

Fig. 7.24: Next step after the performance in figure 7.23
Source: Based on review of literature

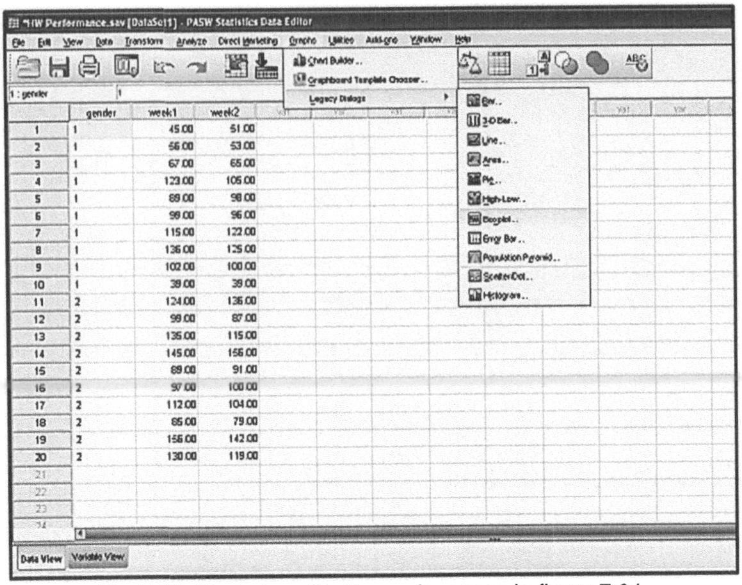

Fig. 7.25: Next step after the performance in figure 7.24

Source: Based on review of literature

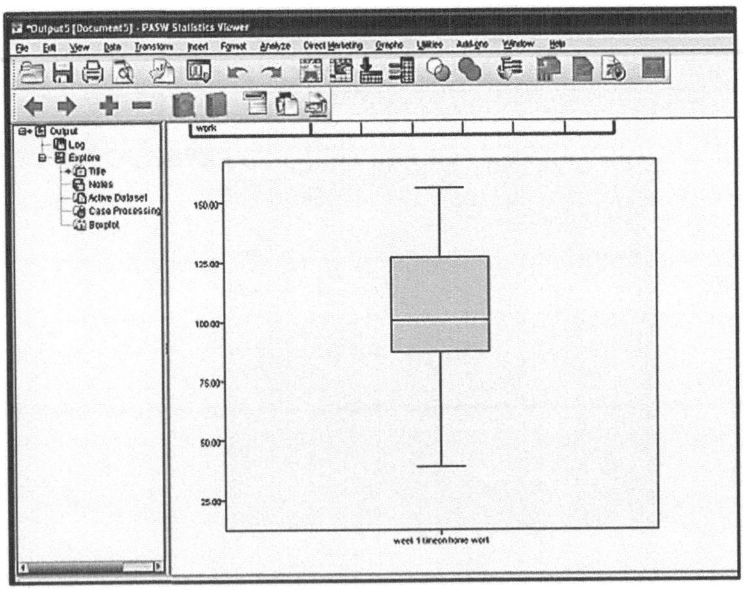

Fig. 7.26: Next step after the performance in figure 7.25

Source: Based on review of literature

- Black line indicates median value.
- Shaded box indicates where 50% of the data falls.
- The lines extending from the shaded box are commonly known as whiskers.

Pages: 85-92
Statistical Tools, Data and Instrumentation in Research and Science
Edited by: Er. Chhavi Kumar 'Bharti'; Dr. Prasann Kumar and
Dr. Pawan Kumar 'Bharti'
ISBN: 978-93-88854-51-1
Edition: 2020
Published by: Discovery Publishing House Pvt. Ltd., New Delhi (India)

8

Leaf Area Index
Process based Model

Prasann Kumar[1,2*] and Shipa Rani Dey[1]

GRAPHICAL ABSTRACT

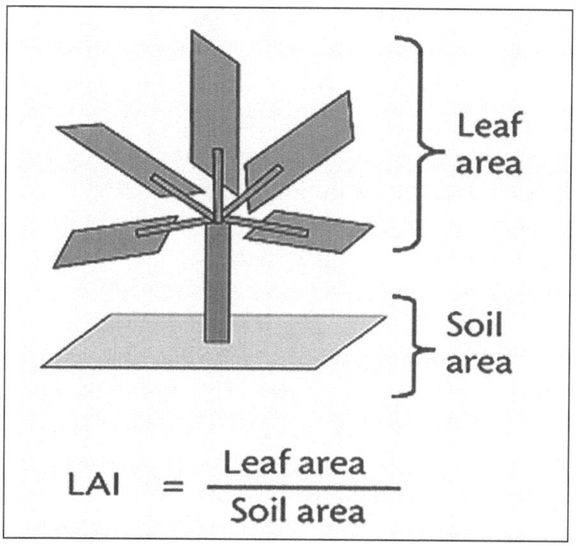

Keywords: Area, Critical, Index, Leaf, Production

[1] Department of Agronomy, School of Agriculture, Lovely Professional University, Jalandhar - 144 411 Punjab (India)
[2] Divison of Research and Development, Lovely Professional University, Jalandhar - 144 411 Punjab, (India)

INTRODUCTION

LAI is a dimensionless variable and was first defined as the total one-sided area of photosynthetic tissue per unit ground surface area. For broad leaved trees with flat leaves, this definition is usable because both sides of a leaf have the same surface area. However, if foliage elements are not flat, but wrinkled, bent or rolled, the one-sided area is not clearly defined. Rapid, reliable and objective estimations of Leaf Area Index (LAI) are essential for numerous studies of the atmosphere, as LAI is very often a critical parameter in process-based models of vegetation canopy response to global environmental change. This paper compiles current knowledge concerning the use of direct and indirect methods for LAI determination. The emphasis will be on techniques, theories and instruments. The same problem exists for coniferous trees, as needles may be cylindrical or hemi-cylindrical. Some authors therefore proposed a projected leaf area in order to take into account the irregular form of needles and leaves. However, in this case the choice of projection angle is decisive, and a vertical projection does not necessarily result in the highest values. consequently defined LAI as the maximal projected leaf area per unit ground surface area. Within the context of the computation of the total radiation interception area of plant elements, and based on calculations of the mean projection coefficients of several convex and concave objects of different angular distributions, Lang and Chen and Black suggested that half the total interception area per unit ground surface area would be a more suitable definition of LAI for non-flat leaves than projected leaf area. Their theoretical reasoning behind abandoning the projection concept was that the latter has neither physical nor biological significance, whereas the total intercepting area has a physical meaningand the total area has a biological connotation (e.g. gas exchange). Still other definitions and interpretations of LAI have been proposed. These vary depending on the technique used to measure LAI.The LAI of vegetation depends on species composition, development stage, and seasonality. Furthermore the LAI is strongly dependent on the prevailing site conditions and the management practices. The sum of these factors, combined with the difference in assessment methods, may therefore lead to widely varying LAI-values as is demonstrated in the relevant literature.There are two main categories of procedures to estimate LAI: direct and indirect methods. The former group consists of methods measuring leaf area in a direct way, while the latter group consists of methods where LAI is derived from more easily measurable parameters. In this review article, demonstrated advantages and disadvantages of the more frequently used direct and indirect techniques to estimate LAI in forests will be discussed. Subsequently, the focus will shift to the use of hemispherical photography for indirect LAI determination and innovative ways to alleviate the drawbacks of this particular method will be highlighted.

DIRECT LAI MEASUREMENT

Direct methods are the most precise, but they have the disadvantage of being extremely time-consuming and as a consequence making large-scale implementation only marginally feasible. Precision problems may in this case result from the definition of LAI, the scaling-up method, or from the error accumulation due to frequently repeated measurements.

Harvesting and Non-harvesting methods

LAI can be assessed directly by using harvesting methods such as destructive sampling and the model tree method or by non-harvesting litter traps during autumn leaf-fall period in deciduous forests. As the leaf area is determined through repeated area measurements on single leaves and area accumulation, these methods are hence considered the most accurate and for that reason they are often implemented as calibration tools for indirect measurement techniques. Non-harvest methods consist of leaf litter collection during the leaf-fall period using what is called litter traps. Traps of a predetermined size are hereby placed at any position in the stand, so that a higher litter trap frequency will result in an improved accuracy as the effect of up-scaling becomes less prevalent. Under the appropriate spatial and temporal sampling schemes, litter traps have proven very useful in deciduous forests. The setup is rather simple and therefore attractive, but is nevertheless not applicable to evergreen forests, where the yearly leaf fall is not directly related to yearly biomass accumulation, but to the average life span of leaves and the cumulative climate conditions over that life span. By means of litter traps, it is the integrated measure for LAI over the measurement period that is provided, so it is not an accurate measure at a single moment in time during the growing season and also climate can have an effect on the data from litter traps.

Leaf Area Determination Techniques

After leaf collection, leaf area can be calculated by means of either planimetric or gravimetric techniques. The planimetric approach is based on the principle of the correlation between the individual leaf area and the number of area units covered by that leaf in a horizontal plane. To do so, a leaf can be horizontally fixed to a flat surface, its perimeter can be measured with a planimeter, and its area can be computed from this perimeter assessment. There are different planimeter types on the market for this purpose. A first type is the scanning planimeter that uses an electronic method of rectangular approximation. The area of the leaf is measured as the leaf is drawn through the scanning head. The scanning head can be combined with a transparent belt conveyer with constant speed in order to measure large numbers of detached leaves. Other scanning planimeters make use of a fluorescent light source and a solid-state scanning camera to ²sense² the area of leaves as they move through the instrument.

INDIRECT LAI DETERMINATION

Indirect methods, in which leaf area is inferred from observations of another variable, are generally faster, amendable to automation, and thereby allow for a larger spatial sample to be obtained. For reasons of convenience when compared to the direct methods, they are becoming more and more important. Indirect methods of estimating LAI *in-situ* can be divided in two categories:

1. Indirect contact LAI measurements
2. Indirect non-contact measurements.

These are ground-based measurements that usually integrate over one single stand only.

Indirect Contact LAI measurement methods

Inclined Point Quadrat

This method was developed by Wilson (1960, 1963) and consists of piercing a vegetation canopy with a long thin needle (point quadrat) under known elevation (i.e. theangle between the needle and the horizontal plane when vertically projected) and azimuth angles (i.e. the bearing of the needle from North when horizontally projected) and counting the number of hits or contacts of the point quadrat with ²green² canopy elements. It is the elevation angle that determines the impact of the canopy structure on the number of hits.The determination of LAI of the vegetation by means of this method is then possible using rather simple equations based on a radiation penetration model. When the method is restricted to one single canopy piercing, an elevation angle β of 32.5° is preferable. At that elevation angle, the extinction coefficient K of a leaf population with random azimuth distribution in the canopy is more or less constant (K=0.9) at the different leaf angles α and, under assumption of azimuthal symmetry, LAI can be estimated as follows:

LAI = 1.1´ N (32.5)

where, Better LAI estimations are possible when the needle is repeatedly dropped in the vegetation canopy under varying elevation-angles. The general formula then becomes

Ni = LAI ´ Ki

where, N_i is the number of contacts of the needle, dropped with elevation i, with the vegetation and K_i the extinction coefficient with elevation i. The crucial element of this method is the ability to assess the number of contacts between the needle and the vegetation canopy without disturbing the latter.The method is attractive because the assumption of random leaf distribution is not necessary and because of its non-destructive character. Bonhomme *et al.* (1974) applied this technique using the gap fraction measurements and found a very good agreement between the actual and estimated LAI values for young crops.

Allometric Techniques

Allometric relations between the leaf area determined via destructive sampling and the basal area of the physiologically active sapwood area have been proposed. Such sapwood-to-leaf-area conversions are based on the pipe model theory that stems and branches are considered an assemblage of pipes supporting a given amount of foliage.Allometric techniques rely on relationships between leaf area as such and any dimension(s) of the woody plant element carrying the green leaf biomass, i.e. stem diameter, tree height, crown base height etc. They found that sapwood area, permeability, and the product of these two variables decreased with depth through the crown of the trees. An additional problem lies in the fact that sapwood determination is a difficult process in some species due to unclear borders between sapwood and hardwood. In some cases, the method may not be practical, for example in areas with preservation or scientific interests where cutting is prohibited. As a consequence, the assumption of constant permeability and sapwood fraction with height must be rejected for large trees, and the use of sapwood area or DBH to predict LAI may result in considerable LAI overestimation. The literature also reveals that leaf area calculated from non-site-specific sapwood allometrics tends to overestimate LAI when compared to indirect optical estimates even when corrected for clumping and wood interception. Very high correlation coefficients were found between sapwood area and leaf area, between stem basal area leaf and between diameter-at-breast-height (DBH) and leaf area of trees in the same stand. Physiologically, the amount of foliage that can be supported by sapwood decreases as trees approach maximum height, likely because of hydraulic limitations to water transport in tall trees that lead to cavitation of vessels. Whitehead *et al.* documented a linear relation between leaf area and the product of sapwood area and permeability, supporting the hypothesis that the relation between leaf area and sapwood area is governed by the permeability. They are nevertheless suggested to be more appropriate than optical gap fraction based measurements, for stands with high leaf area, because these optical measurements saturate at LAI values of about 5. However, the trade-off is that the use of such allometric equations is restricted because of their site-specificity, as sapwood area/leaf area relationships have been shown to be stand-specific and dependent on season, site fertility e.g. nutrition and soil water availability -, local climate, and canopy structure e.g. age, stand density, tree size and forest management. Computer-tomography could offer a solution but field application is far from operational as yet. The alternative use of pressler cores is possibly inaccurate due to the eventually non-circular distribution of sapwood and hardwood in the stem. Finally, wood permeability is not commonly measured.

Indirect Non-contact LAI measurement methods.

It involves ground-based measurement of total, direct, and/or diffuse radiation transmittance to the forest floor, and it makes use of line quantum sensors or radiometers, laser point quadrat, and capacitance sensors.Optical methods are indirect non-contact methods and are more commonly implemented. They are based on the measurement of light transmission through canopies.One approach applies the Beer-Lambert law taking into account the fact that the total amount of radiation intercepted by a canopy layer depends on incident irradiance, canopy structure and optical properties. In recent years, a range of instruments has been developed to indirectly assess in real time LAI of plant canopies. They can be divided in two main categories: a first group contains instruments that are based on gap fraction analysis, while in a second group instruments based on gap size distribution analysis can be classed. Some instruments allow calculating gap fraction manually (luminous slat), some incorporate canopy image analysis techniques (Digital Plant Canopy Imager CI 100, MVI), while others (Accupar, Demon, Licor LAI-2000 Plant Canopy Analyzer) calculate LAI in a rather simple way by comparing differential light measurements above and below canopy. These instruments have already proven their value in the LAI estimation of coniferous as well as broadleaved stands. When compared to allometric methods, the approach provides more accurate LAI estimates. However, the light measurements required to calculate LAI necessitate cloudless skies, and generally there is the need to incorporatea light extinction coefficient that is both site- and species-specific due to leaf angle, leaf form, leaf clumping, etc.The maximal measurable LAI is generally lower for these devices measuring gap fraction than the one assessed via direct methods, with LAI reaching an asymptotic saturation level at a value of about 5. The likely cause is gap fraction saturation as LAI approaches 5-6 (Gower *et al.*, 1999).TRAC and hemispherical photography study the gap size distribution. Documented research has proven these instruments very efficient and reliable where it concerns the measurement of LAI in forest environments (Welles, 1990). Based on error analysis, Chen (1996) stated that in coniferous stands optical methods, if combined with clumping analysis, hold the potential to provide LAI estimates that are more accurate than direct estimates obtained via destructive sampling techniques.The last step in the interpretation of gap fraction for these methods in terms of LAI is based on relationships between gap fraction and canopy geometry. These relationships are derived from light extinction models, which link LAI and canopy architecture to the penetration of solar radiation through the canopy.

Gap fraction, as a function of zenith angle, is the essence of such mathematical formulas and models. Light extinction models describe the probability of interception of radiation within canopy layers, as well as the probability of sun flecks at the bottom of the canopy. Sun flecks correspond to gaps in the canopy when viewed along the direction of the direct solar beam. The assumption of random spatial distribution of the canopy requires a Poisson model, assuming that projections of leaves are randomly located in the plane of the projection (Welles, 1990). Canopies with clumped or more regularly distributed leaves can be described more adequately by binomial models, respectively using negative or positive binomial probability functions (Neumann *et al.*, 1989). Markov models (Nilson, 1971) are also appropriate. To compensate for clumping effects, Lang and Xiang (1986) proposed a combination of local linear averaging with larger-scale logarithmic-linear averaging of transmittance data.The Poisson model divides the canopy in N statistically independent horizontal layers in which leaves are uniformly and independently spread. These layers are sufficiently thin (ÄL = LAI/N) to make the probability of having more than one contact between incoming light rays and vegetation within one layer small compared to the probability for one contact. As N is allowed to approach infinity, the probability of a ray making exactly n contacts is described by a Poisson distribution. However, this definition is not entirely valid for canopies with clumped leaf distributions, as is usually the case in natural systems. With respect to the practical application, it has been shown that most instruments based on gap fraction assess the effective LAI under the assumption of random spatial distribution of leaves (Dufrêne and Bréda, 1995). It is, however, primarily foliage clustering at the shoot level that invalidates this assumption, resulting in an underestimation of LAI by 30% to 70% (Stenberg, 1996; Nackaerts *et al.*, 1999). It must be said, though, that the phenomenon is less prevalent in broadleaved canopies than in coniferous ones (Chen *et al.*, 1997).Norman and Campbell (1989), on the other hand, indicated that for isolated canopies in open tree stands, the inversion kernel may be more complicated than the one. All models, however, require some information on the distribution of leaf angles and leaf azimuths within the canopy, with the binomial and Markov models also necessitating an additional parameter to describe the canopy orderliness. The occurrence of clumping is not restricted to the shoot level, however, but may also take place at branch and crown level. Various experimental studies already recognized the problem of non-randomness, suggesting correction factors account for clustering or clumping when measuring LAI via optical methods. The limitation of the proposed correction factors is that they are not universally applicable and that they are usually very costly to come by, involving additional intensive sampling procedures and requiring new instrumentation such as, for example, the

TRAC instrument. TRAC measures gap-size distribution and is thus able to determine clumping. Moreover, in case of the introduction of clustering indices or clumping factors, it is the effective foliage area index that is determined instead of the real foliage area. Fractal dimension, which quantifies the deviation from a random needle distribution, is tested recently as a correction factor for needle clumping with LAI 2000 measurements. Unlike other parameters described in the literature that are highly tree species and site-specific, fractal dimension can be easily determined in situ with each LAI measurement. It therefore has the potential to offer an universal solution for correction of LAI measurements.

Surface measurement area method

1. Cut all leaves and measure (volume displacement + scaling by mass)
2. Inclined point quadrats.
3. Direct gap fraction.
4. Diffuse hemispherical.
5. Invert a stand ray tracing model (to complex)
6. Allometric methods (may not be locally representative)

CONCLUSION

Leaf Area Index is an important measure of canopy structure because treemorphology, leaf orientation and distribution influence LAI estimates. Trees of different species can have therefore very different LAI values. Clumping of needles or leaves affect LAI estimation in conifer species and to a lesser extent in deciduous species and seems to be the main cause factor of errors in the LAI estimation. This review demonstrates that all methods have specific problems and limitations, the decision which method to use depends on lots of factors as there are: the accuracy needed, time period of measurements, the scale factor of the research, the budget available for the measurements, etc.

REFERENCES

https://en.wikipedia.org/wiki/Leaf_area_index

https://land.copernicus.eu/global/products/lai

https://www.researchgate.net/.../How_do_I_calculate_leaf_area_index_at_regular_tim..

https://www.usgs.gov/media/.../changes-canopy-cover-nasa-modis-leaf-area-index-dat...

https://www.tandfonline.com/doi/abs/10.1080/2150704X.2017.1415472

https://gis.stackexchange.com/.../how-to-calculate-lai-leaf-area-index-using-remote-se...

sciencenetlinks.com/student-teacher-sheets/surface-area-leaf-teacher-sheet/

https://www.kisspng.com/png-leaf-area-index-canopy-analyser-measurement-plant-12

https://www.kisspng.com/png-leaf-area-index-definition-logo-explanation-single-594.

Pages: 93-100
Statistical Tools, Data and Instrumentation in Research and Science
Edited by: Er. Chhavi Kumar 'Bharti'; Dr. Prasann Kumar and
Dr. Pawan Kumar 'Bharti'
ISBN: 978-93-88854-51-1
Edition: 2020
Published by: Discovery Publishing House Pvt. Ltd., New Delhi (India)

9

Open Educational Resources for Agricultural Science

Prasann Kumar[1,2*] and Shipa Rani Dey[1]

GRAPHICAL ABSTRACT

Keywords: Agriculture, Deans, Education, Opportunities

[1] Department of Agronomy, School of Agriculture, Lovely Professional University, Jalandhar - 144 411 Punjab (India)
[2] Divison of Research and Development, Lovely Professional University, Jalandhar - 144 411 Punjab, (India)

To familiarize the faculty about Open Educational Resources and efforts made by Indian Council of Agricultural Research in this direction.

1. What are Open Educational Resources (OER)
2. Why do we need OER
3. What opportunities are available
4. Overview of higher education in Agriculture
5. Deans Committee Recommendations and ICAR initiatives
6. Conclusion
7. Did you find what you were looking for effective curriculum delivery.

What are open educational resources?

- Open Educational Resources (OER) are educational materials and resources offered freely and openly for anyone to use and under some license to adapt, copy and redistribute. OER can include course syllabi, presentation slides, image collections, animations, videos, textbooks, research papers and self-assessments.
- The term "open educational resources" was first adopted at UNESCO's 2002 Forum on the Impact of Open Courseware for Higher Education in Developing Countries.

OER and OCW

- "OER" is largely synonymous with another term: Open CourseWare (OCW), although it is more specific structured subset of OER.
- An Open CourseWare is defined by the OCW Consortium as 'a free and open digital publication of high quality university-level educational materials.
- These materials are organized as courses, and often include course planning materials and evaluation tools as well as thematic content.

The Trend towards openness

- Open Source Software
- Open Access to Research
- Open Educational Resources

Open Educational Resources (OER)

- Digital educational materials that may be freely
- accessed,
- reused,
- modified
- and shared.
- Open educational resources (OER) are any resources available at no cost that can be used for teaching, learning, or research.

- The term can include textbooks, course readings, and other learning content; simulations, games, and other learning applications; syllabi, quizzes, and assessment tools.
- OER typically refers to electronic resources, including those in multimedia formats, and such materials are generally released under a Creative Commons or similar license that supports open or nearly open use of the content.
- OER can originate from colleges and universities, libraries, archival organizations, government agencies, commercial organizations such as publishers, or faculty or other individuals who develop educational resources they are willing to participate.
- 2002 FORUM on the Impact of Open CourseWare for Higher Education in Developing Countries
- Declaration
- Participants expressed:
- "their satisfaction and their wish to develop
- together a universal educational resource for
- the whole of humanity, to be referred to
- henceforth as Open Educational Resources"
- (Massachusetts Institute of Technology, USA) MIT was the first institution to offer Open Courseware Project in 2002 with 50 courses, and by early 2015 was offering extracts from more than 2000 courses with free lecture notes, tests and videos.
- Connexions, at Rice University followed
- Open Learning Initiative (OLI, Carnegie Mellon University, USA) – Offers large number of courses
- The Open University, UK – Courses and course material available
- iTunes U numerous universities make their content available, in the form of lectures, videos, films and other resources. You can download the content in different formats, such as PDF or MP3.
- Having access to an institution's course resources is not equivalent to taking a course at that institution, but users can take advantage of that access to supplement or direct their own learning.
- The UK Open University has been developing high quality distance learning materials for 40 years.
- 'The philosophy of Open Content is entirely commensurate with The Open University's mission to equalise access to high quality educational opportunities ... particularly among educationally marginalised groups'.

Why is OER significant

- Educational resources developed in an open environment can be vetted and improved by a broad community of educators, resulting in materials that represent what the educational community sees as most valuable.
- By providing educators with new access to educational material, open resources have the potential to spur pedagogical innovation, introducing new alternatives for effective teaching.

What are the disadvantages of OER

- Like all educational resources, the quality of OER can be uneven and depends largely on their sources. Some OER are simply ineffective at presenting content in a valuable manner, and not all OER collections have a feedback mechanism by which users can share their evaluations about the quality of a resource.
- Whenever content is shared, and especially when it can be modified, questions arise over intellectual property and copyright concerns.

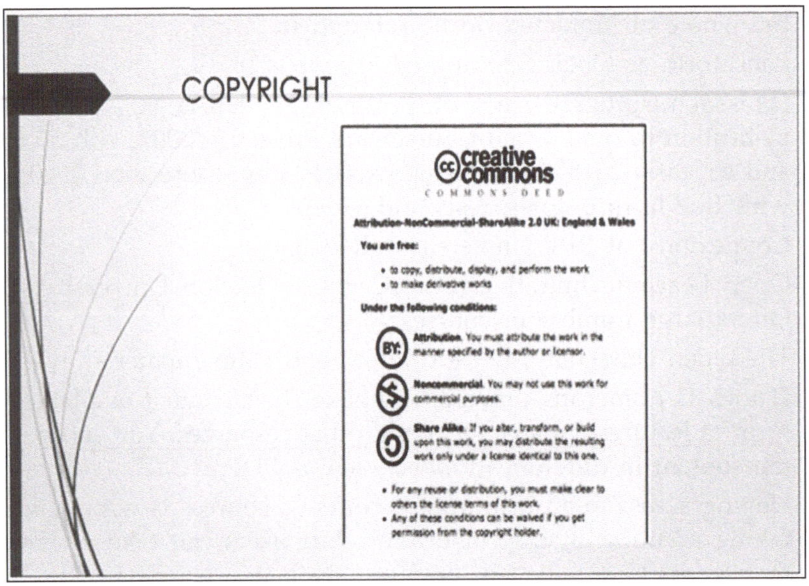

Fig. 9.1: Copyright

Source: Based on review of literature

- Commonwealth of Learning (COL)
- Directory of Open Educational Resources(DOER)
- National Repository of Open Educational Resources (NROER) by Ministry of Human Resource Development offers educational resources in multiple languages.

- You can access educational videos, audio, images, documents and interactive modules. Information about NROER and resource contribution is also available.
- Open Text Book

  A registry of textbooks that anyone can access, reuse and redistribute

  Book Sprint

  http://iquaid.org/2010/03/26/observe-the-operating-room-wiki2xml-sprint-for-foss-textbook/
- P2PU is an initiative designed to promote direct teaching/learning opportunities. You can participate as a student by signing up for a course or as a teacher by designing and running a course.
- Free Technology Academy

  The Free Technology Academy has announced the availability of *Introduction to Free Software,* one of a series of modules teaching/learning modules which intend to support university level courses that use free software to teach computer and technology concepts.
- Wikipedia is made up of people just like you: students, professors, and everyday experts and fans. With about 10,000 articles added to Wikipedia each week, there are plenty of opportunities to join this global community. How Wikipedia Works explains how you can make the Web's go-to source for information even better.
- **How Wikipedia Works**
- An digital version of How Wikipedia Works by Phoebe Ayers, Charles Matthews, and Ben Yates has recently been under the [GFDL](http://howwikipediaworks.com/apf.html).
- You can read the book online, or download an 8mb zip file of the HTML.
- **Wikibooks**
- **WikiEducator – Free Textbooks**
- ***Subjects***
- ***Blogroll***
- California Open Source Textbook Project (COSTP)
- Community College Consortium for Open Educational Resources (CCCOER)
- Connexions
- Free Culture Free Text Book Mailing List
- Free High School Science Texts (FHSST)
- Global Text Project
- OER Commons

- Open Book Project
- Open Knowledge Definition (OKD)
- Open Knowledge Foundation
- Open Textbooks Project on MERLOT
- The Assayer
- The Free Textbook Project

Future Implications of OER

Infusion of OER into higher education is the subject of some debate.

- Radical viewpoints - OER movement will lead to a future in which all of the components of an education will be available online for free and that learners will have the opportunity to construct a course of study—though it might not be called a "degree"—from the wide and growing pool of open content.
- Others envision a less disruptive future for OER, suggesting that the model for higher education will persist in a form not wholly different from what it is today, but enhanced with high-quality, open, digital content.

Let us perform the Activity of redesigning OER material of your interest

- Find some OER material (for example, from one of the sites in this Activity that interests you, or that you think you might like to develop. It could be on a topic you know about, or something completely new.
- Decide who your learners are – what they already know (if anything) about the topic you've chosen, what might get them interested.
- Now that you've found the material, and have decided on your learners, set out what you see as the material's strengths and weaknesses.
- What's missing? Does it go into too much detail, or not enough? If the material's on a topic that is completely new to you, you can test it against your own requirements: does it help *you* learn.

Indian Agriculture – Salient Features

- Agriculture employs over 650 million people- mostly poor & marginalized
- Supports 18% of the world human population
- Third largest food producer at 250 MT
- First in milk production (220 MT)
- Second largest in fruit (45 MT) and vegetable (91 MT) production
- 2nd in rice (100 MT)and 3rd in wheat (90 MT) production
- Largest NARS in the world

Deans Committee on Agricultural Education in India

- Fixes Norms, Standards, Academic Regulations and UG Curricula and Syllabi
- Fourth Deans Committee – Chairman Dr. N.C.Mehta
- Now Fifth Deans Committee – Chairman Dr. R.P. Singh
- Sub Committees have also been formed
- Biotechnology – Dr. B.S. Dhillon (PAU)
- Home Science – Dr. Raghuvanshi (GBPUAT)

Educational Training in Agriculture

SAUs, provide hands on experience and rural awareness to the students to become effective professionals and entrepreneurs:

- Student READY (Rural Entrepreneurship and Awareness Development Yojana)
- RAWE (Rural Agricultural Work Experience)
- Experiential Learning courses
- KrishiVigyanKendras (640+) impart training annually to about 50,000 farmers, farm women, and rural youth and grass root level extension workers.

ODL Mode

- IGNOU - The School of Agriculture of IGNOU runs 17 programmes
- e- gyankosh is their open source
- ODL at TNAU Certificate courses
- The School of Agriculture of YashwantraoChavanMaharathwada Open University (YCMOU), Nasik offering certificate and diploma programmes in agriculture
- The National Institute of Open Schooling (NIOS) offering about 12-15 certificate courses

AGRICULTURE SECTOR SKILL COUNCIL

About 1% is trained in agriculture and allied fields. In a corrective measure, Agriculture Sector Skill Council (ASCI) was formally set up in 2012 as an affiliate body of National Skill Development Corporation. The objective is to train, certify and accredit 56.5 million workforce comprising of farmers, wage workers, entrepreneurs and extension workers, over 10 years through its training partners in PPP framework.

Digital India

- Approved on 20 August 2014. Comprises various projects worth over Rs one lakh crores to transform the country into a digitally empowered knowledge economy.

- About a third of India's 252 million internet users, and a fourth of mobile internet users, are in rural areas. But internet penetration in villages, at 8.6% compared to 37.4% in cities

National Knowledge Network (NKN)

- Initiated in 2010 with an outlay of Rs. 60,000 crores
- Interconnect over 1500 institutions of higher learning and research in the area of agriculture, education, health, e-governance and Grid Computing with a high speed data communication network to facilitate knowledge sharing and collaborative research.

CONCLUSION

- Huge need and a great potential for use of OERs
- Repurposing and localization of content have greater relevance in agriculture
- Lack of digital content – major drawback
- Poor use of ICT in the system
- Awareness & appreciation of OERs is growing
- Encourage OER development & sharing
- Innovative delivery mechanisms- e.g. MOOC

REFERENCES

https://libraryguides.unh.edu › Research Guides › Open Educational Resources

https://pitt.libguides.com/openeducation/biglist

https://link.springer.com/article/10.1007/s10499-019-00355-9

https://www.tandfonline.com/doi/full/10.1080/02680510802627860

https://www.oercommons.org/browse?f.search=Physics

https://www.mdpi.com/2227-7102/9/2/103

https://libguides.humboldt.edu › Research Guides › Open Educational Resources (OER)

Pages: 101-108

Statistical Tools, Data and Instrumentation in Research and Science

Edited by: Er. Chhavi Kumar 'Bharti'; Dr. Prasann Kumar and Dr. Pawan Kumar 'Bharti'

ISBN: 978-93-88854-51-1

Edition: 2020

Published by: Discovery Publishing House Pvt. Ltd., New Delhi (India)

10

Computational Biology

Prasann Kumar[1,2*] and Shipa Rani Dey[1]

GRAPHICAL ABSTRACT

Keywords: Biology, Computational, Design, Economy

[1] Department of Agronomy, School of Agriculture, Lovely Professional University, Jalandhar - 144 411 Punjab (India)

[2] Divison of Research and Development, Lovely Professional University, Jalandhar - 144 411 Punjab, (India)

INTRODUCTION

Computational Biology

- Access to biological data, analysis of data.

Biological data

- DNA sequence, structure
- RNA sequence, structure
- Protein sequence, structure
- Protein complex/protein protein interactions
- Metabolic pathways
- Chemical/ligands
- Literature
- Drugs ...

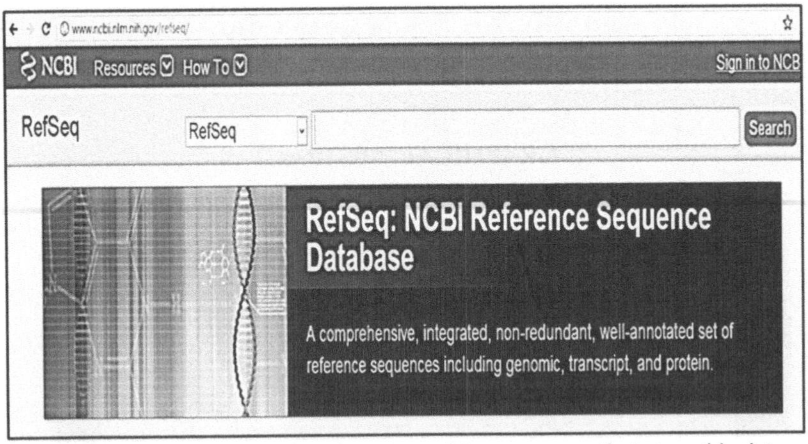

Fig. 10.1: Let us get introduced to some of the resources that store this data

Source: Based on review of literature

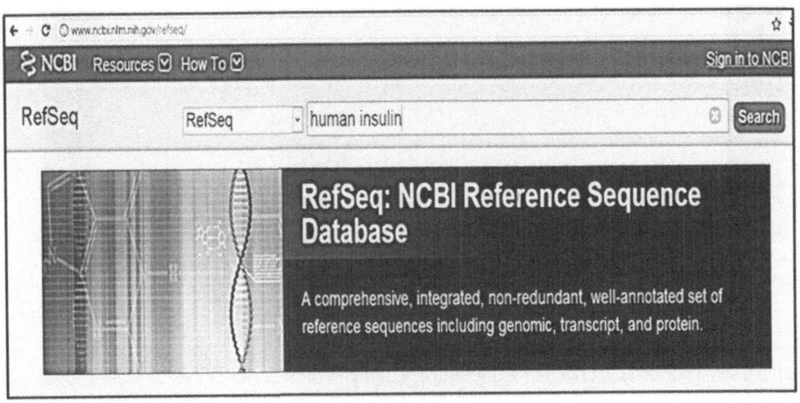

Fig. 10.2: RefSeq

Source: Based on review of literature

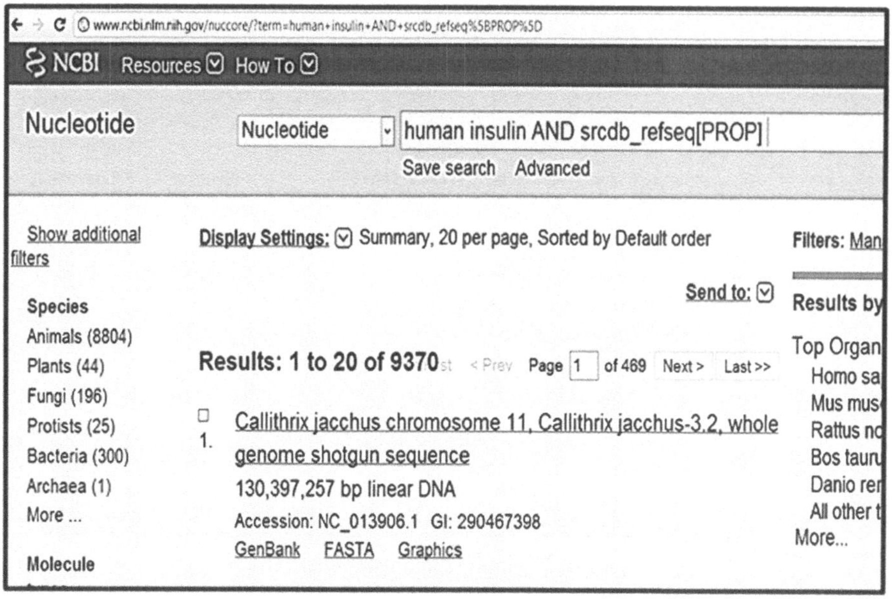

Fig. 10.3: Nucleotide

Source: Based on review of literature

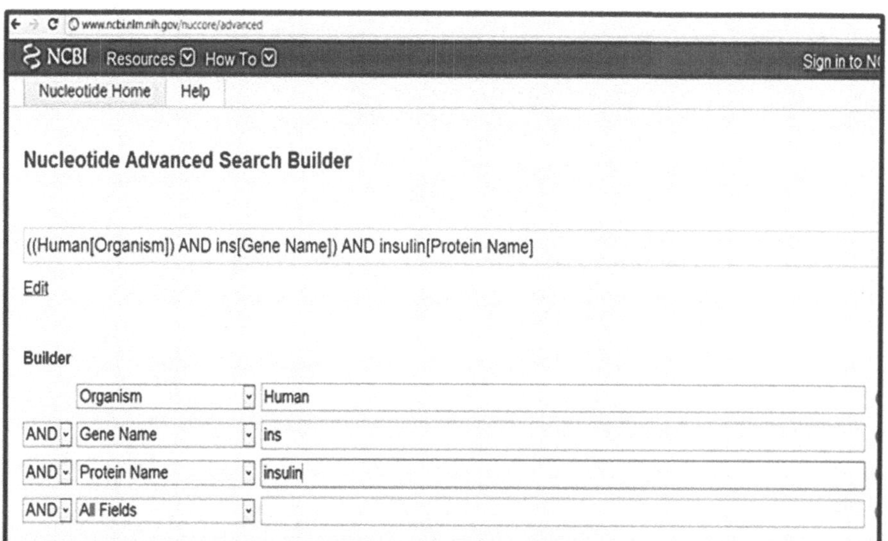

Fig. 10.4: Nucleotide Advanced search Builder

Source: Based on review of literature

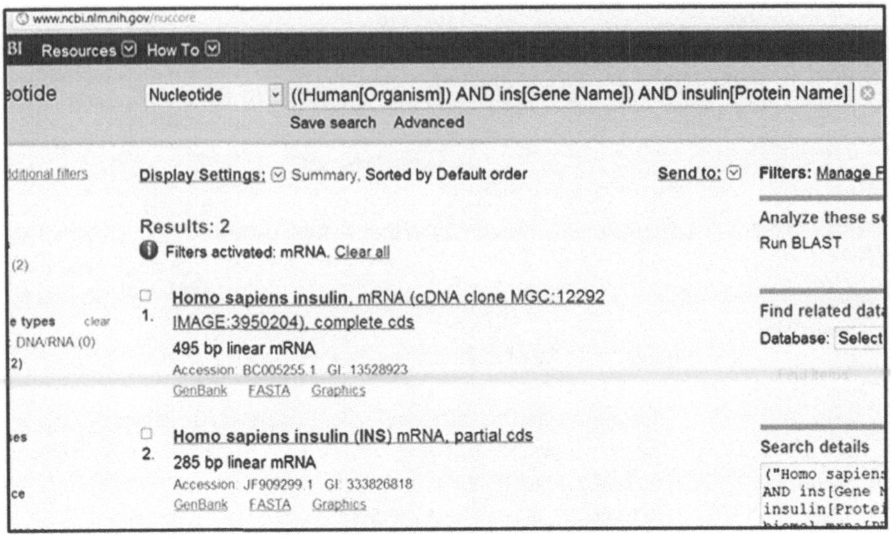

Fig. 10.5: Human Organism AND Ins

Source: Based on review of literature

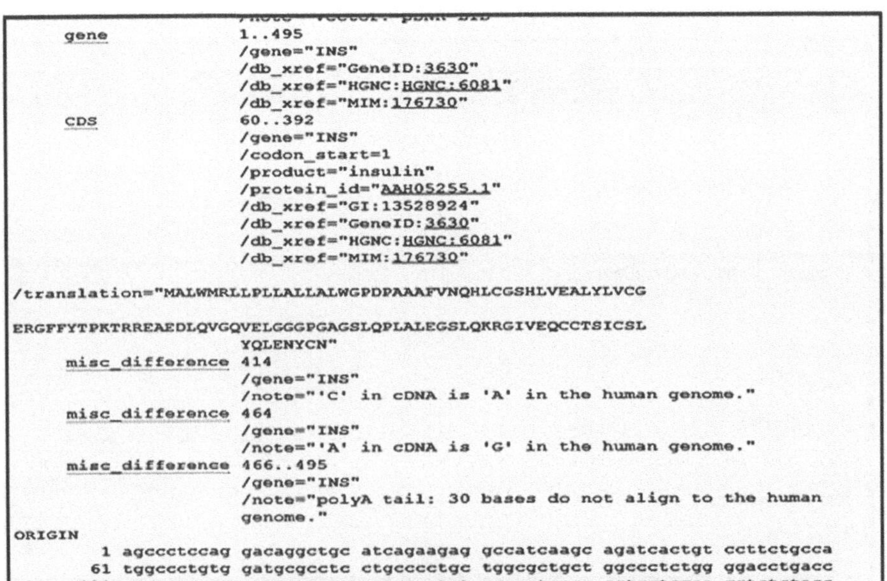

```
     gene            1..495
                     /gene="INS"
                     /db_xref="GeneID:3630"
                     /db_xref="HGNC:HGNC:6081"
                     /db_xref="MIM:176730"
     CDS             60..392
                     /gene="INS"
                     /codon_start=1
                     /product="insulin"
                     /protein_id="AAH05255.1"
                     /db_xref="GI:13528924"
                     /db_xref="GeneID:3630"
                     /db_xref="HGNC:HGNC:6081"
                     /db_xref="MIM:176730"
/translation="MALWMRLLPLLALLALWGPDPAAAFVNQHLCGSHLVEALYLVCG

ERGFFYTPKTRREAEDLQVGQVELGGGPGAGSLQPLALEGSLQKRGIVEQCCTSICSL
                     YQLENYCN"
     misc_difference 414
                     /gene="INS"
                     /note="'C' in cDNA is 'A' in the human genome."
     misc_difference 464
                     /gene="INS"
                     /note="'A' in cDNA is 'G' in the human genome."
     misc_difference 466..495
                     /gene="INS"
                     /note="polyA tail: 30 bases do not align to the human
                     genome."
ORIGIN
        1 agccctccag gacaggctgc atcagaagag gccatcaagc agatcactgt ccttctgcca
       61 tggccctgtg gatgcgcctc ctgcccctgc tggcgctgct ggccctctgg ggacctgacc
      121 cagccgcagc ctttgtgaac caacacctgt gcggctcaca cctggtggaa gctctctacc
```

Fig. 10.6: Some information reported in the record

Source: Based on review of literature

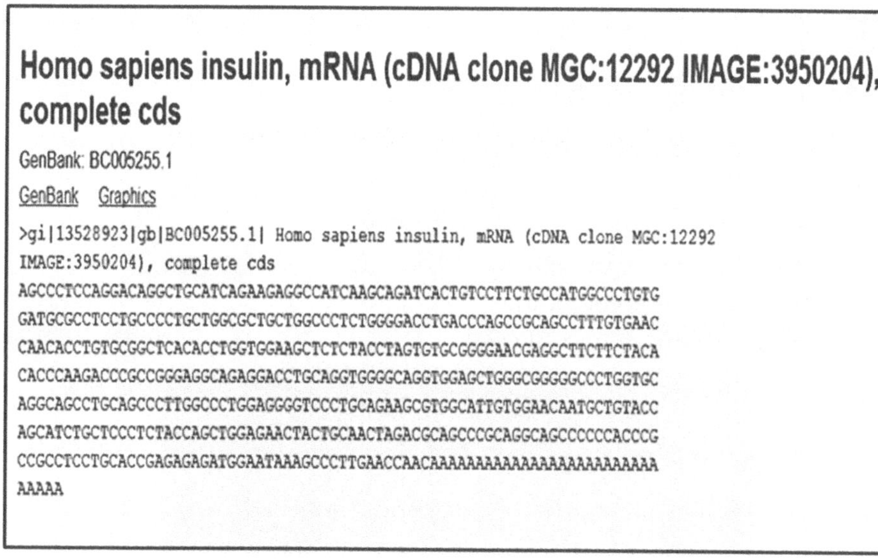

Homo sapiens insulin, mRNA (cDNA clone MGC:12292 IMAGE:3950204), complete cds

GenBank: BC005255.1

GenBank Graphics

```
>gi|13528923|gb|BC005255.1| Homo sapiens insulin, mRNA (cDNA clone MGC:12292
IMAGE:3950204), complete cds
AGCCCTCCAGGACAGGCTGCATCAGAAGAGGCCATCAAGCAGATCACTGTCCTTCTGCCATGGCCCTGTG
GATGCGCCTCCTGCCCCTGCTGGCGCTGCTGGCCCTCTGGGGACCTGACCCAGCCGCAGCCTTTGTGAAC
CAACACCTGTGCGGCTCACACCTGGTGGAAGCTCTCTACCTAGTGTGCGGGGAACGAGGCTTCTTCTACA
CACCCAAGACCCGCCGGGAGGCAGAGGACCTGCAGGTGGGGCAGGTGGAGCTGGGCGGGGGCCCTGGTGC
AGGCAGCCTGCAGCCCTTGGCCCTGGAGGGGTCCCTGCAGAAGCGTGGCATTGTGGAACAATGCTGTACC
AGCATCTGCTCCCTCTACCAGCTGGAGAACTACTGCAACTAGACGCAGCCCGCAGGCAGCCCCCCACCCG
CCGCCTCCTGCACCGAGAGAGATGGAATAAAGCCCTTGAACCAACAAAAAAAAAAAAAAAAAAAAAAAAA
AAAAA
```

Fig. 10.7: Homo sapiens insulin, mRNA (cDNA clone MGC: 12292 IMAGE: 3950204)
Source: Based on review of literature

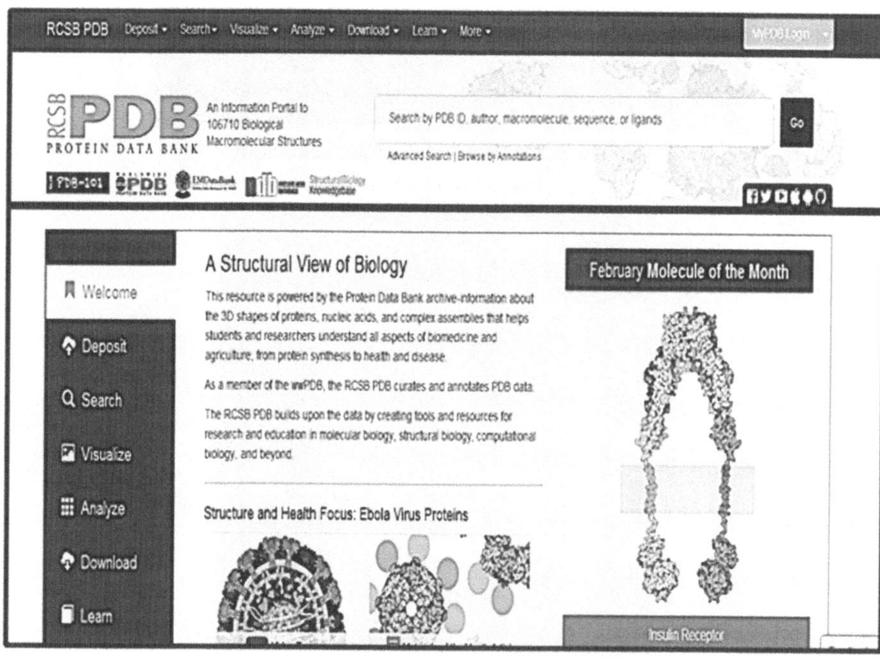

Fig. 10.8: Resource for protein, nucleic acids, viral structures (PDB)
Source: Based on review of literature

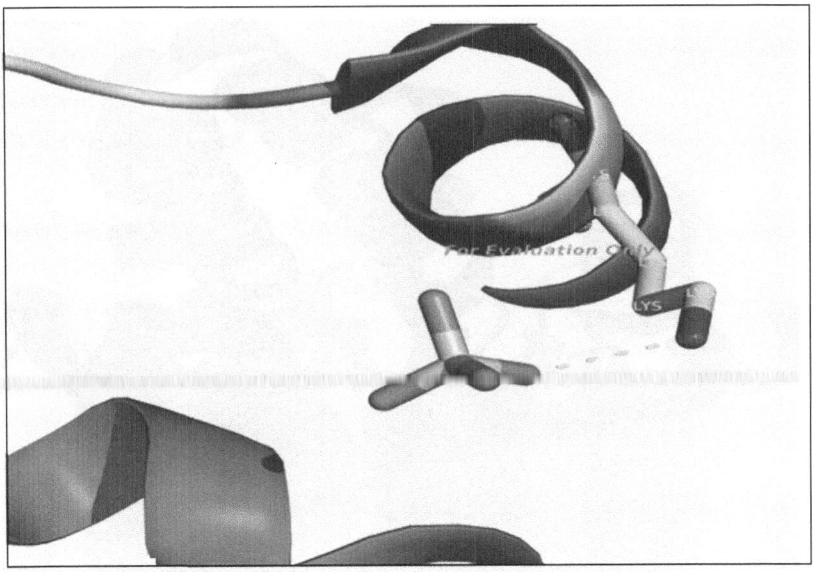

Fig. 10.13: Interaction analysis between ligand and protein
O^- of SO_4 andN^+ of Lys located at a distance of 2.8Å.
Source: Based on review of literature

CONCLUSION

- Access to biological data, analysis of data.

REFERENCES

https://en.wikipedia.org/wiki/Computational_biology
www.cbd.cmu.edu/about-us/what-is-computational-biology/
https://www.nature.com › subjects
https://www.britannica.com/science/computational-biology
https://biology.mit.edu/faculty-and-research/areas-of.../computational-biology/
https://towardsdatascience.com/computational-biology-fca101e20412
https://www.imsc.res.in/computational_biology
https://researcher.watson.ibm.com/researcher/view_group.php?id=137
https://online.lewisu.edu/.../computational-biology-and-bioinformatics-two-fields-cha...
www.frontiersin.org/Bioinformatics_and_Computational_Biology/archive
https://www.springer.com/series/5769
https://brilliant.org/courses/computational-biology/
https://journals.plos.org/ploscompbiol/
www.dbtindia.nic.in/?page_id=1266
https://www.forbes.com/sites/quora/2016/11/.../what-do-computational-biologists-do/
www.jcbose.ac.in/computational-biology
www.sciencepublishinggroup.com/journal/index?journalid=1
https://www.journals.elsevier.com/computational-biology-and-chemistry

Pages: 109-123

Statistical Tools, Data and Instrumentation in Research and Science

Edited by: Er. Chhavi Kumar 'Bharti'; Dr. Prasann Kumar and Dr. Pawan Kumar 'Bharti'

ISBN: 978-93-88854-51-1

Edition: **2020**

Published by: **Discovery Publishing House Pvt. Ltd., New Delhi (India)**

11

Energy Dispersive X-ray Spectroscopy

E Lokesh Goud[1], Prasann Kumar[1,2]

ABSTRACT

Energy Dispersive X-Ray spectroscopy is an analytical technique helps us to analysis the elemental composition in samples depending up on the characteristic x-ray generated from sample under analysis that containing of elements with atomic number greater than3(Z)>3.

Keywords: *Agriculture, Biotic, Crop, Dispersive, Energy.*

INTRODUCTION

The basic principle of EDX for the works has been given below in the form of flow chart.

Bombardment of electron beam on sample containing elements from electron source

⇩

Emission of electrons due to incidence of electron beam

⇩

Creation of holes in inner shell

[1] Department of Agronomy, School of Agriculture, Lovely Professional University, Jalandhar - 144 411 (Punjab) (India)

[2] Divisions of Research and Development, Lovely Professional University, Jalandhar - 144 411 (Punjab) (India)

⇩

Emission of X-Raysdue to filling of hole by higher energy shell electron

⇩

Detector creates pulse charge by absorbing emitted x-ray

⇩

Preamplifier converts charge pulse into voltage pulse

⇩

Elemental analysis from electrical signal

Flow Chart: Flow chart of EDX

Source: Drawn by authors, 2019

Multichannel analyser (MCA)or Computer assisted X-Ray analyser(CXA) are used to control all the above mentioned parts.

INSTRUMENTATION OF THE EDAX

The instrument mainly composed of four components:

- Electron beam source
- X-Ray Detector
- Pulse processor
- Analyzer

Source of electron beam:

- Electron Gun: Cold Field Emitter
- Thermionic Electron Emission

COLD FIELD EMITTER

Uses the strong electric field is known as Extraction voltage to extract the electrons from a filament. Cold gun needs only a small electron source and can generate high current and brightness this process is temperature independent suited for imaging that requires high resolution and high magnification.

However cold gun needs to be periodically flashedit means that the cold filament needs to be heated up in order to restore the emission current to decrease contamination.

THERMIONIC ELECTRON EMISSION

In this method electron gun generates electrons by a heating a solid until the electrons are emitted this process creates steady beam of electrons because it runs at high temperatures it does not need to be flashed. Even though it does not usually achieve as high of resolution and magnification as a cold gun but increased beam stability makes hot gun more suited for EDS.

Sample used in EDX must havefollowing properties:

- Conductivity
- Homogeneity
- Stability
- Polished/Porous

CONDUCTIVITY

Electrons that are emitting from the source needs a path to travel through the sample. The conductive samples allow the electrons to travel through it but nonconductive samples or insulated samples needs a path to be created to travel through the sample. Charging of the sample occurs if the taken sample is nonconductive and if it does not have the sufficient path for the electrons to travel to the ground. Sample charging is commonly explained as buildup of electrons in the particular sample taken for the analysis. Sample charging in sample have huge negative effects on EDS during the imaging charging will leads to the not only the formation of deformities in the image but also unusual contrasting. The charge build up in the sample due to non-conductivity can also deflect the primary beam electron beam incidents on the sample. The deflection of theprimary beam have the ability to change the accuracy of the voltage applied to the sample under analysis as it is important to collecting the accurate data. The path can be created in insulated samples by considering the two methods. First method by the coating the insulated materials with the conductive materials like Gold. Secondly by the painting the insulated material with conductive substances like carbon or silver paint or tape to make a path through the insulated material (Figure 11.1).

HOMOGENEITY

A Homogenous samples are easier to analyze as the concentration of the particle in sample are distributed same all over the sample which results in the reading from the one end of the sample will give results which are equal to the results from the another end of the sample.In Non-homogenous samples the distribution of the particles are in the random manner, the random distribution of particles in sample affect the accuracy of the analysis. While analyzing the non-homogenous samples we have to remember that we have to take the average of the several areas to collect accurate data (Figure 11.2).

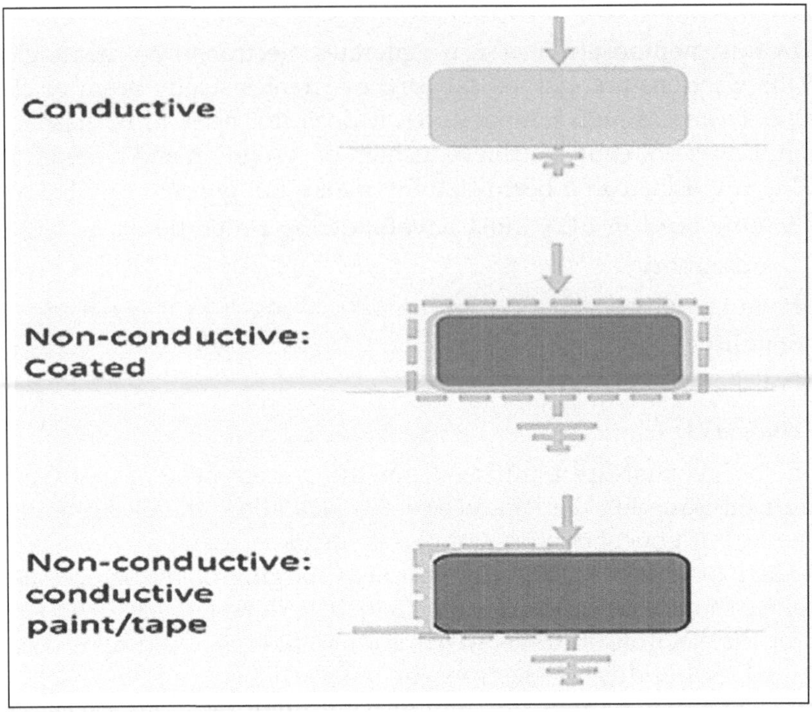

Fig. 11.1: Showing the conductive sample,
Nonconductive sample coated with gold and conductive tape or paint
Source: Based on review of literature, 2019

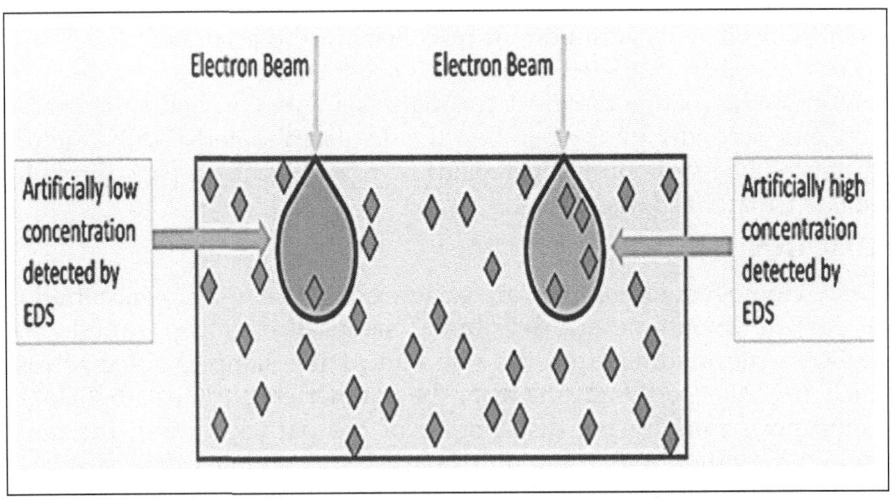

Fig. 11.2: Indicating the elemental distribution in Non-homogenous sample
Source: Based on review of literature

STABILITY AND POROSITY

The sample taken for analysis must be stable in the nature or environment to run EDS, it means that the sample under analysis should not be outgassing, melting or changing the state during the analysis.

SAMPLE SURFACE SHOULD BE SMOOTH AND POLISHED

The exiting surface for X-rays should be have smooth or polished area as the as the variations in the topography of sample can affect the path of x-rays.It is also consider that sample should be cleaned before placing the sample in the microscope (Figure 11.3).

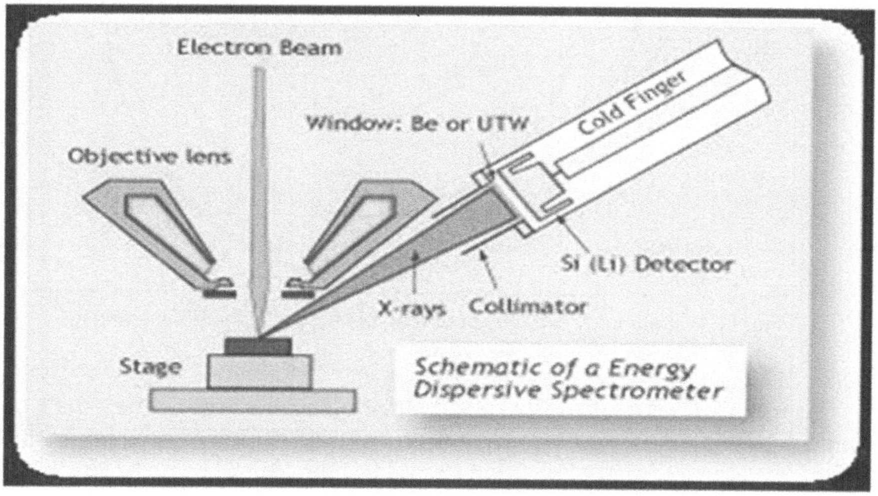

Fig. 11.3: indicating working process of Energy Dispersive X-Ray Spectroscope
Source: Based on review of literature

In EDX as beam of electrons from electron source incident on the atoms present in the smooth and polished surface of the homogenous sample, the electrons present in the inner shell of atom get excited and creates hole in inner shell then electron from higher shell fill the hole in inner shell by releasing energy in the form X-rays. Energy released is expressed in eV (electron volts) energy released is equal to energy difference between the two levels.The characteristic x-rays formed is called on the basis of movement of electrons of higher energy shell to lower energy shell in which the electron hole occurred because of excitation of electrons like k alpha and k beta. Example: if electron comes from L shell to K Then it is named as K alpha, if it comes from M shell to K shell it is known as K beta.X-rays with K-beta radiation have more energy than K-alpha radiation.

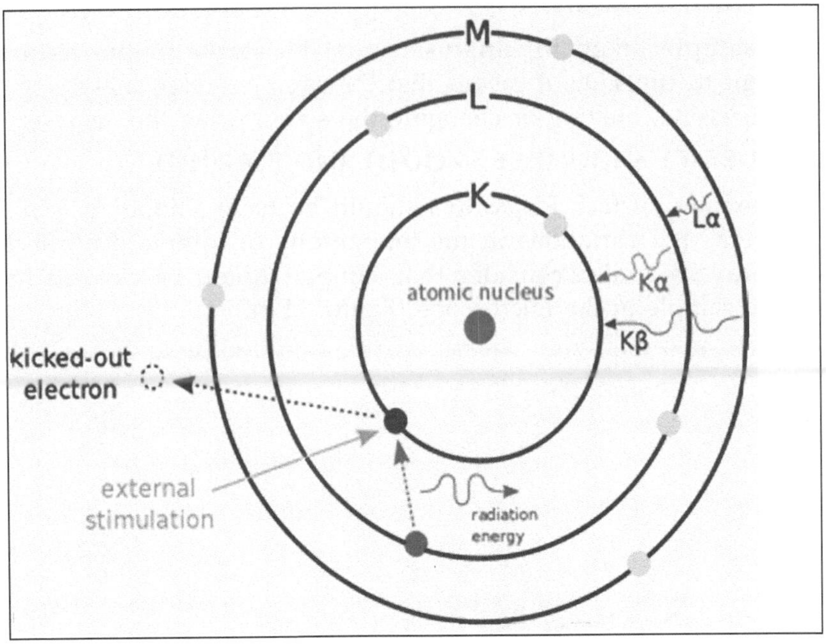

Fig. 11.4: The energy difference between M and K is higher than L and K

Source: Based on review of literature

Figure 11.4, indicating the removal of electrons from inner shell of an atom by the incidence of beam ofelectrons and filling the holes in lower shells by electrons of higher shells by releasing the energy in the form of x-rays.When we are using a microscope the emission energy is related to the voltage that we are applying therefore we have to apply an appropriate kilovolts so we can get ample x-ray from sample. Typically for the most of the samples 20-25 Kilovolts is used but for the samples of film or thin layer of powder 10-15 kilovolts are used.

X-RAY DETECTORS

The detectors are used in energy dispersive x-ray spectroscopy to convert the energy in the x-rays to the proportional voltages. Detectoris present in the end of the long arm in the sample chamber of main instrument. The voltage signals are very noisy and have to undergo shaping and noise reduction and finally output is 1/9 nice smooth looking signal measured in counts. The noise in the signal is minimized by the averaging the signal over a period of time known as Processing time, as the processing time increases the noise in the signal is reduced. Even though the longer processing decreases the noise in the signal it increases the dead time, Dead time is related to input and output rates of the detector, the input rate at which the x-rays pulses are detected and the output rate is the rate at which pulses are sent to the computer for the analyzation when the input rate is greater than output rate it leads to the pulse pile up (it can be explained it by taking the water bottle with a hole if water is going faster than water can flow out of the hole then there will be of a build up of water inside the water bottle, same in the manner the pulses are piling up at the detector and they are just waiting to be processed). Dead time is the time where pulses are not measured it is used as a tool to combat pulse pile up with that time a pulse will hit the detector and then the dead time is started stopping more pulses from being measured and pilling up, once the pulse is converted into voltage signal and has a noise removed the dead time will stop, allowing a new x-ray to the detector. Dead time also increases the amount of signal that is rejected for this we have an automatic compensate on for this in the form of live time the clock for live times moves slower than real clocks, so equipment that we had like to collect the signals during the processing time of 100 seconds it will take actually longer than 100 seconds for the life time we completed this is because the time is extended to compensate for the output rate being less than the input rate by the degree of dead time, when the dead time becomes greater than 60 percentage results in rejection of many signals and results are obtained inaccurate. The result of EDS is overlay of all the signals on the graph of counts versus energy levels, Counts are number of X-rays that are processedby the detector, the larger the counts stronger the data is and less likely data is effected by the noise. Ideal requirement of counts should be more than that of 10000 counts for accurate data. We can increase the number of counts in our signal by voltage, working distance, processing time, acquisition time The X-ray counts (which is abundance of emitted X-Rays)versus X-Rays energies are measured by EDS Detector. At finally an energy dispersive x-ray spectroscopy is a solid device which is based on lithium drifted silicon. AS X-Rays strike the surface of detector charge pulse is created which is equal to energy of incident x-ray incident on detectors. Range of x-rays from 100 electron volts to 20 kilo electron volts are readily measured with a Si (Li) detector and this measuring range can be extended to 100 kilo electron volts with an High purity Germanium detector. Now a day's detector consists of high resistivity silicon chip gain more popularity known as Silicon drift detector and the electrons moves towards the collecting anode because of the presence of low capacitance of this anode it utilizes the shorter processing time and allow extremely high throughput. Silicon drift detector has the capability of producing high count rates and processing. Silicon drift detector provides higher resolution even at high count rates. It has higher processing power which results in the reduction of time utilized for processing x-ray (decreased death time). This detector is operated and stored at high temperatures and eliminating the necessity of liquid nitrogen cooling. We can use the large silicon drift detector chips of size equal to or more than 40 mm^2 as the chip capacitance is not dependent on the area of the detector, detector with large chip not only increases more count rate but also reduces the damage on the sample. Poor quantum efficiency suffers the detector with silicon based technologies when the energy in the x-rays more than of 30 keV due to reduction in the detector stopping power,For the x-ray processing of higher energies detectors made up of high density semiconductors and capability to operating at room temperature are used they may be Cadmium Zinc telluride and Cadmium telluride.

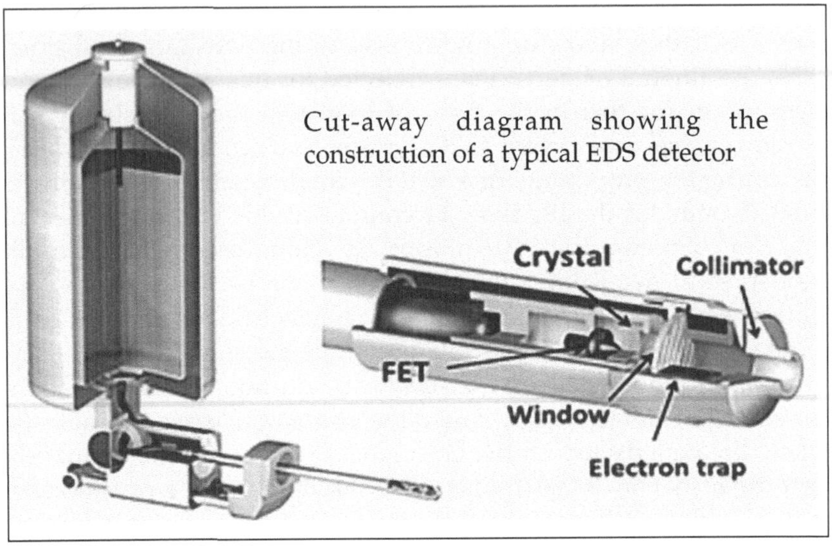

Fig. 11.5: Showing the various parts of the Energy Dispersive X-Ray Spectroscopy

Source: Based on review of literature

Components of Detector

- Collimator assembly
- Electron trap
- Window
- Char F
- Crystal
- FET (Field Effect Transistor)

COLLIMATOR ASSEMBLY

The objective of the collimator to utilize in detector to provide an restrictive aperature to through which x-rays should pass in order to make a way to detector. The collimator helps to detect the x-rays that are being generated due to incidence of beam of electrons on the sample.

ELECTRON TRAP

When the electrons penetrates the detector background artefacts are created. The electron trap contains a pair of permanent magnets which have the main object to deflect the passing electrons and the electron trap that used in detector gives guarantee that only the x-rays should be pass through the detector.

WINDOW

In order to maintain isolation from the microscope chamber to maintain vacuum inside the detector the window is used. As the window is transparent in nature allows low energy x-rays.He is the only material that we are using from many previous years.

CHAR F

Char F in the detector comprises the thin window composed of polymer and the purpose of thischar F totransmit the x-rays from elements that are having the atomic number more than that of Beryllium.

CRYSTAL

In detector the Silicon drifted lithium of around the 3mm thickness is used as a crystal material for small levels of impurity compensation. As the x-rays incident on the silicon drifted lithium crystal in detector the energy in the x-rays get absorbed by a series of ionizations within a semiconductor to generate electron hole pair. Each electron pair is generated by the absorption of the 3.76ev of x-ray radiation. The electrons that are promoted to the conduction band have the tendency to move freely in the crystal lattice. Every excited electrons leaves behind a hole in the valence bond,which acts as a positive charge carrier within the crystal. Whenthe crystals are biased by using the high voltage,the holes moves towards the opposite poles which results in the generation of charge signals that have the size proportional to the incident x-ray energy.

FIELD EFFECT TRANSISTOR

The Field effect transistor designed toperform the initial stage of amplification by measuring the charge released by the crystal due to incident of x-ray and makes total output as voltage output.FET that are using now are integrated with chips to increase the resolution with output which is achieved by reducing the noise by minimizing the capacitance between field effect transistor and anode. The sharp voltage steps are generated by the incident of charge accumulated x-rays on the feedback capacitor during the operation. The step size of the voltage is proportional to the energy of the x-rays incident. In order to avoid the preamplifier saturation, restoration of buildup charge is periodically required. Cryo charge, EDS detector is a self-enclosed vacuum system commonly called as cryo charge that have the liquid nitrogen or cryogenic pumping, The crystal and the field effect transistor are mounted on the cold finger within the cryo charge to reduce noise by cooling as cooling necessary as the detector produces the small charge pulses, at low voltages the resolution of the detector depends upon the noise.By the above information the main purpose of X-ray detector is to absorb the X-rays from sample which are emitted only because of incident of electron beam on sample and to convert them into charge pulses which have the energy equal to that of incident X-rays on detector.

PULSE PROCESSOR

The charge pulse created by detector reaches pulse processor for further amplification. Charge sensitive pre-amplifier that is designed to convert the charge pulse to voltage pulse.

ANALYZER

For the analysis we use the Multichannel analyzer, the energy of x-ray can be obtained by imaging the voltage of charge pulses. The energy is then sent for display. Here data is displayed by using the Histogram by plotting intensity versus voltages.

OPERATION OF EDS SYSTEM

If we are operating the energy dispersive x-ray dispersive system which is used by the many persons, first of all we have to correct the EDS time constant before starting the energy dispersive x-ray measurement here the time constant refers to the processing time for the reduction of noise, shaping time, resolution and counts rate range. We also correct the distance and degree of angle between the specimen and detector if the energy dispersive x-ray spectroscopy is placed on the movable arm for obtaining the effective results. In order to produce the acceptable level of system dead time, we have to select proper beam current, as the EDS detector makes pulse pileup when the incidence of x –rays emitted from the sample are more due to the incidence of the electron beam of high voltage on the sample, it may results in the increase of dead time, for compensating the possible protons lost during the dead time additional time is added at the conclusion of the user specified time so that all the measurements are made on the same live time inorder to achieve constant dose. Increased current beam may results in the increasing the dead time so increased dead time can be controlled by applying the proper beam current. Dead time can be checked timely by altering the beam current and compairing the measured x-ray intensity predicted. There is a chances of appearance of x-ray peaks in wrong locations when the energy calibration is not correct. that may results in the increased failures as the all forms of peak identification expected to be suffer. So it is necessary to perform the EDS energy calibration and it is also important to record the adequate counts in the spectrum.

QUALITATIVE AND QUANTITATIVE ANALYSIS OF DATA

X-Rays generated in a spectrum helps us to carry out qualitative analysis to identify the elements that are present in the sample when the sample is irradiated with high energy beam of electrons in order to perform qualitative analysis we have to follow three methods they are: (1) Point analysis, (2) Line analysis, (3) Mapping. In Point analysis the spectrum is obtained from a point which is radiated with electrons. In line analysis spectrum is obtained from specified line which is displaying one dimensional desired elemental distribution. In Mapping the spectrum is obtained from a specified area displayed two dimensional elemental distribution. It is also called as area analysis. In order to study the particular elemental distribution we use x-ray mapping, for analysis the particular element in the sample, electron beam is scanned over a specified area and characteristics x-rays are acquired. Distribution of particular element is not obtained in case when there is ratio between the peak and background is very low. If the characteristics x-rays of elements of interest are close to those of not required, x-ray mapping does not show the distribution of elements which are not of interest. This occurs only when the energy difference between the desired elements is equal to the spectrometer energy resolution. It takes more time to acquire one x-ray picture as intensities of x-rays are less in comparision to that of secondary and backscattered electrons. Area analysis limits the resolution of x-ray mapping. Analysis area, the electrons get diffused and lose their energy when they incident on specimen by generating characteristics x-rays. The generated x-rays spread over area around of few micrometers under standard operating conditions. So larger area needs to be analyzed in order to examine the particle of the order of few nm range in a scanning electronic microscope image. The analysis area can be reduced by the reducing accelerating voltage. But the accelerating voltage cannot be reduced below a certain level as the generation of x-rays requires high accelerating voltages. We can also reduce the analysis area by reducing thickness of the sample under investigation. Precise elemental distribution can be acquired using the quantitative analysis method even though the ratio between the peak and background is low. Quantitative analysis performed, as the characteristic x-rays intensities are proportional to the particular elements concentration. The concentration of unknown elements in a sample can be obtained by matching the intensities of characteristic x-ray of standard sample with that of the unknown sample. However the,x-ray generated in the sample may be either absorbed within the sample or excite the x-rays from other elements before being emitted in vacuum. In order to perform the quantitative analysis the following requirements are prerequisite. They are surface are of the specimen should be flat or polished, electron probe should be enter the sample in perpendicular direction, distribution of elements in the x-ray generation area should be uniform (Homogenous distribution of elements in sample).

FEATURES OF EDX

Used for analysis of broad range of elements it means the elements in the sample that are ranging from Boron to Uranium can be analyzed.

In histogram X-axis represents the x-rays energy and Y-axis represents X-ray counts.

Sample qualitative compositional data can be known from the respective peak positions with appropriate energies.

- The concentration calculation requires the net count rates and characteristics X-ray energy of a specimen is the marker of specimen atomic number
- The method that used in EDS is Energy dispersive method with a Si (Li)semiconductor detector
- The resolution obtained by the EDS is approximately 130 to 140 electron volts
- The measuring speed is very fast and multi element simultaneous measurement is also possible with energy dispersive x-ray spectroscopy
- The damage and contamination of the sample under observation is very less.
- The detection limit of the energy dispersive x-ray spectroscopy is lies between the 1500 parts per million to 2000 parts per million.

VARIOUS APPLICATIONS OF EDX

1. Identification of heavy metal with the help of EDX

- Toxic substances released by the industry's leading to the increase in environmental pollution.
- As heavy metals are non-biodegradable and have long half life time they can accumulate in ecological systems,Heavy metals became as more problematic pollutants.
- In order to produce the products industries utilizing the resources that contaminated with heavy metals which resulting the accumulation of heavy metals in soils as well as in plants.
- The most commonly released heavy metals from the industries that accumulate in plants causes Toxic and Non Toxic effects are Cadmium,Lead(Pb),Nickel(Ni), and Zinc(Zn).
- The presence of heavy metals in plants creates threshold toxicity and non-threshold toxicity, presence of this elements are non-toxic up to certain level but they became toxic when the accumulation or concentration of heavy metal increases.
- The presence of heavy metal in the plants can be estimated or identified by using the Energy Dispersive X-ray Spectroscopy

which helps in identification of type of heavy metal (Qualitative) and also the amount of heavy metal (Quantity) that present in the sample.

- Management practices like Land usage types and crop rotation types influences the accumulation of heavy metals in Agricultural lands

2. **For identifying the elemental composition of Tissue calcification**
   - Changes in the calcium levels present in the body may leads to the several effects on the tissues of an organism.
   - The diseases like cardiovascular abnormalities and cancer caused due to excess accumulation of organic compounds or minerals in the tissues of the human body.
   - In order to identify the physiochemical processes related with accumulation of organic compounds or minerals are identified by the help of Energy Dispersive X-ray Spectroscopy.
   - Abnormal deposition of calcium salts,along with minor amounts of magnesium, Iron and other mineral salts is called as Pathologic calcifications.

3. **EDX microanalysis for the development of the nanotechnologies**

The substances like TiO_2, FeXOy, carbon, amorphous SiO^2 are safe to humans when they are applied in micrometric range but their application in nanometric scale may induces the deterimental effect on the human health. Nanoparticles are small substances that are less than 100nm in at least one dimension. Nanoparticles gained huge importance in various applications like biomedical imaging, diagnostic labs and drug delivery. In order to address the safety of nanoparticles it is important to understand biological responses with respect to the nanoparticles. Silver nanoparticles are gaining importance in large range of applications like wound dressing and textiles and also for the food processing and packing of food. Vaccines and drug delivery were perfected by the use of nanotechnologies because they have the properties to give protection and specific delivery cargo to immune cells.For the effective use of nanoparticles in bio medical purposes and medical applications we required to have an idea on the nanoparticles potential toxicity and this can be observed by the use of energy dispersive x-ray spectroscopy.

PARAMETERS OF ENERGY DISPERSIVE X-RAY SPECTROSCOPY

Count rate for obtaining good quality spectrum.If the sample consists largely of high energy peaks more than 1 kilo electron volts, the period at which incident x-rays not measured (Dead time) is to be at 20-40 percent,pulse processing time should be at the range of 50-100 micro seconds and count rate per seconds should be in the range of 500-2500 counts per second this are considered as good numbers but in case where the spectrum is dominated by the lower energy peaks it mean less than 1 kilo electron volts then count rate per second should be in the range of 500-1000 counts per second and pulse processing time of 100 microseconds is considered. Accelerating voltage: The ratio of accelerating voltage used to the critical excitation energy of a given line for an element is called over voltage. Over voltage for the higher energy line is at least 2 but it should greater than of 10-20 times lowest energy line of interest.The takeoff angle relates with the sample working distance sample tilt, detector position and detector angle. The range of typical takeoff angle ranges between the 25 to 40 degrees. By increasing the takeoff angle we can enhance or increase the sensitivity for the low energy x-rays or signals that are characterized by high absorption. Some detectors are do not require sample tilt that are placed at the angle of 35 degrees above the horizontal. Sample in tilt position for horizontal entry detector to achieve an optimum take off angle.

LIMITATIONS

There are energy peak overlaps among different elements particularly those corresponding to x-rays generated by emission from different energy level shells like K, L, M in different elements. We can observe the energy peak overlapping in Manganese-k alpha and Chromium-k beta and various lines in Beryllium. User has to apply deconvolution methods to peak separation when individual peaks corresponds to many different elements at higher energies.For actual chemical analysis Energy dispersive X-Ray spectroscopy is more lessley used.Energy Dispersive x-ray spectroscopy is not suitable for detection of elements like Hydrogen Helium, Lithiumin sample as their atomic number is less than 3.For the detection of elements that are with atomic number below the sodium the detectors used in the Energy Dispersive x-ray spectroscopy is equipped with Be window. Dependingup on the instrument and operating conditions for detection light elements we use the polymer based thin windows.

CONCLUSION

By the use of EDS we can able to find out the different type of elements and amount or quantity of elements that are present in the sample when the atomic number of the elements present in the given sample is more than 3 as silicon lithium detector contains beryllium window. To obtain the best results there should be balance between count rate and resolution. By the extending the period of measuring each x-ray spectral resolution can be improved. When the two photons reaches the detector they are not measured as separate event rather they are added to the energy histogram as one single count making resultant peak distorted, in order to avoid pilling up it is advised to maintain dead time below 30 percent. Energy Dispersive X-ray spectroscopy gain importance in the development of nano particle technology, for finding out or measuring the bio accumulation ratio of heavy metals in plants and it is also gaining more importance in the various biological applications.

REFERENCES

https://en.wikipedia.org › wiki › Energy-dispersive_X-ray_spectroscopy
https://www.sciencedirect.com › topics › chemistry › energy-dispersive-spect.
https://www.sciencedirect.com › topics › materials-science › energy-dispersiv...
https://www.mee-inc.com › hamm › energy-dispersive-x-ray-spectroscopy...
https://cfamm.ucr.edu › documents › eds-intro
www.charfac.umn.edu › instruments › eds_on_sem_primer
https://chem.libretexts.org › ... › Spectroscopy
https://serc.carleton.edu › research_education › geochemsheets › eds
https://blog.phenom-world.com › Blog
www.intertek.com › analysis › microscopy › edx

Pages: 124-132

Statistical Tools, Data and Instrumentation in Research and Science
Edited by: Er. Chhavi Kumar 'Bharti'; Dr. Prasann Kumar and
Dr. Pawan Kumar 'Bharti'
ISBN: 978-93-88854-51-1
Edition: 2020
Published by: Discovery Publishing House Pvt. Ltd., New Delhi (India)

12

Infrared Spectroscopy
An Overview

Yaman[1], Prasann Kumar[1,2]

ABSTRACT

Infrared spectroscopy deals with the measurements of the radiations which are absorbed or transmit within the infrared region of the electromagnetic spectrum. In the electromagnetic spectrum there is the distribution of all the radiations according to their wavelength and frequency. The molecules which are infrared active changes their dipole moment when absorption taking place and provide functional group and fingerprint characteristic of the substance present in the given sample from infrared spectrum. Infrared spectroscopy involves dispersive and FTIR instruments. In the dispersive type there is the use of monochromator which separate the infrared radiations into individual frequency which is then detect by the detector. While FTIR uses Michelson interferometer, core of this instrument and all the frequencies of infrared radiations obtained by detector simultaneously. Dispersive spectroscopy is the older technology. Hence FTIR spectroscopy is more preferred in modern day because of rapid scanning speed over the dispersive type.

Keywords: *Agriculture, Biotic, Crop, Density, Infrared, Spectroscopy.*

INTRODUCTION

Interaction between matter and light is known as spectroscopy. Infrared spectroscopy uses the infrared region of electromagnetic spectrum for the determination of functional group and structures of molecule. When

[1] Department of Agronomy, School of Agriculture, Lovely Professional University, Jalandhar - 144 411 (Punjab) (India)
[2] Divisions of Research and Development. Lovely Professional University, Jalandhar - 144 411 (Punjab) (India)

exposed to infrared radiation then sample molecule selectively absorb radiation of specific wavelength which changes the state of atoms within molecule. There is change in the frequency and amplitude of molecular vibrations which can be measured by producing infrared spectrum.

There are three IR regions viz. near, mid and far which can be defined as:

- **Near infrared region (12500-4000 cm^{-1}):**
  - Wavelength ranges from 0.7-2.5 micrometers
  - Near to visible red region
  - Used in fibre optic communication and night vision devices
  - Used in agriculture, textile industries, medicinal and pharmaceutical advances
- **Mid infrared region (4000-400 cm^{-1}):**
  - Wavelength ranges from 2.5-25 micrometers
  - It provides structural information for organic molecules
  - It gives information about the molecular motions, functional group and fingerprint of specific compound
  - FTIR spectroscopy most preferred the use of mid infrared region for carrying out information
- **Far infrared region (400-10 cm^{-1}):**
  - Wavelength ranges from 25-1000 micrometers
  - This region is particularly useful for inorganic studies

Why Infrared spectroscopy

- Infrared spectroscopy is widely use for the determination of structure of molecules because most of the molecules are infrared active.
- Infrared spectroscopy is very useful method for the qualitative analysis of different kinds of the materials.
- There is infrared spectrum having the presence of peaks of different sizes has direct indication about the amount of required material present in the given sample.

ELECTROMAGNETIC SPECTRUM

It is the distribution of entire electromagnetic radiation according to frequency or wavelength. All the electromagnetic radiation travel in form of wave at the speed of light. All these waves are different from each other in length and frequency.The electromagnetic spectrum from the lowest to the highest frequency or longest to shortest wavelength consists of radio waves, microwaves, infrared rays, visible light, ultraviolet rays, X-rays and gamma rays. We can use all the wavelengths and frequencies of electromagnetic radiation for spectroscopy (Figure 12.1).

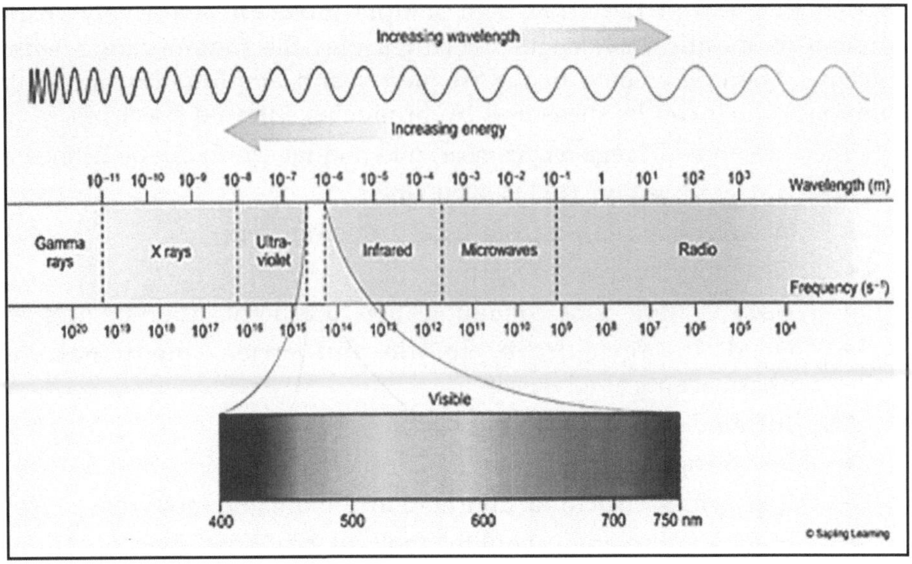

Fig. 12.1: Electromagnetic Spectrum

Source: Based on review of literature

TYPES OF RADIATION

➢ **Radio waves:**

- These are use in the radio communication, satellites, mobile phones and televisions
- These are also use for navigation such as in global positioning system (GPS) and in remote control

➢ **Microwaves:**

- Microwaves use in oven for cooking food
- These are useful for communication and transmit information because they have the ability to penetrate clouds, smoke and light rain
- They can be used in radar which helps in weather forecasting

➢ **Infrared radiation:**

- IR light discovered in 1800 by Sir William Herschel
- It is between the microwaves and visible light
- Classified as near infrared rays (NIR), mid infrared rays (MIR) and far infrared rays (FIR)
- Used in remote sensing and TV remote

➢ **Visible light:**

- It is the part of electromagnetic spectrum which can be seen by human eye

- Visible light consist of different colors (VIBGYOR) having specific wavelength with different types of photons according to their color
- Among VIBGYOR, red and blue light is most important for agriculture which encourage flowering and vegetative growth of the crops respectively

➢ **Ultraviolet rays:**

- These are the rays which coming from the sun causing sunburns and skin cancer
- Ozone layer present in the stratosphere which protect us from harmful UV rays
- UV light use in the powerful telescopes to see the stars in space

➢ **X-rays:**

- X-rays were discovered by Wilhelm Roentgen who is German scientist and got nobel prize for his discovery in 1901
- It has capacity to penetrate the skin and muscle and produce the medical images of body

➢ **Gamma rays:**

- These are the shortest waves with high frequency and energy
- In chemotherapy there is use of gamma rays
- Gamma rays can be used for the treatment of cancer

ELECTROMAGNETIC RADIATION AND SPECTROSCOPY

Spectroscopy is interaction between matter (atoms, molecules) and electromagnetic radiation. There is presence of different radiations in the electromagnetic spectrum and all the radiations have specific type of interaction with molecules, compounds and atoms. Hence different types of spectroscopy are:

➢ **Absorption**

Absorption means when the incident electromagnetic radiation is absorb by the molecules. Absorption takes place only when the energy of light matches with the energy of molecule. Absorption is measured by transmittance percentage that how much of radiation is pass through the molecule with the help of infrared spectra. Spectroscopy which includes absorption are infrared spectroscopy (IR spectroscopy) and ultraviolet-visible spectroscopy (UV-Vis spectroscopy).

➢ **Emission**

It means when the material itself emit the electromagnetic radiation which can be measured by fluorescence spectroscopy.

➢ **Scattering or Diffraction and Reflection**

It studies that how much of the incident radiation is reflected, diffracted and scattered from the matter. For example X-ray crystallography works on this phenomenon for determining the arrangement of atoms in molecule.

➢ **Inelastic Scattering**

In this when the electromagnetic radiation interacts with matter, after that wavelength and frequency of that incident light is changed due to oscillation of light and molecular vibration. This phenomenon is observed in Raman spectroscopy.

INFRARED ACTIVE MODES

In the molecules there is presence of bonds which absorb infrared light more strongly because of the similar energy. The molecules which are infrared active changes their dipole moment periodically when vibration taking place in the molecules then this type of vibration known as infrared active. Vibration that are infrared active are stretching and bending modes. In the bonds if the polarity is more then greater is the IR light absorption. For example: Carbonyl bond which is more polar then greater is the absorption and in alkynes there is carbon-carbon triple bond which is less polar thus absorption is less.There are some vibrations which are infrared inactive because there is no change in the dipole moment of the molecules and therefore there is no absorption of IR light.

Types of vibrations:

➢ **Symmetrical stretching vibration:** The atoms present in the molecule move in the same direction from the central atom.

➢ **Asymmetrical stretching vibration:** In this stretching one atom moves away from central atom while other moves towards the central atom.

➢ **Rocking vibration:** In this vibration atoms in the molecule swing back and forth from the central atom just like pendulum in the clock.

➢ **Scissoring vibration:** In this two atoms in the molecule approach each other with respect to central atom.

➢ **Wagging vibration:** In wagging two atoms move to same direction out of the plane from central atom.

➢ **Twisting vibration:** This vibration also occur out of the plane in which one atom move up while other move down with respect to central atom.

ABSORPTION CONSIDERATIONS

There is a source which transmit the infrared radiation of all the wavelengths. Some of the infrared radiation absorbed by the sample and some are pass through it. Absorption takes place only when the energy of infrared radiation matches with energy of molecules. Then transmitted radiationis detect by the detector resulting to give an IR spectrum for the sample. With the help of this spectrum absorption and transmittance can be measured. There is unique IR spectrum for each particular type of samples (gas, liquid and solid). The amount of IR radiations which are absorb or transmit by sample can be measured by some equations which as follow:

➢ **Transmittance can be calculated by following equation:**

$\%T = I/I_0 \times 100$

Where:

I = Intensity of the radiation leaving the sample

$\mathbf{I_0}$= Intensity of the incident radiation

➢ **Absorbance can be calculated by following equation:**

Beer Lambert law:

$A = \log_{10} (I_0/I)$

= □lc

where

□ = Molar absorptivity ($Lmol^{-1}cm^{-1}$)

l = Length of path travel by light (cm)

c = Concentration of solution ($molL^{-1}$)

INFRARED SPECTRUM

IR spectra shows the absorption band that enable to determine the functional groups which are present in the molecules. IR spectra show the result in the form of peaks. Each peak in the spectra represent the presence of a particular functional group. IR spectra represents the percent transmittance against the wavenumbers (Figure 12.2). There are two regions in the IR spectrum which are follows:

➢ **Functional group region:** Stretching vibration occurs in functional group region.

➢ **Fingerprint region:** Bending vibration occurs in this region.

- Wavenumbers of IR region ranges from 10 to 12500 cm^{-1}
- Most of the analyses takes place with in mid infrared region ranges from 400 to 4000 cm^{-1}

Relationship between wavenumber and wavelength given as follow:

□ = 1/□

where: □ is wavenumber and □is wavelength

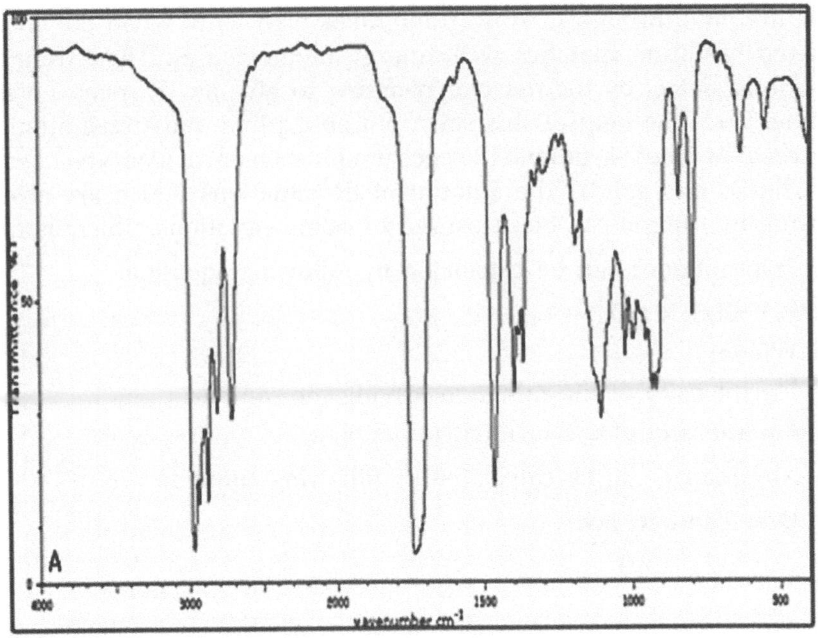

Fig. 12.2: Infrared spectra

Source: Based on review of literature

INFRARED INSTRUMENTS

Infrared spectrometers categorized into two classes:

- Dispersive instruments
- Fourier transform instruments

DISPERSIVE INFRARED INSTRUMENTS

These instruments are also called grating or scanning spectrometers. This is the older technology. In this instrument when the source emits the infrared radiation which is then separated into individual frequencies with the help of a prism or grating. After that there is presence of detector which detect the individual frequencies which has passed through the sample. Then there is formation of spectrum which gives information about the given sample.

There are two types of dispersive infrared instruments:

- Single beam infrared instrument
- Double beam infrared instrument

Single beam infrared instrument: It includes an infrared source, a monochromator and a detector. In it source emit infrared radiations and passes through the sample. After that radiation interact with the monochromator which separate broad infrared radiation into narrow infrared radiation and then detect by the detector. But in single beam IR instrument stability of infrared source and detector changes with time and measurement of sample and blank does not take place simultaneously. These limitations of single beam IR instrument minimize by the double beam IR instrument.

Double beam infrared instrument: This instrument uses two beams of light which is able to measure the sample and reference simultaneously. Chopper is also use in this instrument which control the radiation path. In this instrument infrared radiation is splits into two radiations and one beam of light is passed through the reference while other passes through the sample. Here reference is use to eradicate the absorption which is caused by the water vapour in air (Figure 12.3).

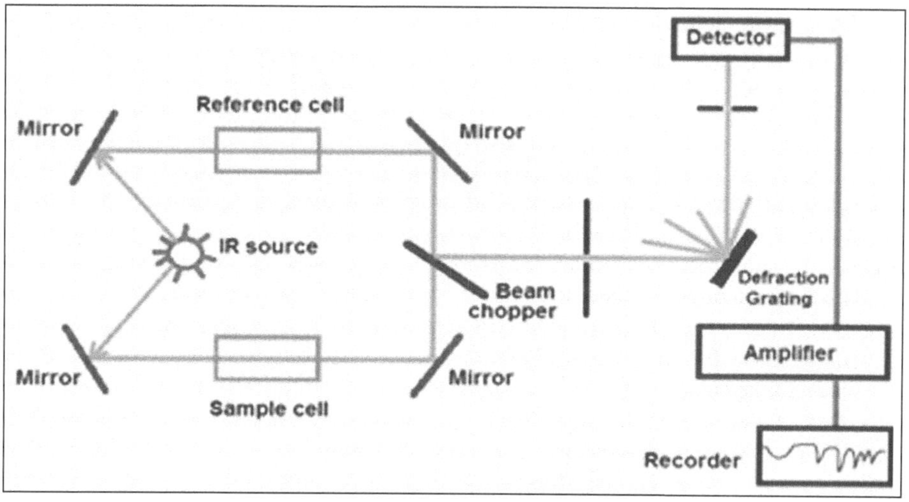

Fig. 12.3: Double beam infrared instrument
Source: Based on review of literature

Applications of IR spectroscopy:

- With the help of this we can identify the structure and functional group of the molecules. Structure of molecule can be identify by the fingerprint region of the spectra.
- Infrared spectroscopy is use to identify the samples of substances which are organic and also determine whether they are identical or not. If they are identical then there will be same infrared spectra.
- This instrument also used to determine the fat, lactose and protein content in the milk.
- IR spectrum also determine the presence of impurities in the particular compound.
- IR spectroscopy use for the analysis of food products for any contamination.

Among these two instruments Fourier transform is more preferred over the dispersive type because of the following reasons:

- Fourier transform is non destructive technique
- Scanning speed is very high with in few seconds
- It provides more accurate and precise measurement
- In this there is only one moving part that is mirror as compare to dispersive type
- All the frequencies of radiation fall on the detector simultaneously while in dispersive type only narrow frequency fall on the detector
- High sensitive and faster while other is time consuming
- Data collection is easier
- Sample is not subject to thermal effects in FTIR
- Stray light does not affect detector since all the signals are modulated

REFERENCES

Kealey, D. andFifield, F. W. "Principle and Practice of Analytical Chemistry" Chapter 7 and 9. Fifth Edition. Blackwell Science Ltd. UK 2000.

Larkin, P. J. " Infrared and Raman Spectroscopy. Principles and Spectral Interpretation" The Netherlands. Elsevier 2011.

Mohamed, M. A., Jaafar, J., Ismail, A. F., Othman, M.H.D., Rahman, M.A. " Fourier Transform Infrared spectroscopy" Universiti Teknology Malaysia, Johor Bahru, Johor, Malaysia.

Pavia, D. L., Lampman, G. M. and Kriz, G. S. " Introduction to spectroscopy. A guide for student of organic chemistry" Thompson Learning. United States of America 2001.

Raphael, Linker. " Application of FTIR Spectroscopy to Agricultural soils analysis". Faculty of Civil and Environmental Engineering Technion – Israel Institute of technology.

Theophanides, T. "Introduction to Infrared spectroscopy". National Technical university of Athens, Chemical Engineering Department, Radiation Chemistry and Biospectroscopy, Zografou campus, Zografou, Athens Greece.

Pages: 133-141
Statistical Tools, Data and Instrumentation in Research and Science
Edited by: Er. Chhavi Kumar 'Bharti'; Dr. Prasann Kumar and
Dr. Pawan Kumar 'Bharti'
ISBN: 978-93-88854-51-1
Edition: 2020
Published by: Discovery Publishing House Pvt. Ltd., New Delhi (India)

13

Fourier Transform Infrared Spectroscopy
An Overview

Yaman[1], Prasann Kumar[1,2]

ABSTRACT

Fourier transform infrared spectroscopy which is used to determine functional group and structures of molecule with molecule's characteristics absorption of infrared radiation and provide information in form of peaks. It can be used for the analysis of any sample whether it is in gas, solid and liquid form. Most important component of FTIR is Michelson Interferometer which splits one beam of light into two beams which create constructive or destructive interference which is detected by photoconductive detector. Then interferogram of sample signal is converted into infrared spectrum with the help of Fourier transform installed in computer and then interpretation of the infrared spectrum. FTIR spectroscopy use in the field of agriculture provide huge advantage because of its rapid determination of the soil and plant samples with respect to the nutrients and toxic elements in samples. FTIR spectroscopy also reduces the cost of analysis because it is able to measure several properties from one infrared spectrum as compared to conventional laboratory techniques.

Keywords: *Analysis, Beam, component, Density, Spectrum*

INTRODUCTION

FTIR is the most preferred method of infrared spectroscopy. FTIR spectroscopy is very powerful instrument for the determination of functional

[1] Department of Agronomy, School of Agriculture, Lovely Professional University, Jalandhar - 144 411 (Punjab) (India)
[2] Divisions of Research and Development. Lovely Professional University, Jalandhar - 144 411 (Punjab) (India)

group in the molecule. It is very useful for identifying the chemicals which are either organic or inorganic. With the help of this instrument we can find out the information about the sample with the help of infrared spectrum which is obtained from interferogram. Interferogram is function of the position of mirror which is moving and pattern formed by wave interference. Then there is decoding of interferogram with the help of Fourier transform installed in computer and displays the spectrum. Hence Fourier transform infrared spectroscopy refers to a development in manner in which data collected and converted from an interference pattern to a spectrum. FTIR is able to identify the unknown materials and quality or consistency of the given samples. It is also very useful in agriculture such as analysis of soils for nutrients and to determine the concentration of particular element in the given plant sample.

HISTORY OF IR AND FTIR SPECTROSCOPY

IR Spectroscopy

Infrared spectroscopy history started with Sir Isaac Newton (1643-1727). He is the father of optics. Study of light is known as optics. Newton gives his first course about optics at Cambridge University in 1669. He published his first article about the study of light in 1672. He also established the mathematical rules for the measurement of the refraction of light. The study about the light or optics started by Sir Isaac Newton but also complemented by Frederick William Herschel (1738-1822) who discovered the infrared light. He was born in Hanover, Germany. He was professionally devoted himself to music but his interest also in mathematics and astronomy. In 1871, he also discovered Uranus planet with help of telescope which is built by himself. He had very good knowledge of optics and mathematics. One day he imagined that there can be the existence of other components out the visible region of the sunlight. But this region is not visible to human eye. So he created an experiment to find out this invisible region by placing the blackened thermometer bulb just below the red color of the light beam. He observed that temperature of the thermometer increased up to the room temperature. He called it as "infrared region" of the light spectrum. After that Herschel made another discovery in March 1800. He just assumed that if he would place a sample in the path of the infrared light then what will be the result there. So he placed a sample and observed that there is changing in part of spectrum because some part of infrared light is absorbed by the sample. In this way he defined "infrared spectroscopy".

FTIR Spectroscopy

In 1890s, Albert A. Michelson invented the interferometer which is known as Michelson's Interferometer core of the Fourier transform infrared spectroscopy. Earlier in 1940's infrared spectroscopy was not much popular and its use was limited because of some limitations. After some time there is development of dispersive spectrophotometer, due to this infrared spectroscopy came into widespread use.'Lord Rayleigh'(1892) a scientist who discovered that spectrum and its interferogram related to Fourier Transform. Fourier Transform is the mathematical process which is required to convert raw data into actual spectrum. Fourier transform is given by 'Jean Baptiste Joseph Fourier' (1768-1830) who was the French mathematician and physicist. In 1949, 'Peter Fellgett' who was astrophysicist successfully convert interferogram to spectrum and produce first Fourier transform infrared spectrum. At that time computers were large and expensive and takes 12 to 13 hours for transforming an interferogram to spectrum. In 1966 there was the two scientists Cooley and Tukey who developed an algorithm which quickly convert interferogram to spectrum. Fast fourier transform (FFT) method on which modern FTIR works developed by Cooley and Tukey.However firstly there was very large and costly FTIR spectroscopy present in the few laboratories. After that there was development in the technology which reduces the size and cost and at the same time increase the availability of FTIR spectroscopy.

Working Principle of FTIR spectroscopy

FTIR spectroscopy works on the principle of Fourier transformation in which interferogram is converted to spectrum. Interferogram is generated by the interference pattern of the waves. Infrared spectrum represents the percent transmittance when plotted against the wavenumbers and provide information of the given sample. FTIR principle also involves the study of interaction between the matter and infrared region of the light when emit by the source. When sample is placed in the path of infrared light then molecules are excited to higher vibrational state by absorbing infrared light but at a certain frequency. There are bonds in the molecules which vibrate at a specific frequency and only absorb that part of infrared light by which its frequency is matched. Then it gives the functional group and fingerprint region in the spectra about the composition of sample.

Components of FTIR spectroscopy:

1. IR source
2. Michelson Interferometer
3. Sample compartment
4. Detector
5. Computer

IR Source

Infrared radiation is emitted by the source. There is an aperture through which infrared radiation is passed and controls the amount of radiation which has to be reach the sample.

Common IR sources are:

- Globar which is also known as silicon carbide rods of 5-10mm width and 20-50 mm length. These rods are heated (1300 K) by passing an electric current through it and able to emit large amount of infrared radiation. Previously there was the requirement of cooling the globar with water but after that there is development in metal alloys which leads to the production of globar which do not required water for cooling.
- Nichrome and Kanthal wire coils which do not require cooling. These coils emit lower amount of infrared radiation as compare to globar.
- Nernst Glowers, which is not able to emit infrared radiation above 2000 cm^{-1}.

Michelson Interferometer

It was discovered by Albert Abraham Michelson and got Nobel Prize in 1907. This interferometer is the core of FTIR spectroscopy. Without it FTIR system would not exist. Interferometer consist of three parts which are beam splitter, a movable mirror and a fixed mirror.

- **Beam Splitter:** It is Nicol Prism which is made up of two calcite prism connected with the help of Canada balsam. This prism allow only the extraordinary rays and reflects the ordinary rays about 50%. Beam splitter placed an angle of 45^0 in the interferometer. Source emits IR radiation which strikes on the beam splitter and this beam of light is divide into two beams. One beam of light is transmitted through the prism to fixed mirror and other beam is reflected to the movable mirror. Then these two beams again recombines at the prism and pass through the sample and then detect by the detector where difference in intensity of two beams are measured as function of difference in path.
- **Movable mirror:** This mirror moves few millimeters from the beam splitter and varies the optical path difference (OPD) between two beams of light.
- **Fixed mirror:** This mirror having high reflective surface.
    - When the distance between two mirrors from beam splitter is equal then distance travelled by the two beams of light is same which is called zero path difference (ZPD) and hence radiations recombined at the beam splitter in phase known as constructive interference.
    - When movable mirror moves known as mirror displacement then in this case extra distance has to be travel by one beam of light which is known as optical path difference (OPD) and hence radiations are recombined not in phase known as destructive interference.

Interferometer signal

Constructive interference: It takes place when optical path difference (OPD) or mirror displacement (Ÿ) equal to integer multiple of Z and crest of the wave overlap with crest and trough overlap with trough. Under this condition maximum intensity signal is observed by detector.

Destructive interference: When optical path difference (OPD) or mirror displacement (Ÿ) equal to half multiple integer of Z and crest of wave overlap with trough. Under this minimum intensity signal is observed by detector.Since mirror move back and forth and hence intensity of the signal increases or decreases which give rise to the cosine waves. Due to the interference pattern of the waves gives an interferogram.

Sample Compartment

It is the compartment where the given sample is placed. Samples may be solid, liquid and gas. After the interferometer the beam of light is passed through the sample. Some amount of light is absorbed by the sample and some is transmit through it. Sample absorb only that part of infrared radiation by which its frequency or energy is matched.

The Detector

It is use to detect the transmitted infrared radiation from the sample and having final measurement of the beam of light. In FTIR two types of detector are most widely used which as follow:

- Photon Detectors (Mercury Cadmium Telluride)
- Pyro Electric Detectors (Deuterated Triglycine Sulphate)

Photon Detectors: The materials used in these detectors are semiconductors. Semiconductors are the insulators when there is no radiation falls onthem but when the radiation is fall on them then they become conductors. They have very fast response to the infrared radiation. Materials such as Mercury cadmium telluride, indium antimonide, indium gallium arsenide and lead selenide are the semiconductors which are used.

Pyro Electric Detectors: Materials which are used in these detectors are insulators, ferroelectric materials and semiconductors. Materials such as lithium tantalite, deuterated triglycine sulphate and strontium barium niobate.

Interferogram: The detectors which are used specially designed to determine the interferogram signalin energy versus time for all the frequencies. Interferogram is the end result of the whole process before analyze by the computer. All the infrared frequencies encoded in the interferogram. Interferogram is function of the position of moving mirror which contain all the information about infrared frequency emit from the source (Figure 13.1).

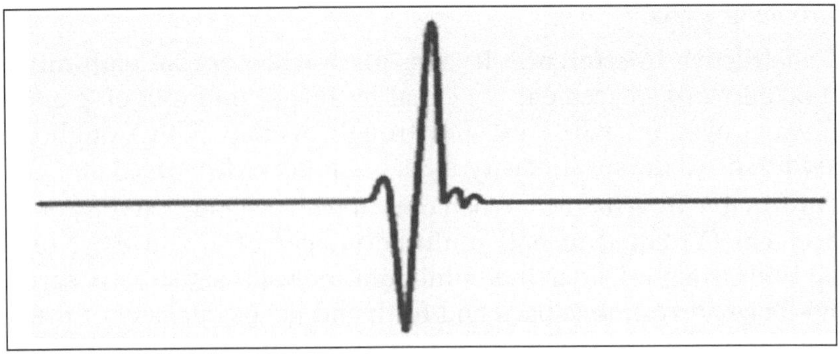

Fig. 13.1: Interferogram

Source: Based on review of literature

Computer

In the computer Fourier transform is installed in which there is decoding of the interferogram to infrared spectrum which enables the user for interpretation and find out the required result from the spectrum. Infrared spectrum represents the percent transmittance against the wavenumbers. Infrared spectra shows the result in form of peaks. Each peak in the spectra represents the presence of a particular functional group. There is presence of two regions in infrared spectra which as follows:

- Functional group region
- Fingerprint region

Generally FTIR spectroscopy works mostly in the mid infrared region (4000-400 cm^{-1}). Hence in this region there is appearance of absorption band which are used to determine functional group exist in molecules or not (Figure 13.2).

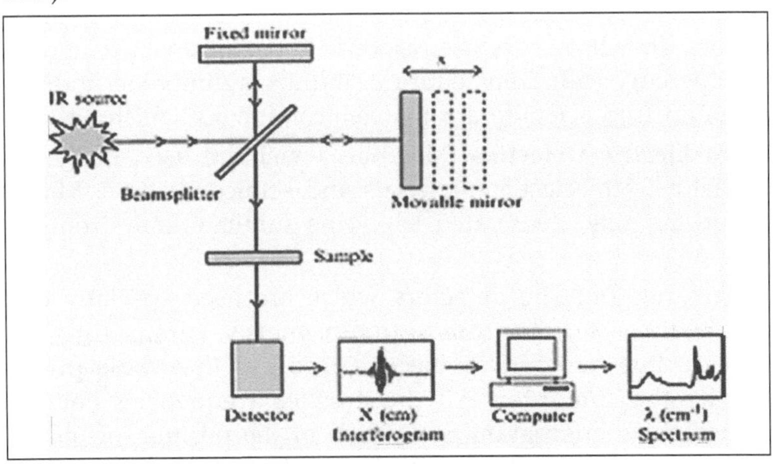

Fig. 13.2: Schematic diagram of FTIR spectroscopy

Source: Based on review of literature

Sample preparation

To get the informative and meaningful infrared spectrum with sharp peaks proper preparation of sample is required. Samples may be in gas, pure liquid, solution and solid form.

➢ **Liquid form:** There is two sodium chloride plates which are transparent in the region of 4000-625 cm^{-1}. A drop of the liquid sample is put between these two plates and then place these plates in the holder and obtained a spectrum after whole process in the instrument.

When the sodium chloride plates are used then samples should not be mixed with water because these plates are very sensitive to water and as a result these plates will dissolve. There proper handling is very important for avoiding damage. They must be hold from the edges. When spectrum is obtained after that plates should be clean with ethanol and store in a desiccator because moisture present in the air can also damage to the plates. The plates must be clean because damaged plates give bad spectra (Figure 13.3).

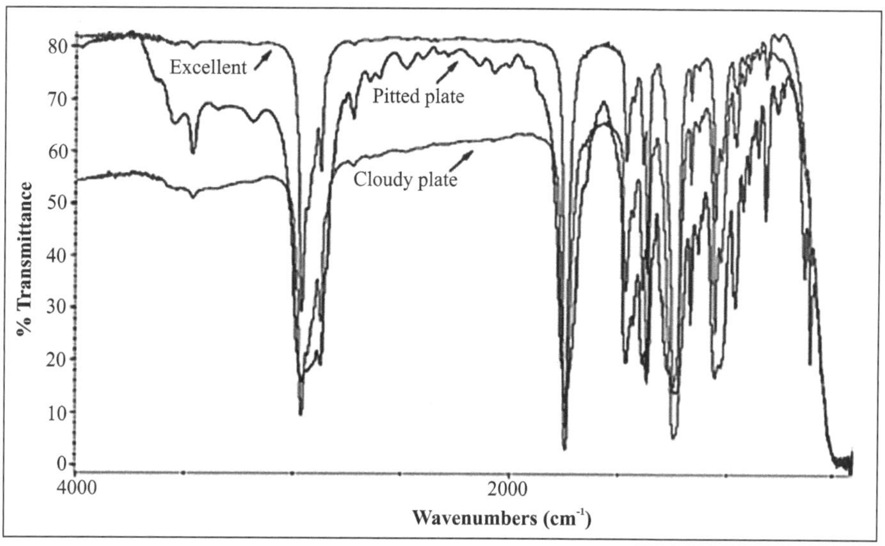

Fig. 13.3: Infrared spectrum from the sodium chloride plates

Solution form: If sample is use in solution form, sodium chloride solution cell is used. In it sample is dissolved in solvent but not in water to form solution and obtained the infrared spectra.

➢ **Solid form:** If the sample in solid form then we two ways to get IR spectra from the sample which as follows:

1. **Use of Nujol Mull:** Nujol is the type of oil which is use to get the infrared spectra of the solid samples. For this we have to take agate mortar and pestle. After that put the solid sample

and drop of nujol in the mortar for grinding. Then take two sodium chloride plates and place resulting material in between them and obtained infrared spectrum.

2. **Use of potassium bromide (KBr) disc:** First of all take solid sample and ground it properly. Then from this ground material take 2mg of sample powder and 300 mg of KBr into agate mortar and together grind them into fine flour. Then this material pressed into the disc by using the hydraulic press and then transfer it into the cylinder bore and get spectra. KBr used as a carrier for the sample and 100% transmittance in the range of 400-4000 cm^{-1}. KBr has the greater transmittance as compare to the sodium chloride.

- **Gas form:** For the gas samples there is presence of cylindrical gas cell which is use for analysis. This cell has an inlet and outlet port with a tap which enable the cylindrical cell to be easily filled with gas which is to be analyzed and obtained the infrared spectra.

Application of FTIR spectroscopy in agriculture:

- **Detect the heavy metal toxicity in the crops:** Due to the development of metal industries and excessive use the fertilizer containing heavy metals viz. phosphatic fertilizers containing cadmium causes toxicity in the crops. Cadmium affects the metabolism of the crops and inhibit photosynthesis, respiration and cell division. FTIR spectroscopy is one of best method for detection of the heavy metal in the crops and also study the changes in the crop due to toxicity.
- **Soil nutrients and organic matter determination:** Soil nutrients such as N, P, K, Ca, S and carbon plays very important for the growth and development of the agricultural crops and for proper functioning. Hence adequate amount of essentialnutrients in the soil is must. FTIR spectroscopy is very useful and rapid method for the determination of agricultural soil analysis for precision fertilization and maintaining sustainability in agriculture.
- **Soil moisture determination:** For the proper growth and development of the crops proper moisture condition should be in the soil. Availability of the nutrients and all the microbial activity in soil depends upon the proper soil moisture condition. Hence use of FTIR spectroscopy provides good results for the determination of the water related soil properties.
- **Identification and detection of fungal pathogens which affects the plants:** Fungi are the pathogens which affects the morphological and physiological functioning of the plants and cause economic damage to farmers. For their proper control, timely identification and detection of these fungal pathogens is must which is possible through the use of FTIR spectroscopy.

CONCLUSION

- FTIR spectroscopy is able to measure all the infrared frequencies which are emitted by source within few seconds.
- The detectors which are used in FTIR are highly sensitive and as a result noise level is lower in this instrument.
- In this instrument there is only one moving part as compare to dispersive instruments by which there is no mechanical damage in the FTIR spectroscopy.
- There is no need of calibration of this instrument by user because a laser is installed in FTIR which automatically calibrate the instrument.
- Data collection is easier in the FTIR spectroscopy.
- In the FTIR spectroscopy there is no threat of thermal effect to the sample.

REFERENCES

Berthomieu, C and Hienerwadel, R. "Fourier Transform Infrared Spectroscopy". ResearchGate.

Griffiths, P.R. and De Haseth, J.A. Fourier Tranform Infrared Spectrometry, Wiley-Interscience. New York.

Mohamed, M.A., Jaafar, J., Ismail, A.F., Othman, M.H.D., Rahman, M.A. "Fourier Transform Infrared Spectroscopy" Universiti Teknology Malaysia, Johor Bahru, Johor, Malaysia.

Raphael, Linker. "Application of FTIR Spectroscopy to Agricultural Soils Analysis". Faculty of Civil and Environmental Engineering Technion – Israel Institute of Technology.

Salman, A. "FTIR Spectroscopy for Detection and Identification of Fungal Phytopathogenes". Department of Physics, SCE – Sami Shamoon College of Engineering, Beer-Sheva, Israel.

Smith, B.C. "Fundamentals of Fourier Transform Infrared Spectroscopy" Chapter 1 to 3. CRC Press. United states of America. Taylor and Francis Group. 2011.

Wei, Z.L., Dong, L. and Tian, Z.H. "Fourier Transform Infrared Spectrometry Study on Early Stage of Cadmium Stress in Clover Leaves". Dezhou University, Shangdong, 253023, China.

Pages: 142-148

Statistical Tools, Data and Instrumentation in Research and Science

Edited by: **Er. Chhavi Kumar 'Bharti'; Dr. Prasann Kumar and Dr. Pawan Kumar 'Bharti'**

ISBN: 978-93-88854-51-1

Edition: **2020**

Published by: **Discovery Publishing House Pvt. Ltd., New Delhi (India)**

14

X-ray Crystallography
An Overview

Jagdish Chand[1], Prasann Kumar[1,2]

ABSTRACT

XRD means X-ray Diffraction based in the concept of Max Von Laue (1912) that all the crystalline substances having the three dimensional structure. Along with spacing "d" between the two planes. This spacing in between the planes is different in all the different crystal and minerals. It helps us in identifying the different substances. In XRD analysis High frequency electrons are bombarded towards the sample generated by a cathode tube and after the incidence they are absorbed by the sample and reflected and scatter back in the form of X rays known as Elastic Scattering. For successful diffraction constructive interference of monochromatic X rays following the Bragg's law ($n\lambda=2d\sin\theta$) *is very important. After diffraction all the constructive X-rays are amplified in a graph at an angle of* 2θ. *According to the different "d" spacing different diffraction peaks are formed which allows us to identify the crystalline substances and minerals either in solid soil or amorphous form. As we know that XRD gives the information about the unit cell dimensions. So it is very helpful for identify the different minerals and composition of medicines because all the medicines are made up of different substances either solid or amorphous form having their own crystal lattice and unique "d" spacing between the planes of crystal. XRD is very unique and powerful technique for solving the problems in pharmaceutical analysis. Although sample preparation and interpretation of S results*

[1] Department of Agronomy, School of Agriculture, Lovely Professional University, Jalandhar - 144 411 (Punjab) (India)

[1, 2] Divisions of Research and Development, Lovely Professional University, Jalandhar - 144 411 (Punjab) (India)

required care and knowledge in this technique but as compared to other instruments like FTIR, DSC/TGA etc. XRD can provide the greater clarity and understanding about the identification of substances used in different medicines in pharmaceutical department.

Keywords: *Three, Dimensional, Energy, Frequency, Scattering*

INTRODUCTION

The emission of X- Ray by the atoms of particular crystal that produces an interference effect, So that the diffraction pattern gives the information on the structure of the crystal or the identity of a crystalline substances. It is very important method of phase identification on the basis of every cell dimension phase contains unique (d- spacing). The d-spacingis the distance between the two planes of every cell all the cell have their own d-spacing. This can help us for phase identification of materials. The diffraction pattern is of every crystal is same as that of fingerprinting in case of human beings (Figure 14.1).

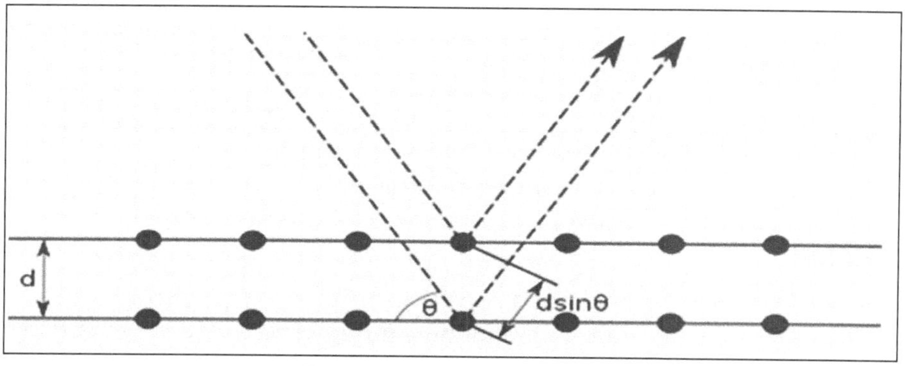

Fig. 14.1: Pattern of diffraction

Source: Based on review of literature

Some important facts about the X-ray:

- X-rays were discovered by WC Rontgen in 1895.
- Maxwell von Lauerelied that X-ray might be the correct wavelength to differentfrom proposed space lattice.
- In June 1912, Von Laue published the first diffraction pattern of (copper sulfate) in proceedings of Royal Bavarian Academy of science.
- Braggs in 1913 used X- rays to solve the first crystal structure, which was the structure of NaCl (Figure 14.2).

What the XRD machine can do:

- It can helps us to identify the crystal structure.
- Also helps us to identify the texture orientation and helps in characterization of polymorphs material.

- Helps in identify the defected portion in the complex material.
- Identify the amorphous materials.
- Useful for quantitative analysis of phase composition.
- It is a powerful tool for material characterization.

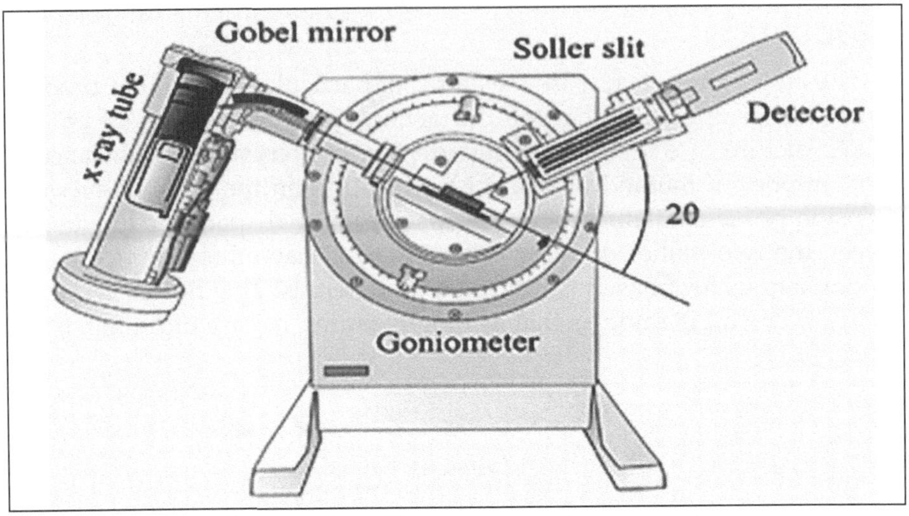

Fig. 14.2: X-ray diffractometer and its component Diffractrometer

Source: Based on review of literature

PRINCIPLE

XRD analysis is based on the constructive interference of monochromatic X-ray and a crystalline sample. The X-ray generated by a cathode ray tube filtered to produce monochromatic radiation collimated to concentrate and directed towards the sample.

Component of diffractometer:

- X-ray source
- The primary optics
- The sample holder
- The secondary optics
- Detector

1. X-ray source

X-ray tube is a common source of x-ray. It is made up of the metals such thatas molybdenum, tungsten, copper, rhodium, silver or cobalt. On the passage of electric through the filament electron are directed towards the sample surface resulting to oscillate the electron of thesample generated a new form of radiation known as X-rays. After the emission all the X-ray are absorbed by the detector.

2. Primaryoptics

On the side of X-ray having 30mm long source, X-ray passes through these slits having 30mm long and 0.05 mm thick and contains closely packed a series of metal plates which refines the rays towards the sample.

3. The sample holder

The sample holder is also known as the sample stage or a goniometer.The sample holder is place where it contains the sample for observation. And the radiationsare directed towards the sample. Sample should be uniformly distributed on the sample stage and size of crystal should be less than 10 mm.

4. The secondary optic

After the emission of X-rays in all directions from the sample secondaryoptics can helps to collect the desirable X-rays, stops the further diffraction and send all the radiations towards the detector.

5. Detector

Emitted X-rays are absorbed by the detector in order to be recorded for subsequent analysis.

There are Three main types of detectors:

- Proportional detector.
- Scintillation detector.
- Solid state detector.

1. Proportional detector

It is most commonly used detector. It consist of Nobel gas filled in a tube and also comprises of thin positively charged tungsten filament. When the radiations are enter in the tube then they ionized the electrons of the gas and electrons are attracted towards tungsten filament with generating a s amount of current according to the amount of electron. Thus this amount of current is used further observation (Figure 14.3).

2. Scintillation detector

It consist of mainly two main parts i.e. Scintillation material and a photo multiplier tube.

SCINTILLATION MATERIAL

When the external nuclear partial or any charged particle enters into the scintillator. Then all the charged particles are absorbed by the gas filled in the scintillator which leads into the emission of photons from the particles and all the photons are absorbed by thephotocathode resulting in the emission of primary electron directed towards the series of dinodes to increase the electric pulse for further observation.

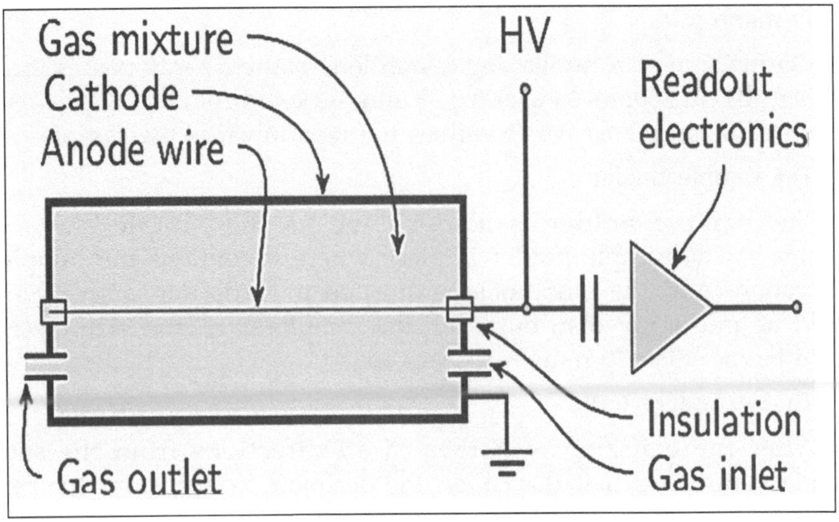

Fig. 14.3: Proportional detector

Source: Based on review of literature

3. Solid state detector

In this type of detector Semiconductor are used for the dectection having properties of both conductors and insulators due to some thermal excitation the electron in balance bend is jumped in conduction bend.Solid state detectors consists of "p- n" junction diode. In "n" type f semiconductors the majority charge carries are electrons and in "P" type of semiconductor the majority charge carriers are holes. Electrons and the holes are opposite charge carriers and diffuse and recombine in a particular zone is known depletion region. This Depletion region has no kind of charge carriers. As a result this depletion region behave as a nuclear detector when any kind of charged particle or alpha particles are enters into this region results into the creation of pairs of free electron and a hole which leads the generation of some kind of electric pulse used for detection of existence of amount of alpha particles (Figure 14.4).

METHODS OF X-RAY DIFFRACTION

1. Powder Method

This method is very good technique to measure the lattice parameter of any crystal (a,b, c). In this method polycrystals are used for diffraction and the value for lattice parameter we get from this method is very accurate and precise. A mono chromatic X-rays is incident towards the sample (in powder for) in a cylindrical containers then the rays are diffracted when it follows the braggs law i.e. ($n\lambda=2d\sin\theta$). Thus diffraction pattern are obtained on photographic film. This diffraction pattern is used for observing the size and shape of crystal.

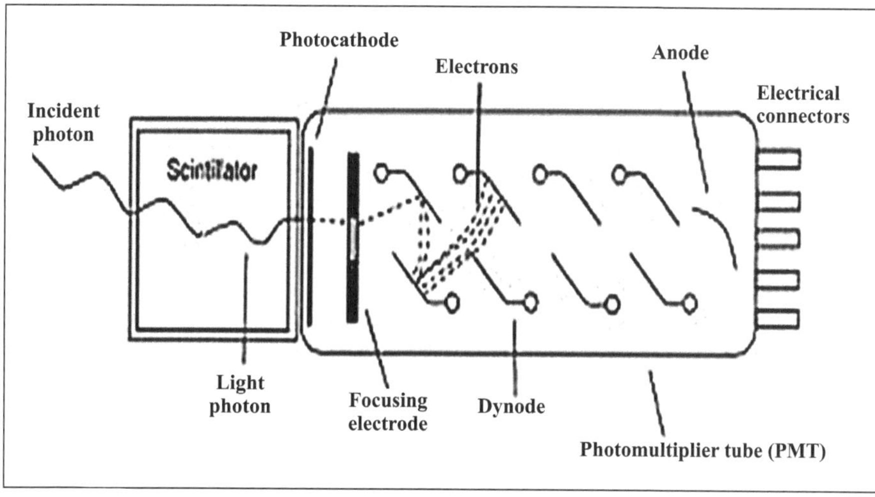

Fig. 14.4: Solid state detector
Source: Based on review of literature

2. Rotating Crystal Method

This method is also used for measure the lattice vectors i.e. (a.b,c,). In this monochromatic crystals are incident on the sample (single crystal) placed in the cylindrical chamber coated with photographic film. Single crystal is inclined with the help of stand in the direction of X-ray. When the ray came in contact with the single crystal the ray get diffracted only when it follows the Braggs law ($n\lambda=2d\sin\theta$) and make the diffraction pattern on the photographic film. And the remaining rays which does not follows the Braggs law passes as it is in the axis of incidence (Figure 14.5).

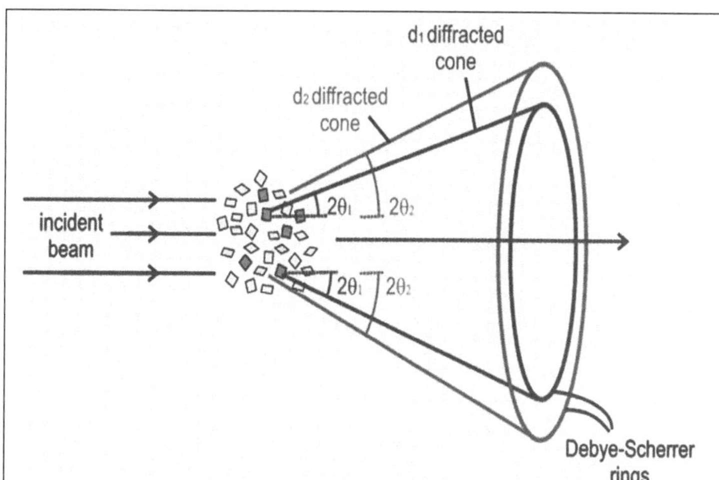

Fig. 14.5: Rotating crystal
Source: Based on review of literature

3. Von Laue method of direction

In this method X-rays are allows to pass through the narrows slits towards the sample (Sample must be a single crystal) and the range wavelength of radiation i.e. (λ= 0.2-2 A). When the rays get came in contact with crystal then the rays get diffracted if only follows the Braggs equation in all directions and final arrangement of atoms are seen on the photographic plate (Figure 14.6).

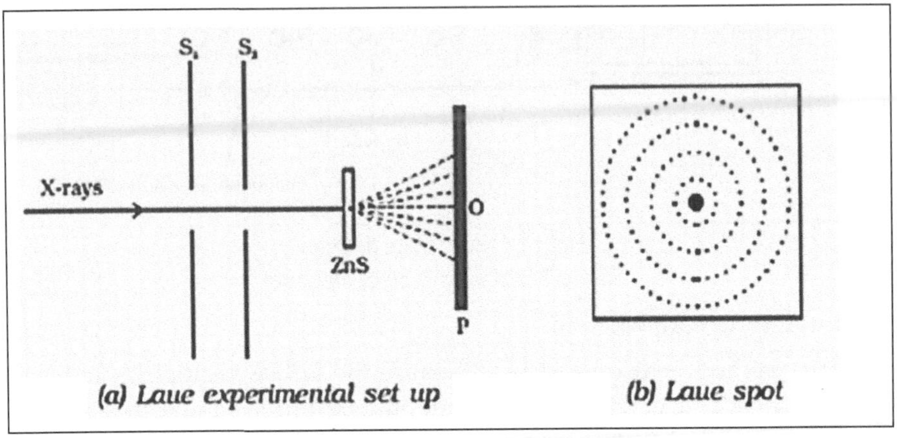

Fig. 14.6: Von Laue method of direction

Source: Based on review of literature

REFERENCES

https://www.iitk.ac.in.ac/che/pdf/resources/XRD_reading materials.pdf.

https://www.youtube.com/edit?o=U&ar1...

https://www.yputube.com/watch?v=178b...

https://www.amazone.in/solid-state-phy...

B.D. Cullity and S.R. Stock, Element of X-ray Diffraction, Pearson, 2001.

Bragg, W.H.; Bragg, W.L.(1913). "The reflection of X-ray by crystal".

Pages: 149-158
Statistical Tools, Data and Instrumentation in Research and Science
Edited by: Er. Chhavi Kumar 'Bharti'; Dr. Prasann Kumar and Dr. Pawan Kumar 'Bharti'
ISBN: 978-93-88854-51-1
Edition: 2020
Published by: Discovery Publishing House Pvt. Ltd., New Delhi (India)

15

Scanning Electron Microscope
An Overview

Poonam Kumari[1], Prasann Kumar[1,2]

ABSTRACT

Scanning electronic microscope is very different microscope having magnification ~1-2 million times and ~0.5nm optimal spatial resolution. It produces images by scanning the samples by electronic focused beam. In this the beam of electrons is produced by the electronic gun when the tungsten wire is heated at high temperature. The electrons flow from cathode to anode through a hole. When electron beam strikes with the sample it produces some X rays, back scattered electrons etc. and they are detected by the detectors and produces image on screen.

Keywords: *Anode, Cathode, Detectors, Electrons, Microscope, Scanning, Tungsten.*

INTRODUCTION

The human eyes have some utmost and can resolve two that are 0.2 mm separated from one another, called as the goals intensity of the human eye. Nonetheless, by the expansion of focal point or gathering of focal points (supported eye), the human eye is empowered for high goals and can resolve the two spots that are nearer than 0.1-0.2 mm from one another. Anything beneath 0.1-0.2 mm requires a type of amplification; consequently, to beat these restrictions of human visual perception, the magnifying lens was created and utilized as a proficient amplifying instrument. Magnifying

[1] Department of Agronomy, School of Agriculture, Lovely Professional University, Jalandhar - 144 411 (Punjab) (India)
[1, 2] Division of Research and Development, Lovely Professional University, Jalandhar - 144 411 (Punjab) (India)

lens has an a lot higher goals and has been utilized as a useful asset for considering or describing a wide scope. This magnifying instrument settling power not just relies upon the number and quality of focal points utilized, yet in addition of light wavelength or source to deliver picture is exceptionally considered. In this manner, magnifying instrument can be partitioned into two classes based on source to create picture, for example optical or light magnifying instrument (OM) and electron magnifying instrument (EM). Both OM and EM have a similar working standard, however the significant distinction is the source, for example OM utilizes obvious light as a source while EM uses centred quickened electrons pillar. Surface examination of the materials can be accomplished through the two magnifying instruments. Be that as it may, the goals of optical magnifying lens is constrained by diffraction properties. Rather, an a lot higher goals information can be accomplished by utilizing one of the electron minuscule strategies. Since electrons have shorter wavelength than noticeable light and in this way are progressively enthusiastic then obvious light photon, a light emission quickened electrons are centered around the outside of materials, in this way making the picture. EM is an imaging apparatus with much better imaging goals when contrasted with OM. The utilization of the quickened electrons bar in EM highlighted by short wavelength causes the diffraction impacts to happen at a lot littler physical measurement, which thusly helps settle nuclear highlights running from nanometre to micrometer molecule size. On account of EM, centered quickened electrons are utilized to see through the example and output materials on a fine and little scale. Thus, it gives pictures of higher amplification with better goals. The primary explanation behind the advancement of electron magnifying instruments was the regions and confinement of OM. Two principle sorts of EM are accessible, checking electron magnifying instrument (SEM) and transmission electron magnifying lens (TEM) [1, 2]. The main EM, for example TEM, was designed in 1931 by Knoll and Ruska in Germany, and as far back as it was considered as a significant instrument that has been utilized to comprehend logical marvels in different fields, for example, nanotechnology, science, prescription and numerous others [1, 2]. The SEM was first presented in 1938 (Von Ardenne), and in 1965 the first SEM instrument came into market.

SCANNING ELECTRON MICROSCOPE (SEM)

SEM is an adaptable propelled instrument which is to a great extent utilized to watch the surface wonders of the materials. The example is shot in a SEM utilizing highenergy electron, and the outcoming electrons/X-beams are investigated. These outcomingelectrons/X-beams give data about geology, morphology, piece, direction of grains, crystallographic data, and so forth of a material. Morphology demonstrates the shape and size, while geography shows the surface highlights of an item or "what it looks like", its surface, smoothness or unpleasantness. Moreover, creation implies components and intensifies that comprise the material, while crystallography implies the course of action of molecules in the materials. SEM is the main mechanical assembly that is fit for accomplishing a point by point visual picture of a molecule with high-caliber and spatial goals of 1 nm [3-4]. Amplifications of this sort of mechanical assembly can reach out up to multiple times. In spite of the fact that SEM is utilized just to envision surface pictures of a material and doesn't give any inside data [2], it is as yet considered as a ground-breaking instrument that can be utilized in portraying crystallographic, attractive and electrical highlights of the example and in deciding whether any morphological changes of the molecule has happened in the wake of adjusting the example surface with different atoms [3]. SEM can give a few subjective data of the example including its geography, morphology, arrangement and crystallographic data. At the end of the day, it gives data about the surface highlights and surface, shape, size and game plan of the particles lying on the example's surface. The sort of components and aggravates the example comprises of and their relative proportions just as the course of action of iotas in the single gem particles and their level of request can likewise be given Thus, SEM is a multipurpose instrument which can look at and investigate the materials with high goals (Figure 15.1).

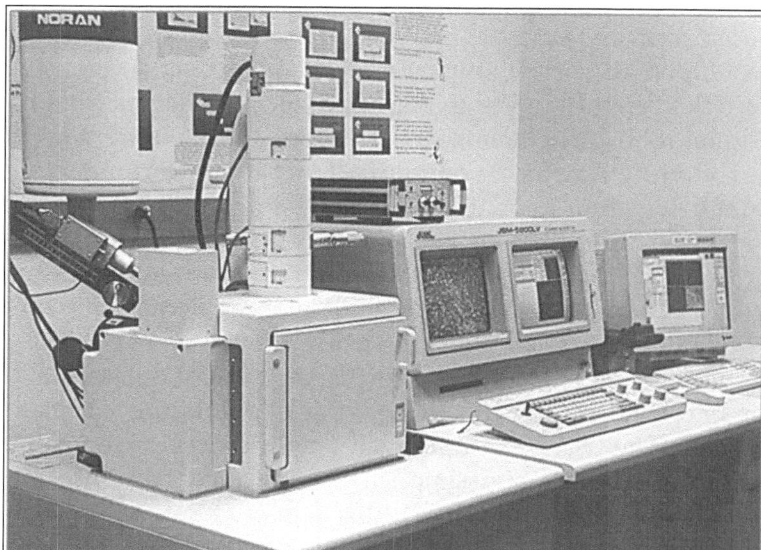

Fig. 15.1: Scanning Electron Microscope

Source: https://d32ogoqmya1dw8.cloudfront.net

Components of SEM

- Electron gun
- Electromagnetic lenses
- Detection of electrons
- Sampling chamber
- Display of images by computer

Electronic gun: Electron gun is a component of Scanning electronic microscope which produces electronic beam and that electrons are emitted by a filament that is cathode which is made from a thin tungsten wire and in size of about 0.1mm and that filament is heated upto the temperature of 2000K. The electrons flows towards positive voltage i.e. anode. On the plate one hole is present which allows electron flow.On a fundamental level, first the firearm discharges the electron shaft which is held inside a vacuum which pursues a vertical travel way through electromagnetic fields and focal points. The electron bar is focussed by target focal point on the example. At that point the focussed bar look over a particular region of the example surface where the focussed pillar is rastered over the outside of the materials with assistance of redirector curls, which is constrained by the output generator. Amplification controls the size of the rastering design. The adjustments in amplification change the size of the rastered territory on the example. At the point when the electron shaft hits the material, this strike creates a colossal number of sign, for exampleelectrons and X-beams are produced from the example. These sign are identified by the identifier (contingent upon thesort of finder) and changed over to signals where pictures are delivered from the signals. The sign that begins from electron-test communication gives itemized data about the material, for example, outer morphology (surface), compound organization and crystalline structure and direction of materials making up the test. The examining electron magnifying lens has a few points of interest since it has a huge significance of field which grants to concentrate more examples one after another. The SEM additionally has a lot of prevalent goals, so barely divided examples can be amplified at many propelled levels. The greater preferred position of SEM is that it gives the analyst substantially more control in the level of amplification as focal points are supplanted by electromagnets. The change of upgraded amplification, greater profundity of centre, prevalent goals and simplicity of test reconnaissance make the SEM one of the most significantly utilized instruments in explore zones these days [1-6]. Electron weapon gives the electron shaft whose vitality can change according to need of material to get a picture with the best goals with least example charging furthermore, harm. The capacity of the electron weapon is to give a huge and stable current in a little pillar. The electron weapon or discharge source is of two kinds, for example thermionic producer and field producer [6]. The fundamental contrast among SEM and FESEM is the kind of producer, for example thermionic producer is utilized in SEM while field producer is the electron firearm used in FESEM (figure 15.2).

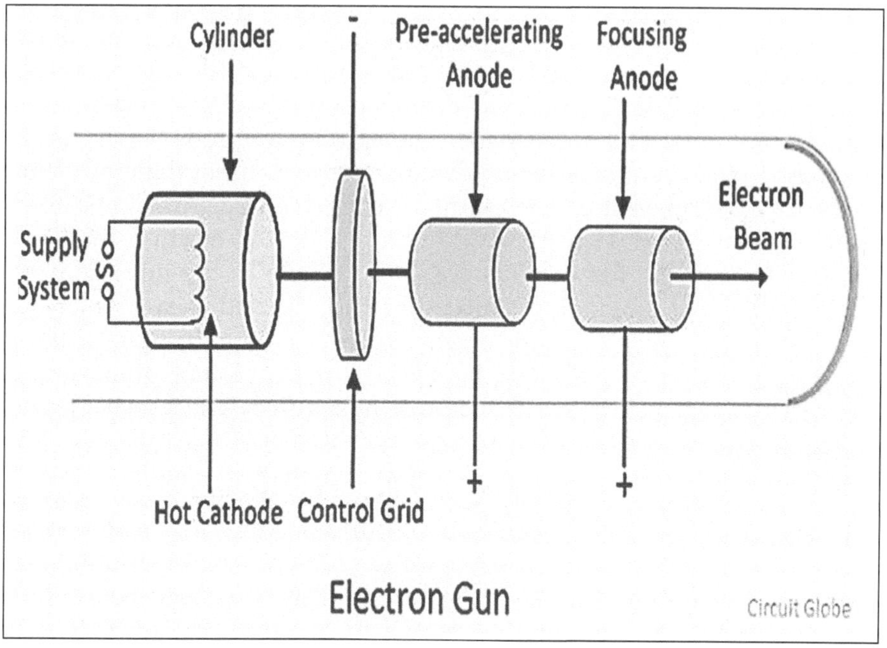

Fig. 15.2: Electron Gun of SEM

Source: https://circuitglobe.com/wp-content/electron-gun.jpg

ELECTRO MAGNETIC LENSES

Section with Lenses and Apertures, Condenser focal point, filtering loops, stigmator curls and target focal point and the gaps in the section center the electron shaft onto the outside of example. Every focal point comprises of copper wire conveying direct current encompassed by an iron cover. Along these lines, electromagnetic focal point contains copper wire curl inside an iron shaft piece. These curls make attractive field when applying current through the loops, and this attractive field join the electron pillar. When an electron goes through an electromagnetic focal point, it faces two vector powers at a specific minute [5]: (i) a power parallel to the Z-hub of the focal point and along these lines is spoken to by Hz that causes spiraling of the electrons while going through the perspective; (ii) A power parallel to the span of the focal point and in this way is spoken to as HR, which causes centering of the electrons while going through the viewpoint At the point when an electron is going through the viewpoint, it will encounter a power parallel to the Z-hub, and this power will ask the electron to winding through the perspective. This spiraling makes the electron experience another power parallel to the sweep of the focal point, and this power pack the pillar towards the Z-pivot. The attractive field doesn't stay homogeneous. It stays solid near the drag while feeble in the focal point of the hole. In this way, those electrons which pass near the inside experience less power and are less firmly redirected, while those electrons which are passing the focal point a long way from the hub experience more power and are all the more unequivocally avoided. Consequently, electromagnetic focal point produces electromagnetic fields which have pivotal and spiral parts. The spiral part keeps the electrons in helix way. In the event that the bar distance across is littler than the element, in such a case, highlight on the example surface can be settled, and for this reason, it is an absolute necessity to consolidate the electron bar. In this way, electromagnetic focal points are used to help in the demagnification of the shaft. Field emanation source has little hybrid measurement, and consequently the shaft buildup to a lower level is vital in light of the fact that in such a case the test will be significant for picture preparing, and that is the reason the FESEM is the most noteworthy goals instrument [5].

Condenser Lens

The condenser focal point merges the cone of the electron shaft to a spot beneath it, before the cone flares out again and is combined back again by the target focal point what's more, down onto the example. This underlying union can be at various statures, for examplenear the focal point or further away. The closer it is to the focal point, the littler the spot width at the purpose of combination. The further away, the bigger the width of this point. Thusly, the condenser focal point right now controls this underlying spot size and is alluded to as the spot-size control. The width of this underlying combination (moreover called a hybrid point) influences the last width of the detect the pillar makes on the test. The condenser focal point decreases the measurement of the test. Changing the current in the condenser focal point will bring about changing the distance across of the pillar and can get a bar with a little distance across. A littler test breadth and limited bar will empower better goals. In any case, the disadvantage of a tight bar is more awful sign to-agitating proportion, while on account of shaft with enormous breadth, the sign to-agitating proportion will be better. The source size of the FEG is nearly little with the goal that the measure of demagnification important to create little test sizes is not as much as that of other electron sources [5-7].

Scanning Coils

Filtering curls which are likewise called pillar diversion loops are utilized to check the test surface, and the current in these loops is expanded so as to get a higher amplification. The job of the filtering loops is to redirect the electron bar above the item in a crisscross example, and with assistance of this sweep development, the production of the picture happens on the screen in synchrony. The invigorating rate on the screen and measure of commotion in the picture relies upon the sweep speed. If there should arise an occurrence of moderate sweep, the reviving will be moderate; the sign will be high while the agitating will be low. On the other hand, if the sweep is quick, the reviving will be quick, the sign will be low while the agitating will be high. Examining loops for the most part contain upper and lower curls, which maintain a strategic distance from the formation of a roundabout shadow at low amplification [5-7].

Objective Lens

The target focal point is the most reduced focal point in the segment which concentrates the test on the example. The target focal point is utilized to concentrate the pillar on the example. Coarse centring of the example should be possible by picking the working separation (WD = separation between the base of the target focal point and theexample), centring the target focal point to match with this worth and afterward changing the physical tallness of the example to bring it into centre. Fine centring can be along these lines done exclusively with the goal lens. WD should be diminished for an example to be all around centred. In the event that the WD is less, it implies that the example is at a higher position and near the target focal point. In this way, more prominent power is expected to divert the electron shaft by target focal point. The most brief WD creates shaft with the littlest breadth and gives the least fortunate profundity of field in this way getting a picture with the best goals [5-7] (Figure 15.3).

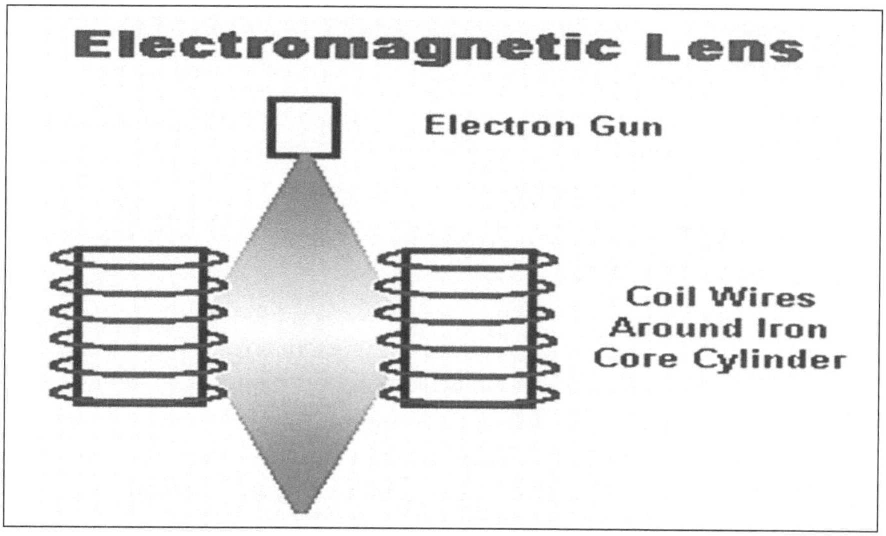

Fig. 15.3: Electromagnetic lens of SEM

Source: https://d80d238b-a-62cb3a1a-s-sites.googlegroups.come

INTERACTION BETWEEN ELECTRON AND SAMPLE

In scanning electronic microscope, a very high beam of electron strikes on the sample and produces images by sample scanning. Scattered back or secondary electrons produced when they strikes with sample. The detectors which are present there collects the signals and display them in the form of image on the screen. Depending upon the density and voltage of the sample, microns penetrates in the sample and then various signals are produced in the sample. There are multiple factors on which resolution of the Scanning electronic microscope depends that is volume and size of the sample. It provides resolution below 1nm (Figure 15.4).

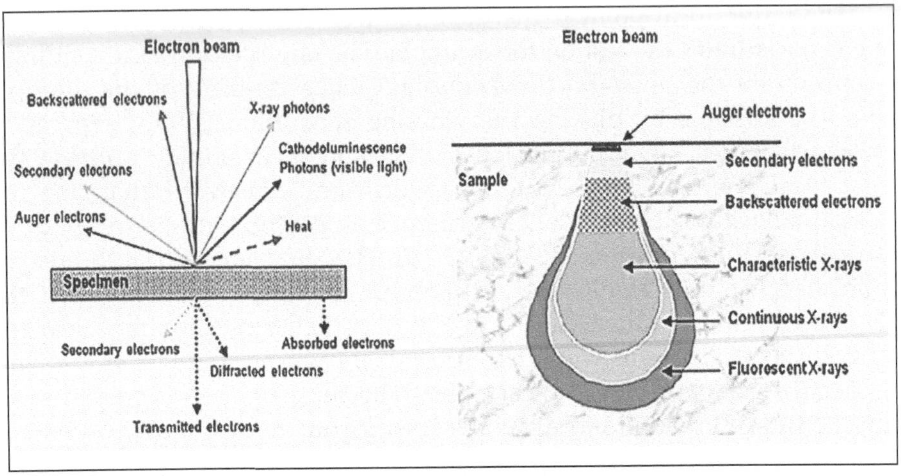

Fig. 15.4: Interaction between electron and sample

Source: https://www.researchgate.net

ELECTRON SOURCE

The thermionic heating is a source by which electrons are produced.1-40KV voltage is required to accelerate these electrons.

There are three types of electron sources i.e.

1. Tungsten filament
2. Field emission gun
3. Sodium state crystals

1. **Tungsten filament:** It is V shaped inverted wire,100um long, made up of tungsten. It produces electrons when heated resistively.
2. **Field emission gun:** It is less than 100um having sharp tip, made up of tungsten. It produces electron beam by field electron emission. It has a good focusing and emission ability due to its small tip.
3. **Sodium state crystals:** It has 5-10 times more brightness and life than tungsten. It is thermionic emission gun and also known as Lanthanum hexaboride (LaB_6) or Cerium hexaboride (CeB_6).

WORKING PRINCIPLE

When a specimen is hit with the beam of electrons known as the incident beam, it emits X rays and three kinds of electrons i.e. primary, backscattered and secondary electrons and auger electrons. The detectors present in this detects the rays and form images in computer. Resolution depends on the electron size and wavelength of electrons.When tungsten wire is heated by current the electron gun produces the electron beam of electrons. That beam is speed up by some positive charge i.e. anode, then the beam of electrons moves through electromagnetic fields towards the sample. The coils produces beam and scans the sample in raster pattern. X ray, backscattered electrons and secondary electrons are produced when it touches to the sample surface. After that the scattered electrons are collected and converted to signals and them image is produced in the computer screen. And the leftover X rays and back scattered electrons produces other images (Figure 15.5).

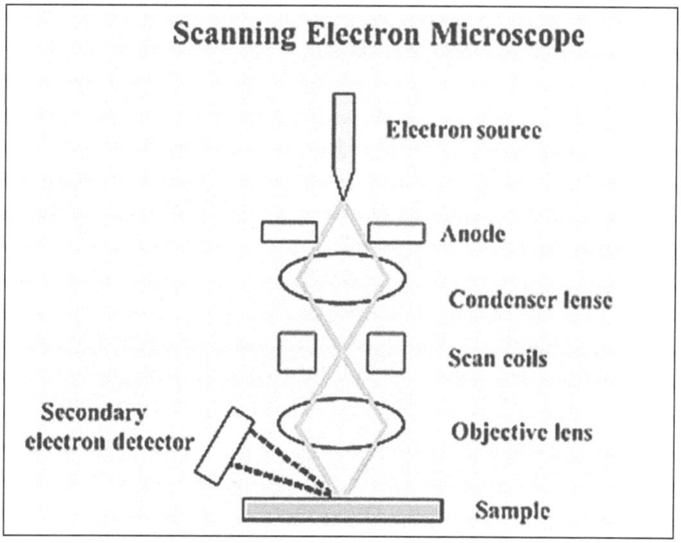

Fig. 15.5: Schematic diagram of SEM
Source: https://blog.phenom-world.com

Sample Preparation

- Remove all water, solvents, or different materials that could vaporize while in the vacuum.
- Firmly mount every sample.
- Non-metallic examples, for example, plants, what's more, earthenware production, ought to be coated with electrically conductive materials.

Advantages of SEM

1. It is based on advanced computer technology.
2. It is use and environmental friendly.
3. It requires very less time to analyse the samples.
4. It takes less than 5 minutes to analyses SEI, BSE and EDS analysis.
5. 3-D imaging can be done.

Disadvantages of SEM

1. Size of SEM is very big.
2. Cost is too high.
3. Maintenance is difficult.
4. It requires circulation of cool water.
5. Constant voltage is required.
6. Special training is required to operate SEM.
7. Extremely sensitive to vibration.
8. Causes risk of radiation exposure.

REFERENCES

1. Alyamani, A., & Lemine, O.M. (2012). FE-SEM Characterization of some Nanomaterial. In V. Kazmiruk (Ed.), Scanning Electron Microscopy. InTech. London.
2. McMahon, G. (2007). Analytical Instrumentation: A Guide to Laboratory, Portable and Miniaturized Instruments (1st ed. p. 296). Chichester: Wiley.
3. Goldstein, J.K., & Yakowitz, H. (1975). Practical Scanning Electron Microscopy: Electron and ion Microprobe Analysis (p. 582). New York: Plenum Press.
4. Brabazon, D., & Raffer, A. (2010). 3 – Advanced Characterization Techniques for Nanostructures. In W. Ahmed & M.J. Jackson (Eds.), Emerging Nanotechnologies for Manufacturing (pp. 59-91). Boston: William Andrew Publishing.
5. Zhou, W., Apkarian, R.P., Wang, Z.L., & Joy, D. (2006). Fundamentals of Scanning Electronmicroscopy. In: Scanning Microscopy for Nanotechnology (pp. 1-40). New York: Springer.
6. Sant'Anna, C., Campanati, L., Gadelha, C., Lourenco, D., Labati-Terra, L., Bittencourt-Silvestre, J., Benchimol, M., Cunha-e-Silva, N. L., & De Souza, W. (2005). Improvement on the Visualization of Cytoskeletal Structures of Protozoan Parasites using High-resolution Field Emission Scanning Electron Microscopy (FESEM). Histochemistry and Cell Biology, 124(1), 87-95.
7. Lloyd, G.E. (1987). Atomic Number and Crystallographic Contrast Images with the SEM: A Review of Backscattered Electron Techniques. Mineralogical Magazine, 51(359)

Index

D

E

F

G

H

I

❑❑❑❑❑